Microsoft®
Excel 2010
2-in-1

by Richard Rost

ALPHA

A member of Penguin Group (USA) Inc.

This, my first real book, is dedicated to my wife, Michele. She has been patient and understanding over the past 20 years, and has given me the space to pursue my own projects (some good, most disastrous) instead of making me get a real job.

ALPHA BOOKS

Published by the Penguin Group

Penguin Group (USA) Inc., 375 Hudson Street, New York, New York 10014, USA

Penguin Group (Canada), 90 Eglinton Avenue East, Suite 700, Toronto, Ontario M4P 2Y3, Canada (a division of Pearson Penguin Canada Inc.)

Penguin Books Ltd., 80 Strand, London WC2R 0RL, England

Penguin Ireland, 25 St. Stephen's Green, Dublin 2, Ireland (a division of Penguin Books Ltd.)

Penguin Group (Australia), 250 Camberwell Road, Camberwell, Victoria 3124, Australia (a division of Pearson Australia Group Pty. Ltd.)

Penguin Books India Pvt. Ltd., 11 Community Centre, Panchsheel Park, New Delhi—110 017, India

Penguin Group (NZ), 67 Apollo Drive, Rosedale, North Shore, Auckland 1311, New Zealand (a division of Pearson New Zealand Ltd.)

Penguin Books (South Africa) (Pty.) Ltd., 24 Sturdee Avenue, Rosebank, Johannesburg 2196, South Africa

Penguin Books Ltd., Registered Offices: 80 Strand, London WC2R 0RL, England

Copyright © 2011 by Richard Rost

International Standard Book Number: 978-1-61564-0-744
Library of Congress Catalog Card Number: 2010910370

13 12 11   8 7 6 5 4 3 2 1

Interpretation of the printing code: The rightmost number of the first series of numbers is the year of the book's printing; the rightmost number of the second series of numbers is the number of the book's printing. For example, a printing code of 11-1 shows that the first printing occurred in 2011.

Printed in the United States of America

Note: This publication contains the opinions and ideas of its author. It is intended to provide helpful and informative material on the subject matter covered. It is sold with the understanding that the author and publisher are not engaged in rendering professional services in the book. If the reader requires personal assistance or advice, a competent professional should be consulted.

The author and publisher specifically disclaim any responsibility for any liability, loss, or risk, personal or otherwise, which is incurred as a consequence, directly or indirectly, of the use and application of any of the contents of this book.

Most Alpha books are available at special quantity discounts for bulk purchases for sales promotions, premiums, fund-raising, or educational use. Special books, or book excerpts, can also be created to fit specific needs.

For details, write: Special Markets, Alpha Books, 375 Hudson Street, New York, NY 10014.

Publisher: *Marie Butler-Knight*

Associate Publisher/Acquiring Editor: *Mike Sanders*

Senior Managing Editor: *Billy Fields*

Development Editor: *Ginny Bess Munroe*

Senior Production Editor: *Janette Lynn*

Copy Editor: *Krista Hansing Editorial Services*

Cover Designer: *Rebecca Batchelor*

Book Designers: *William Thomas, Rebecca Batchelor*

Indexer: *Heather McNeill*

Layout: *Brian Massey*

Proofreader: *Laura Caddell*

the
cultural

How

50 Million People

Are Changing

the World

praise for *The Cultural Creatives*

"There is a quiet revolution of values afoot in America with the potential to change the planet. Ray and Anderson have done a splendid job defining and interviewing the cultural creative revolutionaries, astounding us with the good news that we are not lone voices crying in the wilderness, but a vanguard of hope over 50 million strong."

JOAN BORYSENKO, PH.D., author of
A Woman's Book of Life and *A Woman's Journey to God*

"When people identify themselves as cultural creatives through reading this book, the transformation of society will be accelerated. The book itself will be a force for change."

JEAN SHINODA BOLEN, M.D., author of
Goddesses in Everywoman and *The Millionth Circle*

"*The Cultural Creatives* provides a vital mirror for a multifaceted 'social uprising of wellness' to see itself as a powerful movement, to gain the collective authority and a shared sense of direction required to seed the culture with health and vitality in the third millennium."

BARBARA MARX HUBBARD, author, speaker,
and president, Foundation for Conscious Evolution

"Paul Ray and Sherry Ruth Anderson eloquently envision that, as the media fog clears, seemingly isolated islands of progressive change prove to be towering peaks of a big mountain chain. This book grounds that vision convincingly, and the world grows more hopeful for it."

KENNY AUSUBEL, author of *When Healing Becomes a Crime*
and *Restoring the Earth* and founder of the Bioneers Conference

"Paul Ray and Sherry Ruth Anderson's research shows that we are not alone in our yearning for a sane, sustainable future and that human creativity can actually shift the course of events. . . . This is a landmark book which deserves to be a landslide success."

VICKI ROBIN, coauthor of *Your Money or Your Life*

"Paul and Sherry give life and character to a great social movement before it has even recognized itself. . . . This is but a stepping stone along the path of human emergence, not the end point, and the authors offer good counsel on how to navigate even further."

CHRIS COWAN, founder of the National Values Center

Introduction

Even though the title of this book says "Complete Idiot's Guide," you are *not* an idiot. Technology can sometimes make all of us *feel* like idiots, but you're not alone. It happens to everyone.

Picking up this book, however, is the first step in understanding Excel—so instead of feeling like an idiot, you'll feel that wonderful sense of accomplishment that comes from learning something new and applying that knowledge to get something done.

The favorite part of my years of teaching Excel in the classroom was seeing the "ah ha!" moment when the lightbulb turned on as the student learned that new concept. Mission accomplished. Brain expanded.

Who This Book Is For

This book is written for the novice to intermediate-level Excel user. If you've never used Excel, that's just fine. Make sure you start with Chapter 1 and don't skip anything. The first couple chapters are designed as a simple walk-through for the beginning Excel user.

Don't forget to watch the video tutorials included on the enclosed CD. These video lessons give you a nice, detailed introduction to Excel, to help you get started.

If you have a little Excel experience under your belt, feel free to skim Part 1 and then get started learning new material in Part 2.

What Is Covered in This Book

This book does not cover everything that Excel can do. I would need a few *thousand* more pages to cover all of that material. Instead, I have tried to include everything you will need to know to effectively and efficiently work with Excel.

Excel can do some pretty incredible things. Unfortunately, most people use only half of what Excel is capable of. It's that half that this book focuses on. You will learn a lot about the important Excel features that people use every day. In fact, there's probably still more material in this book than you may ever need to know. We save the really advanced, nerdy stuff for the next book.

Extras

Sprinkled throughout the book, you'll find sidebars of information that can help you navigate Excel.

> **DEFINITION**
>
> Excel has lots of terms that you might not be familiar with. The Definition sidebars will help you to understand all the spreadsheet lingo.

> **NOTICE**
>
> In case there is more information that you should be aware of regarding a specific topic, a Notice sidebar will point it out for you.

> **TIP**
>
> The Tip sidebars are filled with lots of little useful tidbits of information. Don't skip these!

> **WARNING**
>
> There are many common mistakes that people make when using Excel. The Warning sidebars will help you to avoid these pitfalls.

What Version of Excel You Should Have

This book is written specifically for Microsoft Excel 2010. If you're using Excel 2007, you'll notice some minor differences, but you should still be able to follow 90 percent of the topics in this book. The changes from 2007 to 2010 aren't very drastic, and I've outlined what's new in Appendix A.

If you're using Excel 2003 and earlier, this book is definitely not for you. Microsoft made very extensive changes to the interface in Excel 2007. While the core functionality of Excel is still the same as it has been for years, all the menus were completely redesigned in Excel 2007.

What's on the CD

On the CD that's enclosed with the book, you will find all the sample spreadsheet files that I use in the book. Not every chapter has sample files, but for those chapters that mention a sample sheet, you will find it in the appropriately titled chapter folder.

For beginning students, and at least for the first couple chapters, it's really *to your benefit* to re-create the spreadsheets on your own rather than just loading them off the CD. You have so much to gain from taking the time to *practice* building spreadsheets. I show you how to do everything step by step in the chapter text, so just follow along with me and do everything I do, and you'll be just fine.

Later, when we get into more advanced material, feel free to load up the sample sheets, just so you don't have to sit there typing rows upon rows of bogus sample data.

Also on the CD, you'll find more than 90 minutes of video tutorials on Microsoft Excel. These tutorials are designed for the novice user, to get you started with Excel. Some things are just so much easier to *show* than to explain when writing a book. Pop in the CD, install the tutorials, relax, and enjoy as I show you how to use Excel with these easy-to-follow video lessons.

What You'll Find in This Book

This book is divided into seven parts. Each part covers similarly related topics. Again, if you're a novice user, make sure you read Part 1. Beyond that, I highly recommend you read the chapters in order, as some of the material builds on the topics in previous chapters. However, if you must skip around to find something you need to know *now*, I've done my best to refer back to topics that were covered in earlier chapters.

- **Part 1, The Basics,** is designed for the absolute beginner who is using Excel for the very first time. You get a complete walkthrough of the Excel interface, and you build your first simple spreadsheet.

- **Part 2, Working with Data,** teaches you the fundamental operations you need to work with an Excel spreadsheet. You learn about navigating the Excel interface, working with the Ribbon and different sheet tabs, and understanding the different types of data (text, numbers, dates, and so on). This part also covers basic math calculations; introduces functions and formulas; and offers help with using the Clipboard, sorting, executing find and replace, printing, and working with files (saving and loading).

- **Part 3, Formatting,** is all about making your spreadsheets look professional. You learn about fonts, colors, borders, cell formatting, techniques for manipulating columns, conditional formatting, styles and themes, page layout, and headers and footers.

- **Part 4, Illustrations,** covers just about everything you can insert into one of your spreadsheets. You learn how to work with pictures, ClipArt, shapes, SmartArt, screenshots, text boxes, WordArt, and, of course, charts.

- **Part 5, Formulas and Functions,** is a guide to most of the functions you'll ever need. You learn about relative and absolute references, named cells and ranges, techniques for working with data on other sheets, and formula errors. Complete chapters cover each of the various types of functions that work with text, date and time, logic, lookups, math and statistics, and finance.

- **Part 6, Data Analysis,** teaches you how to organize your data so that it makes more sense. You learn about filtering, organizing your data into tables, and creating PivotTables.

- **Part 7, Miscellaneous,** covers a few topics that didn't fit easily into another part. It covers reviewing your spreadsheets and customizing the Excel interface.

A Note About My Writing Style

You might find that my writing style is a little different from other authors who write computer books. I have a tendency to write like I'm speaking to a classroom. This is from my years of experience in the training room. I personally think that it makes for a more enjoyable book, especially when you're trying to learn something new. I've done my best to make this less of a reference book and more of a step-by-step learning experience. I hope you enjoy it.

Additional Resources

Want to learn more about Excel? Have questions that aren't answered in this book? Visit my website at www.CIGExcel.com for additional resources on Excel, tips and tricks, a user forum, more free video tutorials, and a link to e-mail me your questions.

Acknowledgments

I've been a "lone gunman" for most of the projects I've worked on in the last 20 years, but putting together a project like this book is truly a team effort. My thanks go to Mike Sanders over at Alpha Books for lending his guiding hand. I'd also like to thank Ginny Munroe for her editing genius. Special thanks go out to Bob Diforio for getting me started on this project and offering his years of experience for my benefit.

Special Thanks to the Technical Reviewers

The Complete Idiot's Guide to Microsoft® Excel 2010 2-in-1 was reviewed by experts who double-checked the accuracy of what you'll learn here, to help us ensure that this book gives you everything you need to know about Excel 2010. Special thanks are extended to Robert Deveau and Andrew Knowles.

Trademarks

All terms mentioned in this book that are known to be or are suspected of being trademarks or service marks have been appropriately capitalized. Alpha Books and Penguin Group (USA) Inc. cannot attest to the accuracy of this information. Use of a term in this book should not be regarded as affecting the validity of any trademark or service mark.

The Basics

If you're new to Microsoft Excel, read the chapters in this part carefully—they're designed to give the novice an introduction to using Excel. If this is your first time using Excel, or if you haven't used Excel 2010 or 2007 yet, don't skip this part!

In Chapter 1, you're introduced to the different parts of the Excel interface, including the Ribbon, and you learn the basics of working with spreadsheets: working with rows, columns, and cells.

In Chapter 2, you build your first Excel spreadsheet. You learn the proper way to input data, edit that data, format your cells, save your spreadsheet to disk, load it back up again, and print your worksheet.

This part is the perfect guide to "getting started" with Excel. It covers everything you need to know to build a short, simple spreadsheet in very little time.

Getting Started with Excel

In This Chapter

- Tips for starting Microsoft Excel
- Parts of the Excel interface
- The Ribbon
- Parts of a spreadsheet

In this chapter, you learn how to start Microsoft Excel. You take a quick tour of the Excel interface so you become familiar with all the parts of the screen. You also learn about the big monster group of commands called the Ribbon. Finally, you learn about the parts of a spreadsheet, such as rows, columns, and cells.

Opening and Starting Excel

Let's get started by opening Microsoft Excel and learning about the Excel interface. Whether you're using Windows 7, Vista, or XP, you should be able to find Microsoft Excel by clicking your Windows **Start** button. Click on **Programs** (or All Programs), click **Microsoft Office**, and then find **Microsoft Excel 2010**.

After clicking Microsoft Excel 2010, you will briefly see a small welcome screen, and then Microsoft Excel loads.

The Microsoft Excel Interface

At first glance, Excel looks a little scary. There's a lot of stuff on the screen—buttons, menus, drop-down boxes, commands, and options. Don't be intimidated. Excel is a lot easier to use than it looks at first.

Figure 1.1

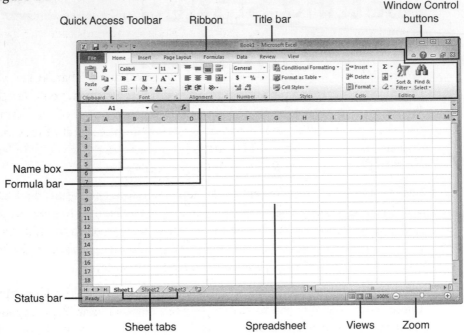

The components of the Excel interface.

Following are the components of the Excel interface shown in Figure 1.1:

- **Title bar:** Across the top of the Excel screen, you'll see the Title bar. Mine says "Book 1—Microsoft Excel."

- **Window Control buttons:** In the upper-right corner of the window, you'll find the Control buttons: Minimize, Maximize, and Close. Minimize enables you to send the Excel window down to the Windows taskbar at the bottom of your screen. Maximize makes Excel fill your entire screen. And, of course, the Close button closes Excel.

  Unlike in Microsoft Word, you'll find two sets of Minimize, Maximize, and Close buttons in Excel. The upper set of buttons is for the entire Excel application, whereas the lower set of buttons controls the spreadsheet itself.

- **Ribbon:** Sprawled across the top of the Excel window is the Ribbon. This is Microsoft's new menu system and was introduced in Office 2007. It replaces the archaic menus from previous versions that were harder to use. The Ribbon makes it much easier to find commonly used commands, and it's dynamic, so it changes based on what you're currently doing in Excel.

- **Quick Access Toolbar:** In the upper-left corner of the window, you'll find the Quick Access Toolbar, which contains commonly used commands. By default, you can see the Save, Undo, and Redo commands. You can easily add your own favorite commands to this toolbar.

- **Formula bar:** Under the Ribbon, you'll find the Formula bar. When you're typing data, a formula, or a function into your spreadsheet, you'll see that the formula also displays in the Formula bar. The purpose of the Formula bar is to enable you to see the formula itself, while the result of that formula displays in the spreadsheet. This may sound confusing, but you'll understand it better after you learn about formulas and cells a little later.

- **Status bar:** Across the bottom of the Excel window, you'll find the Status bar. The Status bar displays Ready when it's ready for you to enter data. As you're entering data, it displays Enter. If you select a bunch of numbers on your spreadsheet, you'll see some interesting information about those numbers, such as their average, count, max, sum, and so on.

- **View buttons:** In the middle of the Status bar, you'll find the View buttons. These buttons enable you to switch between Normal view, Page Layout view, and Page Break Preview mode.

- **Zoom controls:** In the bottom-right corner of the Excel window, you'll find the Zoom controls. These enable you to zoom into or out of your spreadsheet. This is especially handy if you can't read the tiny numbers on your screen.

Ribbon Commands

As mentioned earlier, the Ribbon contains most of Excel's popular commands, which are grouped into different tabs. These tabs further organize commands into groups that make it easy to find exactly what you're looking for.

- The *File tab* contains commands for saving and opening files, printing your sheets, customizing Excel, and more.

- The *Home tab* is where you find most of the commonly used commands, such as commands for changing font, cell alignment, sorting, and so on.

- The *Insert tab* is where to go if you want to insert pictures, charts, or other objects into your spreadsheets.

- The *Page Layout tab* contains all the commands to adjust your page setup, such as margins, page size, and so on.

- The *Formulas tab* has all of Excel's functions neatly organized into a library. You will learn all about functions and formulas in Part 5.

- The *Data tab* contains many handy features for working with data, such as advanced sorting and filtering. It also contains commands for working with data outside of Excel.

- The *Review tab* has proofing features that are common to most Microsoft Office programs, like Spell-Check, Thesaurus, and Research. You'll also find collaboration tools here.

- The *View tab* enables you to change the way your spreadsheet displays on your screen. You can adjust the zoom ratio, arrange windows, and more.

Now, the Ribbon may change in several ways, depending on your screen size and the task you're currently performing in Excel. For example, if you have a small screen or you have Excel in a small window, the Ribbon buttons may look different. Take a look at the difference between Figures 1.1 and 1.2. These figures show the same Ribbon tab, but the buttons look different because of the size of the windows.

Figure 1.2

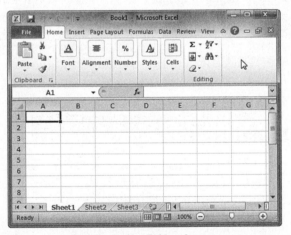

Small window Ribbon buttons.

In addition to changing based on the size of your window, the Ribbon may also change if you're performing different tasks. For example, if you insert a picture by clicking Insert > Picture, the Picture Tools tab displays on the Ribbon (see Figure 1.3). Many other tabs display like this, as you'll see.

Figure 1.3

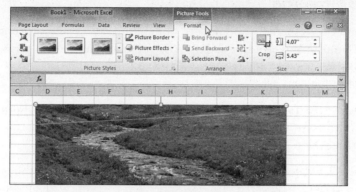

Picture Tools tab.

Each tab on the Ribbon is divided into various groups. For example, the Home tab has groups labeled Clipboard, Font, Alignment, Number, Styles, Cells, and Editing. These groups collect various commands based on their functions. For example, all the commands related to changing fonts (font face, size, bold, color, and so on) are in the Font group.

The Ribbon has lots of different buttons. Don't worry about learning them all at once; we cover them as we go. If you're curious, however, and you want to know what a particular button does, hover your mouse over the button without clicking it—a pop-up message tells you what that button is for. In Figure 1.4, the mouse is over the button to set the fill (background) color of the current cell.

Figure 1.4

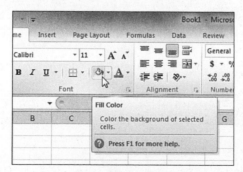

Button Pop-up help.

TIP

Notice in Figure 1.4 that the pop-up tip reads Press F1 for More Help. If you press the F1 key on your keyboard, Excel's Help system displays. We cover Help in more detail later, but just know that Help is always one keystroke away.

Types of Commands

The Ribbon houses many different types of commands. Some commands, such as Bold in the Font group, are simple buttons. You click the button once to turn on the feature, and then you click it again to turn it off.

Other commands might be part of a command button set (see Figure 1.5). For example, the Align Text Left, Center, and Right buttons in the Alignment group are part of a set. You can select only one of those three buttons in the set at a time.

Figure 1.5

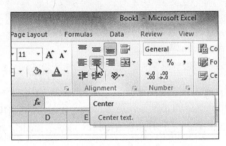

Command button set.

Some of the commands are drop-down menus (see Figure 1.6). For example, to change the size of the font in the current cell, either you click the Font Size drop-down menu and select a value, or you type a value into the box itself.

Figure 1.6

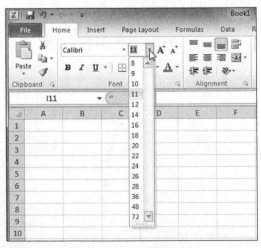

Drop-down menus.

Some of the command buttons also have attached drop-down menus (see Figure 1.7) containing additional options. Notice the down arrow next to the Underline button. If you click that down arrow, you'll see additional underline options display. You can select from a single or double underline.

Figure 1.7

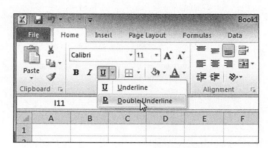

Command buttons with drop-down menus.

Introduced in Excel 2007, some of the commands are grouped into galleries (see Figure 1.8). For example, on the Page Layout tab, you can find a Themes gallery.

Figure 1.8

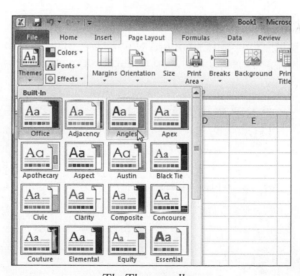

The Themes gallery.

If you look closely, you'll see that some of the groups have little buttons in their bottom-right corner. These are dialog launcher buttons that open dialog box menus with many more commands than you'll find in the Ribbon group. For example, click the dialog launcher button for the Font group (see Figure 1.9).

Figure 1.9

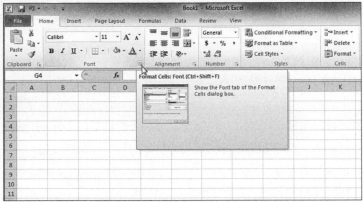

Dialog launcher button in the Font group.

You can see that the Format Cells dialog box has opened to the Font tab. This menu has many more font-formatting options that aren't available on the Ribbon. If you're familiar with older versions of Excel, you might recognize this window (see Figure 1.10).

Figure 1.10

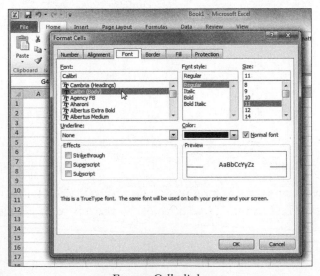

Format Cells dialog.

What Is a Spreadsheet?

The whole purpose of Excel is to enable you to organize and store data in a *spreadsheet*.

> **DEFINITION**
>
> A **spreadsheet** is a grid made up of rows and columns that can contain data; formulas to perform calculations on or manipulate that data; and other types of objects, like pictures.

Rows, Columns, and Cells

Excel organizes a spreadsheet into vertical *columns* lettered A, B, C, and so on. The spreadsheet also has horizontal *rows* that are numbered 1, 2, 3, and so on.

Where a column and a row intersect is a *cell*, and this is referred to by its column and row. For example, Figure 1.11 shows cell B5, where column B and row 5 meet. Your individual bits of data in Excel are stored in cells.

Figure 1.11

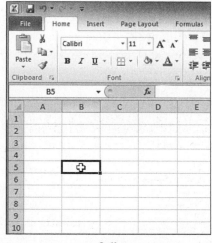

Cells.

You select a cell simply by clicking it with your mouse. You'll find the name of the currently selected cell in the Name box, just to the left of the Formula bar (refer back to Figure 1.1).

Sheet Tabs

When you open Excel, you'll find three different sheet tabs at the bottom of the window (just above the Status bar). That is because Excel stores information in *workbooks* that can consist of one or more *worksheets*. Each "spreadsheet" is considered one worksheet, and these worksheets are gathered into one big workbook. When you save your Excel file, you're actually saving this collection of sheets, called a workbook.

By default, each new workbook file gets three sheets to start. You can add more if you want; you can also delete sheets you don't need. You can rename them, give them colors, and move them. You learn how to do this in Chapter 3.

The Least You Need to Know

- The Excel interface is made up primarily of the main spreadsheet, where you enter your data, and the Ribbon, which contains all the menu items and commands.
- The Ribbon contains many different tabs, groups, and types of commands.
- A spreadsheet consists of rows and columns that intersect in cells. This is where you enter your data and formulas.
- An Excel workbook file can contain multiple worksheets in which you can store data. *Worksheet* is synonymous with *spreadsheet*.

Your First Excel Workbook

In This Chapter

- Typing data for the first time
- Editing your first data
- Doing simple formatting
- Saving, loading, and printing your first workbook
- Using the Excel help system

This chapter is for the first-time Excel user. Here you learn how to enter data into Excel for the first time, edit that data, save your work to a file, load it back up again, and then print your spreadsheet. You also take a quick look at Excel's help system.

Typing Data into a Spreadsheet

Let's get started with a blank Excel workbook. When you open Excel, you should see a plain, empty spreadsheet. Let's begin by entering some sample data, such as a sales summary sheet for a fictional company.

Entering a Column of Data

Before you begin typing, make sure you currently have cell A1 selected. If not, click on cell A1.

TIP

If you don't always want to use the mouse to move around, you can use the arrow keys on your keyboard. Locate the left-, right-, up-, and down-arrow keys—they enable you to move around the cells on your spreadsheet.

Start typing the words **Sales Rep**. Notice that these words display both in cell A1 and in the Formula bar, as shown in Figure 2.1.

Figure 2.1

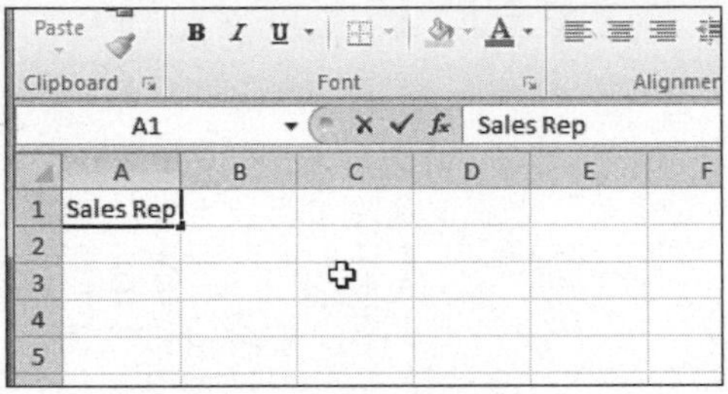

Typing data in a spreadsheet.

When you're finished typing the data for cell A1, press the **Enter** key on your keyboard. This moves the selected cell down to the next row. Now the selected cell is A2.

If you plan to enter data in columns, press Enter to move the selected cell down to the next row after you type the data for each cell. If you plan to enter data across in rows, press the Tab key to move to the right of the cell where you just typed. Just remember: "Enter down, Tab right."

Now let's type the names of the sales reps for the fictional company, pressing **Enter** after each one: Chris, Alex, Jan, and Pat. (See Figure 2.2.)

Figure 2.2

Names of sales reps.

Entering Column Labels

Now that you're done entering sales reps, go to the top of the next column. Click cell B1 or use the arrow keys to move to cell B1.

For this sales summary, the boss wants to see sales data for January through April. So in cell B1, type **Jan** and then press **Tab**. Jan is the label that indicates what data is in the column. Type **Feb**, **Mar**, and **Apr**, as shown in Figure 2.3. Remember to press the Tab key after entering the data in each cell. This will move the selected cell right one column.

Figure 2.3

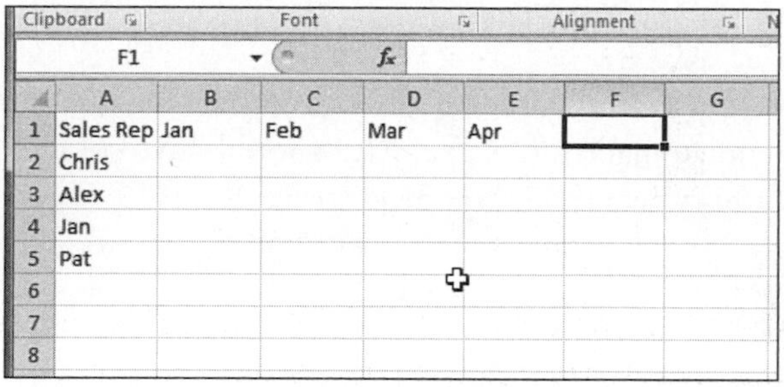

	A	B	C	D	E	F	G
1	Sales Rep	Jan	Feb	Mar	Apr		
2	Chris						
3	Alex						
4	Jan						
5	Pat						
6							
7							
8							

Monthly column labels.

Finishing the Sheet Data

Now type in some sales figures. Use your arrow keys or click to move back to cell B2, and then type some data for each sales rep for each month. The numbers themselves don't really mean anything, but this is great practice for entering real data.

Remember, after you've typed in a column of numbers, you can use either the arrow keys or the mouse to move to the top of the next column. When you're finished, your sheet should look similar to Figure 2.4.

Figure 2.4

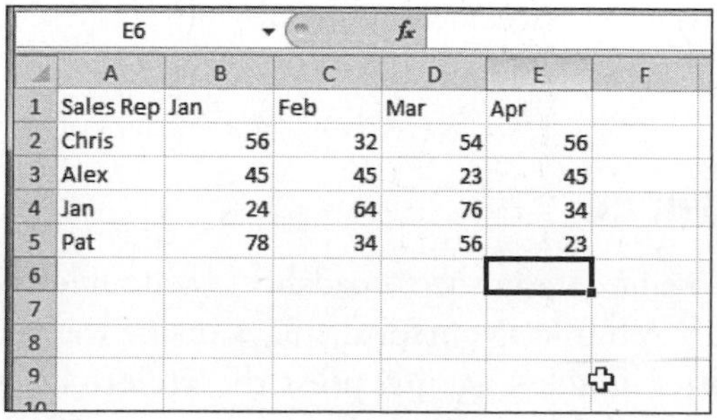

	A	B	C	D	E	F
1	Sales Rep	Jan	Feb	Mar	Apr	
2	Chris	56	32	54	56	
3	Alex	45	45	23	45	
4	Jan	24	64	76	34	
5	Pat	78	34	56	23	
6						
7						
8						
9						

Sales data entered.

Editing Data

Imagine that you've finished entering all the figures for your sales data sheet when you realize that you've made a mistake. Alex should have sold 54 units in February, but you accidentally typed in 45. You need to fix it.

Typing over a Cell

The first—and easiest—method for replacing data in a cell is to simply type over it. In this case, click cell C3 and then type **54** over what's there. The new data that you type replaces the old data. You don't have to delete what's there first.

Editing with the Formula Bar

The next way you can edit data is to click the cell you want to edit and then click the Formula bar. A blinking cursor displays and you can change the data by typing over it, using the Backspace key or the Delete key, if necessary.

Editing a Cell in Place

Finally, you can also edit data in the spreadsheet by double-clicking the cell itself. Double-click cell C3. A blinking cursor displays inside the cell, and you can edit the data. In this case, after double-clicking, press the **Delete** key on your keyboard twice, type **54,** and then press the **Enter** key.

> **TIP**
>
> Here's a quick tip: if you like using the keyboard, you can press the F2 key on your keyboard to edit a cell in place. This is handy if you're moving around with the arrow keys and you don't want to stop to use your mouse to double-click.

Deleting Data and Clearing a Cell

You can delete data (also called *clearing a cell*) from a cell by simply clicking that cell (or moving to it with your arrow keys) and then pressing the Delete key. This effectively clears the data from that cell. Delete **Pat** by clicking cell A5 and then pressing the **Delete** key. Notice that the Pat entry is gone and the cell is empty.

Undoing a Mistake

Now you've realized that you made another mistake. You shouldn't have deleted Pat. You could just type **Pat** in cell A5 again, but there's a quick and easy way to undo your mistake. Take a look at the Quick Access Toolbar at the top of your Excel window. Find the button that looks like a backward-pointing arrow. This is the Undo button, and you can use it to erase your previous actions. If you hold your mouse over it now, it should read Undo Clear (see Figure 2.5), which means that you can undo the previous action (clearing Pat from cell A5) if you click this button.

Figure 2.5

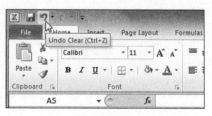

Using Undo.

Click **Undo** and notice that Pat is reinserted into the cell. You can use the Undo button to undo several of your previous mistakes.

Simple Formatting Techniques

Your spreadsheet has all the data you need at this point, but it's not very pretty. Let's take a few minutes to make the sheet look a little more professional.

Aligning Cells

As noted earlier, in Excel, text always lines up on the left side of a cell, whereas numbers and dates always line up on the right. First, let's change the column labels so that the text in them lines up over the data in the cells under them.

Click cell B1 to select the column labeled Jan. On the Ribbon, make sure you're on the Home tab. In the Alignment group, you can see buttons to align the text of a cell to the left, center, or right. Click the **Align Right** button, shown in Figure 2.6. Notice that the label now lines up to the right side of the cell.

Figure 2.6

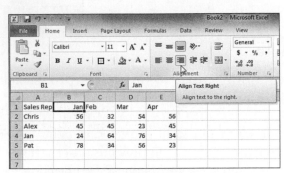

Aligning text right.

Selecting Multiple Cells

You could repeat the steps for cells C1, D1, and E1, but you can also use a shortcut to select all three of those cells and apply the formatting at one time.

Click cell C1, but hold down your mouse button and drag your mouse to the right until all three cells are selected, as shown in Figure 2.7. This is called a *range* of cells.

Figure 2.7

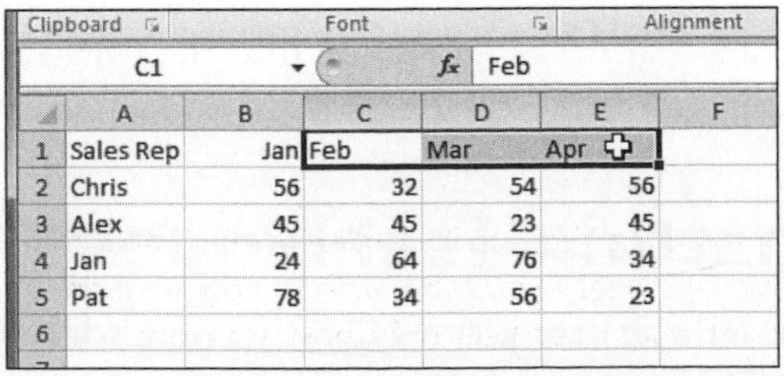

Selecting multiple cells.

Now that all three cells are selected, again click the **Home** tab, click the **Alignment** group, and then click the **Align Right** button. This aligns all three cells at the same time. Your sheet should now look like Figure 2.8.

Figure 2.8

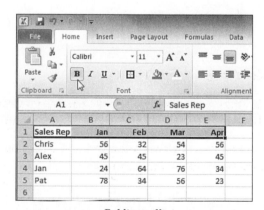

The column labels are aligned.

Applying Bold to Cells

Next, bold all the cells that make up the column header labels. Using your mouse, select cells A1 through E1, and then click **Home > Font > Bold**, as shown in Figure 2.9.

Figure 2.9

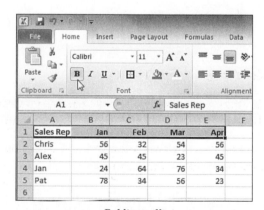

Bolding cells.

TIP

The buttons for Bold, Italics, and Underline in the Font group are known as *toggle* buttons. This means you can switch (or toggle) them on or off. If you decide you don't want these cells to be bold anymore, select the cells and click the Bold button to toggle off that setting.

Save, Load, and Print Your First Workbook

You've done a lot of work in the spreadsheet. It would be a shame if the computer locked up or the power went out and you lost all that work. You need to *save* the workbook file to the hard drive.

Save Your First Workbook

To save your Excel workbook to disk, click the **File** tab and then click the **Save** button, as shown in Figure 2.10.

Figure 2.10

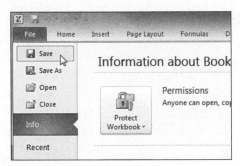

File > Save.

> **TIP**
>
> In addition to the Save command, you can see Save As. This command enables you to specify a different file name for your workbook. Because you haven't saved the workbook yet, the Save As dialog box displays, asking for a file name. After you've initially saved your workbook, clicking Save just saves your work without prompting you for a new file name.

The Save As dialog box displays. By default, Excel tries to save the workbook in your personal Documents folder. In Windows Vista and Windows 7, you can find this in your Users folder, such as:

C:\Users\Richard\Documents

You now have the option to specify a file name for your workbook. By default, Excel tries to save your files as Book1.xlsx, Book2.xlsx, Book3.xlsx, and so on. Notice the *XLSX file extension* at the end of each of these file names. Change the file name to **Chapter 1.xlsx**, as shown in Figure 2.11. Then click the **Save** button.

DEFINITION

Don't worry if you don't see the XLSX after each of your file names. Windows uses **file extensions** to know which program your data file belongs to. Excel 2010 files are generally saved with the XLSX extension. If you don't see this, that's okay—Windows might be hiding it for you. You don't need to type it in.

Figure 2.11

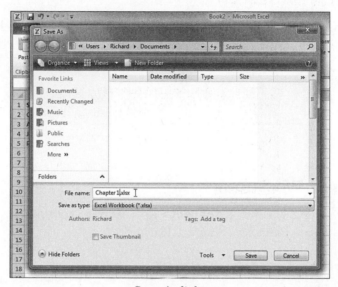

Save As dialog.

Opening a Workbook

Congratulations, you've just saved your first Excel workbook. Now pretend you're going home for the day. You shut down Excel and turn off the computer. The next morning, you want to open your Excel Chapter 1 file. Click **File > Open**.

The File Open dialog box (see Figure 2.12) displays, and you can see all the Excel workbook files that you saved previously. Click the Chapter 1 file, and then click **Open** (or just double-click your file). This is called "opening" or "loading" a file.

Figure 2.12

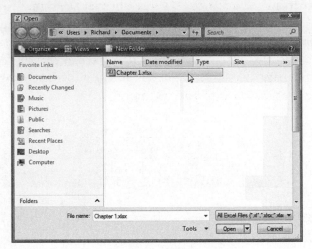

File Open dialog box.

Print Your First Workbook

Now the boss wants a hard copy of your work. To print your masterpiece on your printer, click **File > Print** (see Figure 2.13).

Figure 2.13

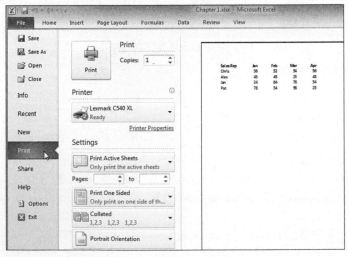

File, Print.

You can see a preview of your printed spreadsheet at the right. To the left of that, you can see options where you can set the number of copies and change which printer you're sending the document to (if you have multiple printers installed on your PC). You can also see other advanced settings where you can change which sheets are printed, collation, page orientation, and so on. Click the big **Print** button (see Figure 2.14) to send your spreadsheet to your printer.

Figure 2.14

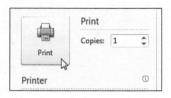

File, Print menu.

Excel's Help System

Finally, if you're in a pinch and you can't figure out what you're looking at on the screen, you can always try to get some help from Excel's Help System. Try looking in this book first (we really do have a nice index), but then try Excel's Help System. Notice the blue circle with a question mark in it in the upper-right corner of most Excel screens. This is the Help button (see Figure 2.15).

Figure 2.15

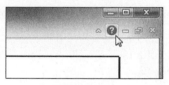

Help button.

TIP

You can also press F1 to access Excel's help.

If you click the Help button, Excel's Help and How-To window displays. Here you can browse and click the help topics, or you can type a keyword into the search box to look for a topic (see Figure 2.16).

Figure 2.16

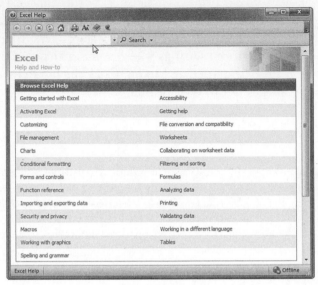

Excel Help.

The Least You Need to Know

- You can enter data into columns in Excel by typing the data into each cell and then pressing Enter after each item.
- You can move around in your sheets using either the mouse or the keyboard arrow keys.
- To edit the contents of a cell, simply double-click the cell; then you can change the data in place.
- Click the **Undo** button to undo your mistakes.
- You can select multiple cells by clicking and dragging with the mouse.
- You can save, open, and print your sheets by clicking the File tab.

Working with Data

Once you've moved beyond the basics, the chapters in this part cover the "nuts and bolts" of working with Excel. We focus on function over format and get down to how Excel really works.

In Chapter 3, you learn more tips for navigating the Excel interface with the keyboard and mouse. We cover some popular keyboard commands and show you how to navigate the Ribbon and work with sheet tabs.

In Chapter 4, we cover the different types of data. You learn the difference between text and numeric data, including currency, decimals, fractions, dates, and times.

Chapter 5 covers calculations and formulas. You explore various math operations, constants, operations with multiple values, and the all-important order of operations.

In Chapter 6, you get an introduction to functions: what they are and what you can use them to do. You also learn about cell ranges. Then we cover five of the most popular functions: SUM, AVERAGE, COUNT, MAX, and MIN. You also learn about the AutoSum and Insert Function buttons.

Chapter 7 is about manipulating data—moving data around. You learn about the Clipboard and how to cut, copy, and paste data. You also learn how to use AutoFill to quickly copy a formula down a column.

Chapter 8 covers organizing data. You learn about sorting data and using the Find & Replace feature.

Chapter 9 covers the new Backstage View, where you can save, load, and print your workbooks.

Navigating the Excel Interface

In This Chapter

- Navigating rows and columns
- Using the mouse
- Using the keyboard
- Working with the Ribbon
- Working with sheet tabs

In Part 1, you learned how to create a simple spreadsheet in Excel. The goal was to get up and running quickly and to see how to set up a simple sheet. Now that you know a little bit about how Excel works, take some time to investigate how to navigate and use Excel.

Column and Row Headers

As discussed earlier, an Excel spreadsheet consists of rows and columns. The columns go across the top of the spreadsheet, starting with A and going to Z. After that, the columns are lettered AA, AB, AC, and so on, up to ZZ. Following ZZ, they're lettered AAA, AAB, and so on. The last column in Excel 2010 is XFD.

Likewise, the spreadsheet rows start at 1 and go to over a million. This is a huge number of potential cells for your spreadsheet. However, if you come anywhere close to using all these cells, you should consider putting your information into a database program, such as Microsoft Access 2010.

Using the Mouse

Because spreadsheets can get very large, it's important to know how to move around in them. Of course, you can click any cell to move to it. The cell you click is the active, or selected, cell.

If you have more data than fits on one screen, you can use the horizontal and vertical scrollbars to move up and down and left and right. To scroll up and down, click on the arrowhead at the top or bottom of the scrollbar. This moves you up or down one row at a time. If you click the box inside the scrollbar, you can drag it up or down to move as far as you want.

TIP

Here's a little trick. Hold down the Shift key and then click and drag the scroll box. This moves up and down several cells at a time. This trick works well when you're working in extremely large spreadsheets.

If you think of the scrollbar as an elevator shaft, with the scroll box as the elevator, you can click inside the shaft above or below the elevator itself to scroll up and down one whole screen at a time.

The horizontal scrollbar works the same as the vertical scrollbar, but it navigates the worksheet left and right instead of up and down.

If your mouse has a scroll wheel, you can use it to scroll up and down. If you press the scroll wheel down as a button, you can drag the mouse in any direction to scroll that direction. In Figure 3.1, you can see how the mouse is used to scroll to the right.

Figure 3.1

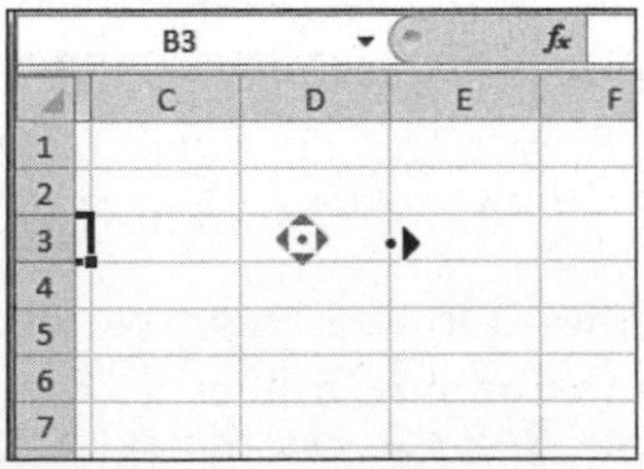

Scrolling with the mouse.

If you hold down the control key (Ctrl) and roll your scroll wheel up, you zoom in on the spreadsheet. Likewise, you scroll down to zoom out.

You can right-click on almost anything in Excel to bring up a shortcut menu. For example, you can right-click on any cell to perform a copy or cut operation, as shown in Figure 3.2.

Figure 3.2

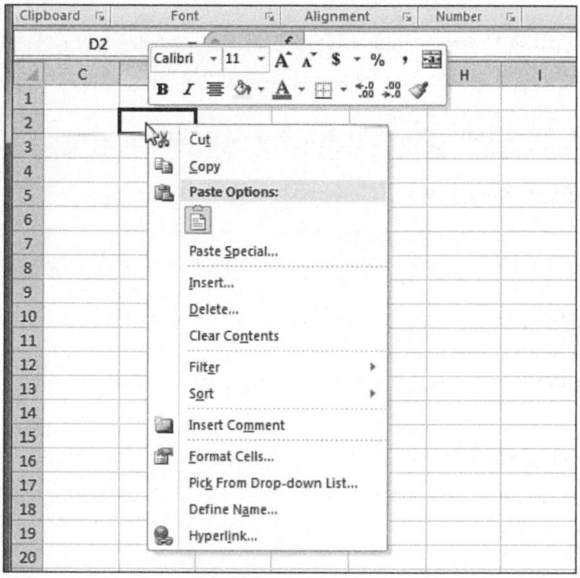

Right-click menu.

You can also right-click on a column header to perform several other actions pertaining to columns. You learn about other shortcut menus in upcoming chapters.

Using the Keyboard

The mouse isn't the only way to move around in Excel. You can do almost everything you need in Excel using just the keyboard. You might not like grabbing the mouse when you're in the middle of entering data—fortunately, different shortcut keys are available.

You already know about the arrow keys. You can use them to move up, down, left, and right in your spreadsheet. You can use the page up (PgUp) and page down (PgDn) keys to move up and down one full screen at a time. If you hold down the Alt key while pressing PgDn, the selected cell moves to the right one full screen. Likewise, Alt+PgUp moves the selected cell to the left one full screen.

The Tab key moves one cell to the right (just like the right-arrow key), and the Enter key moves down one row (just like the down-arrow key).

If you turn on the scroll lock (press the ScrLk key) and use the keyboard to move around your spreadsheet, this keeps the active cell where it is but still lets you view other regions of the spreadsheet. This is great if you just want to take a look at part of your sheet but you don't want to move the selected cell.

Finally, Ctrl+Home moves the selected cell back to the top-left corner of your sheet, which is usually cell A1. Likewise, Ctrl+End makes the active cell the bottom-right corner of the sheet; the exact location depends on how much data is in your sheet.

Table 3.1 summarizes these popular keyboard commands.

Table 3.1 Popular Keyboard Commands

Arrow keys	Up, down, left, right one cell
Tab	Right one cell
Enter	Down one cell
PgUp, PgDn	Up or down one whole screen
Alt+PgUp	Left one whole screen
Alt+PgDn	Right one whole screen
ScrLk+arrow keys	Scroll without changing active cell
Ctrl+Backspace	Locate active cell
Ctrl+Home	Top left of spreadsheet (cell A1)
Ctrl+End	Bottom right of spreadsheet
Ctrl+PgUp/PgDn	Move between sheet tabs

TIP

If you want to return the screen to the active cell, press **Ctrl+Backspace**.

Using the Ribbon

In addition to the standard Ribbon tabs (Home, Insert, Page Layout, and so on), a different, nonstandard tab occasionally displays, depending on what you're doing. For example, if you insert a picture into your spreadsheet, the Picture Tools tab displays.

This is just one of the many *context-sensitive tabs* that pop up from time to time. These tabs (see Figure 3.3) are completely dependent upon what you're doing at that time. In this case, if you click off the picture, the Picture Tools tab disappears. If you click back on the picture, it displays.

Figure 3.3

The Picture Tools tab is a context-sensitive tab.

If you have a smaller screen and you feel that the Ribbon is taking up too much space, you can minimize it by double-clicking any of its tabs. You can also click the Minimize Ribbon (see Figure 3.4) button. Click this button again to restore the Ribbon to normal.

Figure 3.4

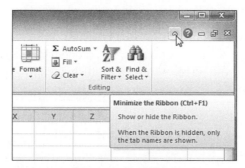

Minimize the Ribbon.

Even though the Ribbon looks like it would be impossible to navigate with the keyboard, it's actually easy. Begin by pressing and releasing the **Alt** key. Notice the little numbers and letters over the Ribbon tabs and the Quick Access Toolbar, shown in Figure 3.5.

Figure 3.5

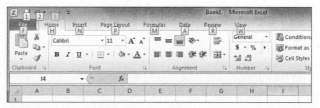

Clicking the Alt key displays numbers and letters on the Ribbon.

Now just press the letter for the tab you want to activate. For example, press **H** to activate the Home tab. You'll see all the different key combinations for the commands on that tab. Press **1** to toggle the Bold setting, or press **AL** to align text left. If you make a mistake, press the escape (**Esc**) key to back up.

You'll find that most of the Ctrl+key shortcuts from older versions of Microsoft Office still work. For example, Ctrl+B, Ctrl+U, and Ctrl+I still make the text bold, underlined, and italic, respectively.

Using Sheet Tabs

Every new workbook in Excel starts with three blank sheets, but you can add more, if you like. You use these different sheets for tracking different types of information in your workbook, such as income on sheet 1 and expenses on sheet 2.

You can also track the same type of information on each sheet but use different sheets for different time periods. For example, you could store all your 2010 sales in one workbook but assign a different month to each sheet. However you decide to lay out your workbook is up to you. Excel is flexible.

The first thing you might want to do is give your sheet tabs meaningful names. For example, if you assign months for each of the sheet tabs, you might want them to read January, February, March, and so on. To rename a sheet tab, double-click it and then type the new name. Press **Enter** when you're finished.

> **TIP**
>
> As with everything in Excel, you have multiple ways to rename a sheet tab. You can also right-click the sheet tab and select Rename.

If you want to add another sheet to your workbook, click the **Insert Worksheet** button, or right-click any sheet tab and select **Insert > Worksheet** (see Figure 3.6).

Figure 3.6

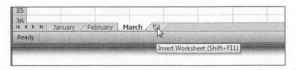

Insert Worksheet.

If you want to move a sheet, just click and drag it wherever you want. For example, if the current month is April and you want to move that sheet to the start of your workbook for easy access, just click and drag the sheet tab to position it in front of January. You'll see a little arrow moving as you drag the sheet tab. (See Figure 3.7.)

Figure 3.7

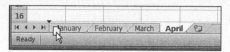

Moving a sheet tab.

When you release the mouse button, the sheet tab moves to its new location.

If you decide that you no longer want a particular sheet, you can delete it. Simply right-click the sheet tab and select **Delete**. Be careful, however—you cannot undo a sheet tab deletion. Make sure you save your work first.

If you want to create a copy of a sheet, right-click the sheet tab and select **Move or Copy**.

The Move or Copy dialog box displays (see Figure 3.8). Make sure you check the box labeled **Create a Copy**. You can optionally choose to move or copy the sheet to a different workbook, or select which sheet you want to place this sheet before. Click **OK** when you're finished.

Figure 3.8

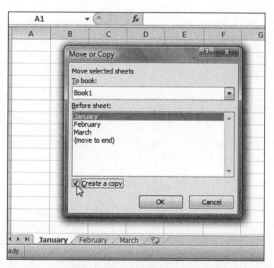

Move or Copy dialog box.

Now you have a copy of the original sheet, with all its data. (See Figure 3.9.)

Figure 3.9

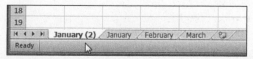

Copy of sheet.

Finally you can change the color of a sheet tab by right-clicking it, selecting **Tab Color,** and then clicking a color. (See Figure 3.10.)

Figure 3.10

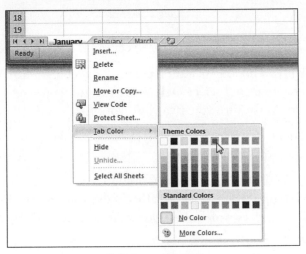

Coloring a sheet tab.

You can see how easy it is to locate the sheet you want by giving each of your sheets a different color.

The Least You Need to Know

- Excel supports more rows and columns than you should ever need for your spreadsheets.
- Many different techniques exist for navigating Excel with both the keyboard and the mouse.
- It's easy to navigate the Ribbon using the keyboard. Begin by pressing the **Alt** key and then follow the numbers and letters that pop up.
- You can rename, delete, move, and copy sheet tabs, and even create new tabs of your own.

Types of Data

In This Chapter

- Text
- Numeric data
- Currency
- Decimals, fractions, and percentages
- Dates and times

In Excel, you can put three types of data into your cells: text, numeric data, and formulas. We look at formulas in more detail in later chapters. This chapter focuses on what you can do with text and the different types of numeric data, such as numbers, fractions, currency, dates, and times.

The Characteristics of Text

The easiest type of data that you can input into a cell is text. Any time you enter data that isn't recognized as another specific data type (such as a date or fraction), Excel treats it as text. Text cells essentially have a value of zero (0) for the purposes of any calculations. Text is always aligned to the left side of the cell.

In Figure 4.1, you see a column of simple text data that represents a list of first names. Notice how the value in cell A1, which is the column label First Name, seems as though it spills over into cell B1. The entire text value is actually stored in A1. This effect is only apparent.

You can widen column A so that it neatly fits all your data. Move your mouse over that border between the column headers A and B. Your mouse changes into a double arrow (see Figure 4.1).

Figure 4.1

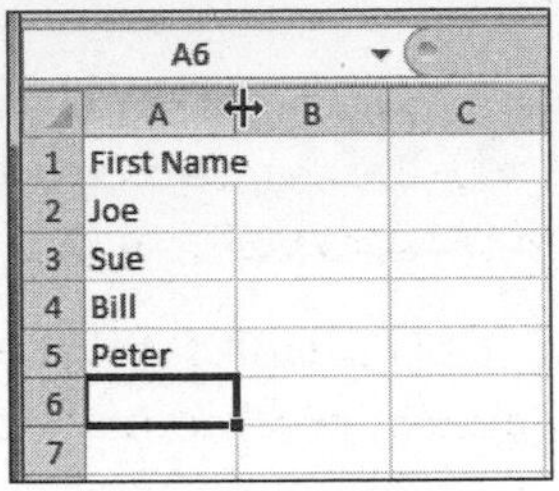

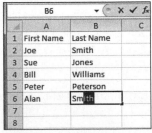

Widening a column.

Now click and drag to the right; this widens column A. Release the mouse when you're happy with the width.

TIP

As with everything in Excel, you can widen a column in different ways. Another method is to double-click that same spot between the two column headers. Excel automatically widens the column to perfectly fit the data. You can also right-click directly on the column A header and select Column Width to manually enter a width.

AutoComplete

Excel has a neat feature called *AutoComplete.* When you're typing data that begins the same as some other data that's already in that column, Excel tries to finish the data entry for you (see Figure 4.2).

Figure 4.2

AutoComplete attempts to complete the entry you're typing.

For example, if you start typing Sm into cell B6, Excel sees the name Smith above, in cell B2, so it tries to AutoComplete that word for you. This is to save time typing. If you like what Excel is suggesting, press Enter at any time, and the rest of the cell is finished for you. If not, press Delete or keep typing.

When to Separate Data

Anytime you have both a number and text that need to be stored together, such as the address 101 Main Street, that value is stored as a text value. This is generally fine for most applications where you store something like a street address.

Exceptions do exist, of course. For example, if you ever think you're going to need to perform calculations on the numeric portion of your data, you should separate it into two cells. You're probably never going to need to add the number values in a street address. However, if you do a lot of mass mailing and you want to sort your customers based on ZIP code, then their street name, and then the number of their house in the street, you might want to consider breaking those into separate cells.

Remember, it's always easier to put the data together later (a process called *concatenation*) than it is to separate it. It's easy to add two text values, such as 101 and Main Street to create 101 Main Street. It's much harder to split 101 Main Street into two cells after you've already created the entries in one cell.

Forcing Specific Formats on Cells

Sometimes you're entering values that Excel might view as numbers but that you really want to be text. The perfect example is a ZIP code or postal code, as in Figure 4.3.

Of course, some countries use letters in their postal codes (like Canada or the United Kingdom). Even within the United States, however, you might want to store your ZIP codes as text so that you can have the ZIP+4 code stored with it.

Figure 4.3

List of postal codes.

NOTICE

If you do a lot of mailing, you might also want to separate the ZIP code and the +4 extension into two cells. Again, it's always easier to combine them later than to try and split them.

Notice that the ZIP code in cell G2 was treated as a number and is aligned to the right side of the cell. G3 is treated as text because it includes letters and spaces. G4 is treated as text because of the hyphen.

Take a look at the Ribbon. On the Home tab, in the Number group, notice the drop-down box with General in it. By default, Excel assigns all the cells in a spreadsheet the General format. This means that Excel will do its best to guess what kind of data you're entering. It's usually pretty good, too. However, sometimes you want to force a specific format on a cell.

If you want to force the data in a specific cell to be formatted a specific way, just click the cell, open the Format drop-down box, and pick a specific format.

For example, format cell G2 as text. Click G2, click the **Format** drop-down box, and then select **Text** from the list of options.

G2 is formatted as text, and the cell is now aligned to the left. Keep in mind that the *value* of the cell hasn't changed; you've just chosen to *format* it as a text value rather than a number.

Leading Zeros

Sometimes Excel treats a text value as a number and then "chops off" the leading zero. For example, one of the ZIP codes of Portland, Maine, is 04100. If you type that into Excel, it gets treated as a number and is converted to 4100.

You can fix this by formatting the entire column as text. Just click the column header G to select the entire column, as shown in Figure 4.4. Notice that your mouse pointer turns into a downward-pointing arrow.

Figure 4.4

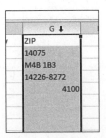

Selecting a column.

Now use the Format drop-down box to change the format of the entire column to Text, as you just did for a single cell. After you change the format, type that leading zero to add it to the entry where Excel deleted it.

TIP

If you know in advance that you're going to be typing in a value that looks like a number, but you want to force Excel to treat it as text, you can type a single quote before the number, like this:

'01400

Excel then treats the value as text, and you won't lose your leading zero.

Ignoring an Error Message

When you store numbers as text, Excel doesn't like it and throws up an error message. This appears as a green triangle in the upper-left corner of the cell (see Figure 4.5).

Figure 4.5

14226-8272
04100

The triangle represents an error.

If you click the cell, you'll see a yellow warning sign display (see Figure 4.6). Click it to see a menu of options. For now, just select **Ignore Error** to make the green triangle disappear.

Figure 4.6

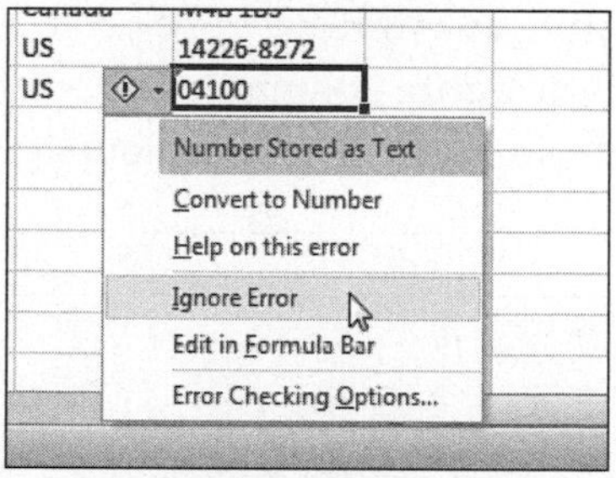

| US | 14226-8272 |
| US | 04100 |

Number Stored as Text

Convert to Number

Help on this error

Ignore Error

Edit in Formula Bar

Error Checking Options...

Ignoring an error message.

Characteristics of Numeric Data

Excel wouldn't be a spreadsheet if you couldn't work with numbers. Numeric data consists of everything that's not text or a formula. It includes dates, times, currency, fractions, percentages, and more. Numeric data is always right-aligned in a cell. Of course, you can change alignment by clicking the Align Left button.

Numbers can be simple integers: 0, 1, 2, 3, and so on. You can have negative values: –1, –2, –3, and so on. You can store decimal point values, such as 50.45. A good example of using numbers is storing a customer's balance.

Currency

You could use just plain numbers to represent each customer's balance, but Excel has a built-in format called Currency that is specifically designed for dollar amounts. Select all of column H by clicking the column header. Then on the Home tab, in the Number group, find the **Number Format** drop-down list. Pick **Currency** from the list of available formats.

You can see that all the numbers have been formatted as dollar values. Each has a dollar sign in front of it and has two decimal places, the default for the Currency format. (See Figure 4.7.)

Figure 4.7

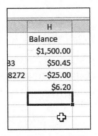

Reformatted values.

If you want to right-align the entire column, click cell H1 (or the column H header) and then click **Align Right** in the Alignment group. (See Figure 4.8.)

Figure 4.8

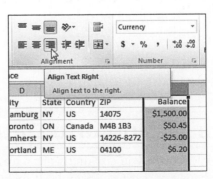

Align Right.

TIP

Another, similar format type is called Accounting. Selecting Accounting makes the dollar signs line up at the left side of the cell and the number portion line up to the right. In addition, negative values show up enclosed in parentheses.

Notice that if you start typing a cell value and begin it with a dollar sign ($), as long as the rest of your cell includes only numbers (and an optional decimal point), Excel automatically changes the format of that cell from General to Currency.

NOTICE

If you like to have Excel automatically treat all numbers that you enter as dollars and cents, you can turn on the option Fixed Decimal Points. Go to **File**, **Options**, **Advanced**. Under Editing Options is **Automatically Insert a Decimal Point**. Set it to two places. Now whenever you type in **100**, you'll get 1.00, and **25** becomes 0.25. This is handy for people who deal with money.

Decimals, Fractions, and Percentages

If you enter a fractional value without a leading zero, such as .5, Excel automatically gives you a zero. If you try entering a value such as 1/2 to represent one-half, Excel converts that to a date, and you'll see 2-Jan.

This is the way Excel treats values entered as digit-slash-digit. If you want to have 1/2 shown as a fraction in a cell, you need to type **0 1/2**.

Notice that the cell displays 1/2, but you can see the true value of the cell in the Formula bar as 0.5. Excel always stores decimal values internally, regardless of what's displayed in the cell itself. If you want to store three-and-one-half and display it as a mixed fraction, you type in **3 1/2**—you then see 3.5 in the Formula bar. (See Figure 4.9.)

Figure 4.9

	Alignment	⌐	Number	⌐	
ƒx	3.5				
G	H		I		J
		Balance	Bathrooms		
5	$1,500.00		0.5		
1B3	$50.45		1/2		
6-8272	-$25.00		⊹ 3 1/2		
0	$6.20		2		

Mixed fraction.

If you want to display a percentage, just type the percent sign (%) after the number. For example, to show 50%, type **50%** into a cell.

Although Excel displays 50% in the cell and the Formula bar, keep in mind that Excel stores percentages internally as fractions of 1. This means that 50% is actually stored as 0.5 in the cell. This becomes important later when you start performing math calculations.

If you type a value such as 25 and then decide you want to show that value as a percentage, you can click on the **Number Format** drop-down menu and pick **Percent**. However, in this case, Excel shows 2500%. Again, this is because Excel considers 1 to be 100%; 25% is actually 0.25.

Again, if you want to format an entire column of numbers as percentages, select the entire column and then click the **Percent** format from the drop-down box.

If you don't want to show those two decimal places for all your percentages, select the column again and click the **Decrease Decimal** button twice. You can find the Increase and Decrease decimal buttons in the Home > Number group. (See Figure 4.10.)

Figure 4.10

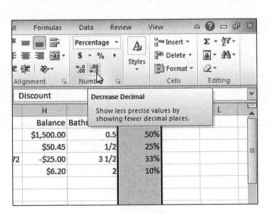

Decrease Decimal button.

Dates and Times

Excel treats date and time values as numbers. This makes it easy to perform calculations on them (such as knowing the number of days between two dates), as you learn later.

All of the following are valid date formats. This list is not exclusive, but these are the popular formats:

- January 1, 2011
- jan 1, 11
- 1/1/11

- 1-1-11
- 1-jan-11
- 1JAN11

- 1/1
- JAN1

Be aware of a few cautions when working with dates. First, if you don't type in a year, Excel assumes that you mean the current year. So if you type just **1/1**, Excel converts that to 1/1/2011 internally and shows 1-Jan in the cell.

If you want to abbreviate a month, always use the three-character standard abbreviation. In this way, jan becomes January, and aug becomes August. Excel dates are not case sensitive, so JAN and jan are essentially the same thing.

If you type in a two-digit year between 00 and 29, Excel converts that to 2000 to 2029. Likewise, if you type in 30 through 99, Excel converts those dates to 1930 through 1999. If you want to override this default setting, make sure you type in four digits for your year.

TIP

You can change the cutoff date for entering two-digit years in Windows. For example, in Windows Vista, click **Start**, **Control Panel**, **Clock Language and Region**, **Change the Date Time or Number Format**, **Date Tab**. In the Calendar section, you'll see where you can change the year range.

Some of the more popular time formats include these:

- 10 am
- 10:05:25 pm

- 10 p
- 18:00

You can specify hours, minutes, and seconds. If you don't specify AM or PM, Excel assumes that you mean A.M. You can type in **10 p** to represent 10 P.M., but keep in mind that you need to have that space in there. Military time (or 24-hour time) is also acceptable.

Most important, you should know that a single cell can store both a date *and* a time. For example, if you want to track when an employee clocked in for work, these are all valid date/time values:

- 1/2 10 am
- 1-Jan 16:00
- 5/1/11 9:00 pm

You can mix and match the way you type in dates and times, and Excel is pretty good at figuring out what you're trying to do. You can use the Format drop-down to pick some of the popular date and time formatting options, such as Short Date (11/5/2011), Long Date (November 5, 2011), or Time (10:05:00 A.M.) if you need to.

Here's one issue that comes up often. Imagine that you type a date in one format, such as 1/1, and it's converted to 1-Jan, which is stored as 1/1/2011. You realize that you wanted this to be 1/1/2009, so you type **1/1/2009** into the field, but Excel still displays 1-Jan.

This is because Excel has already made up its mind on the date format for this cell, and it's going to continue displaying DD-MMM until you change it manually. You can do this using the Format drop-down menu and picking the short date. Remember, you can force Excel to show the years by making sure you type in your dates in the MM/DD/YY format.

The Least You Need to Know

- Any data that Excel doesn't recognize as a specific format is treated as text.
- You use Excel to work with numbers, currency, decimals, fractions, percentages, dates, and times.
- A single cell can store both a date and a time, or either value separately.

Calculations and Formulas

In This Chapter

- Math operations
- Constants
- Tips on working with multiple values
- Order of operations

Microsoft Excel is great for storing information, but its real purpose is to perform calculations and analyze data. In this chapter, you see how Excel performs basic math calculations and you create your first formulas.

How Math Works in Excel

Open Excel to a blank workbook or move to a blank sheet in your current workbook. In cell A1, type the number **10**; and in cell A2, type the number **5**. Now you'll add these two cells together. A *calculation* in Excel is just like the math equations you learned in grammar school, only backward, with the equals sign in front. In traditional algebra, for an addition equation, you would write:

$$X + Y = Z$$

You could flip that around and write:

$$Z = X + Y$$

In Excel, you write calculations, or *formulas*, almost the same way, except that you start with the equals sign and you use the cell names to indicate what you want to add together. For example, to add cells A1 and A2, you put this in cell A3:

$$= A1 + A2$$

You don't need to specify the A3 anywhere in this formula because that's the cell you're placing the value in. Excel adds up the values of whatever is in cells A1 and A2 and places that number in the current cell, A3. (See Figure 5.1.)

Figure 5.1

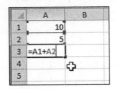

Adding two cells.

As you're typing formulas, you'll notice that Excel colors the different cells you're referencing, along with their cell names in your formula. This makes it easier to see what you're doing so that you don't accidentally type the wrong cell name.

> **WARNING**
>
> Make sure you begin your formula with the equals sign. Every formula in Excel, from the simplest to the most complex, *must* begin with an equals sign.

When you're finished typing the formula, press **Enter** to see the result of the calculation in cell A3. In this case, you see the number 15. Note also that if you click once on cell A3, you still see the result in the cell, but you see the formula you just typed in the Formula bar above the column headers.

One of the nice things about working with Excel is that it automatically recalculates your formulas if the data changes. For example, if you change cell A1 to 12, your answer in A3 is automatically updated to 17. (See Figure 5.2.)

Figure 5.2

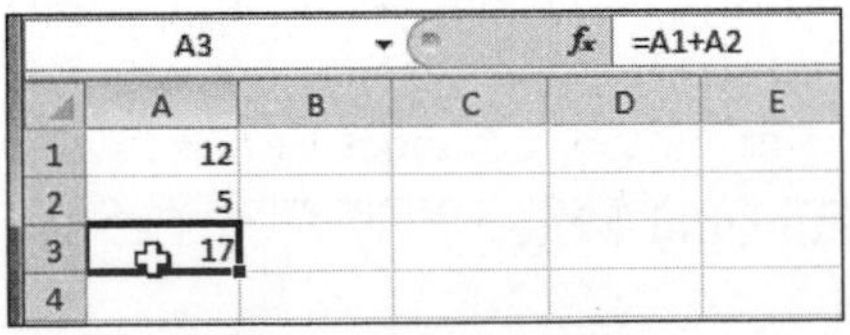

Automatic recalculation.

Assume that you want to subtract the same two numbers. If you decide that you want to switch from addition to subtraction, just edit the formula in the Formula bar. Click cell A3 to select it. Then click in the Formula bar right in front of the plus sign. Press **Delete** to get rid of the plus sign, and replace it with a minus sign. (See Figure 5.3.)

Figure 5.3

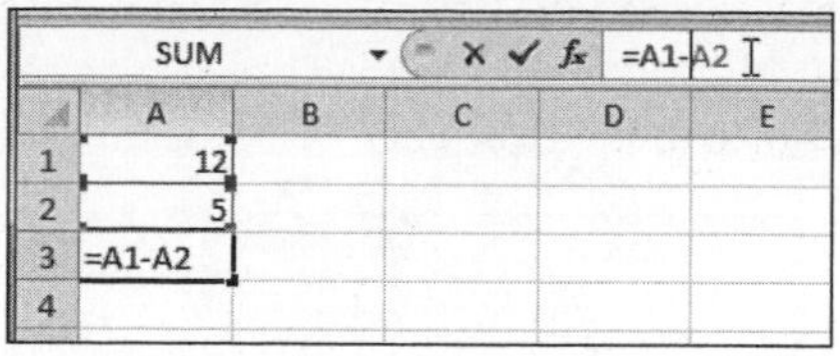

Change to subtraction.

When you press Enter, you now have a subtraction formula instead of an addition formula, and the result of 12 minus 5 is 7. Table 5.1 shows all the basic math operators for addition, subtraction, division, multiplication, and exponentiation (raising a number to a power).

Table 5.1 Basic Math Operators

+	Addition
–	Subtraction
*	Multiplication
/	Division
^	Exponentiation

Constant Values

In addition to using cell references like A1 or B3 in your formulas, you can also use numbers called *constants*. With constants, the values don't change. For example, if you want to multiply the result in A3 by 5, you can put this in cell A4 (see Figure 5.4):

$$= A3 * 5$$

DEFINITION

A **constant** is a value that never changes, such as the number 5. You can use either cell references like "A3" or constant values in your formulas.

Figure 5.4

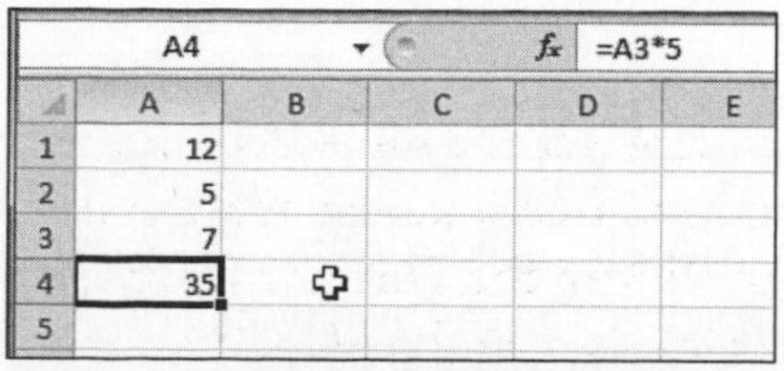

Multiplication.

If you then want to divide that result by 2, put this in cell A5 (see Figure 5.5):

= A4 / 2

Figure 5.5

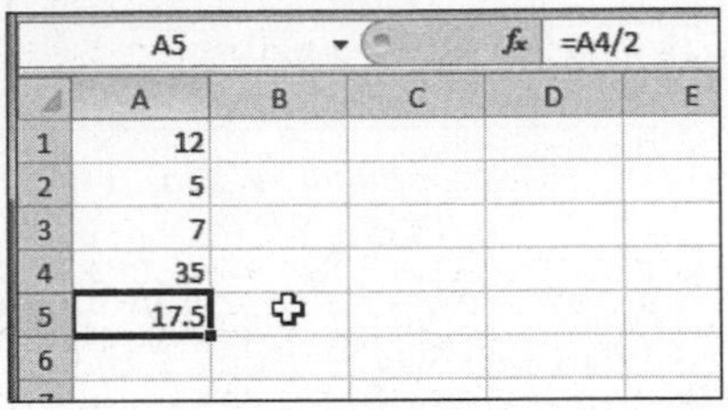

	A	B	C	D	E
1	12				
2	5				
3	7				
4	35				
5	17.5				
6					

A5   *fx* =A4/2

Division.

To raise that number to the third power (the same as saying A5 * A5 * A5) you can use this formula (see Figure 5.6):

= A5 ^ 3

Figure 5.6

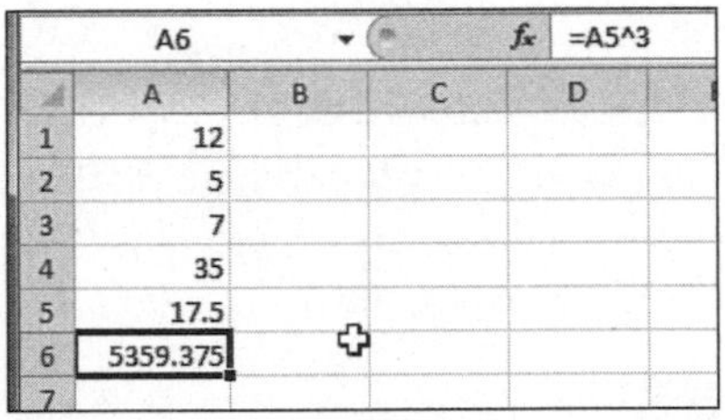

	A	B	C	D	
1	12				
2	5				
3	7				
4	35				
5	17.5				
6	5359.375				

A6   *fx* =A5^3

Exponentiation.

Multiple Values

Now take a look at another example with some basic math calculations. First clear the data out of column A. You can do this by moving your mouse over the column header so that it becomes a downward-pointing arrow. Click to select the column cells, and then press **Delete**.

Now type five test grades for a student. Type **90, 85, 80, 75,** and **73** into column A. To add these five values, you can put the following formula into cell A6:

= A1 + A2 + A3 + A4 + A5

TIP

If you don't want to type the whole formula, you can use a shortcut with the mouse. Type in the equals sign and then click cell A1. Notice that A1 is placed in your formula. Now press the plus key and then click cell A2. Continue doing this until your formula is complete; then press **Enter**.

The correct sum is 403. However, when dealing with test grades, you generally don't want to add them. Instead, you want to find their average. So how do you find an average? To find an average, you add a bunch of numbers and then divide by the total number of values. In this case, you've already added the numbers. You should be able to divide by 5 to get the average. Here's what you might think is the formula:

= A1 + A2 + A3 + A4 + A5 / 5

However, if you go with this formula, the answer is 344.6, which is not correct. What went wrong? If you think back to your high school algebra days, you need to follow a certain rule when performing calculations. It's called the *order of operations*, and it's discussed next.

Order of Operations

The order of operations states that multiplication and division go before addition and subtraction. So in this case, following the order of operations, Excel divided A5 by 5 and then added the rest of the values.

I cover the Order of Operations in more detail in video lesson 10 that you'll find on the CD that came with the book. In a nutshell, Excel will perform calculations inside of parentheses first, then perform exponentiation, followed by multiplication, division, addition, and subtraction in that order of preference.

Table 5.2   Order of Operations

( )	Parentheses (innermost first)
^	Exponentiation
* /	Multiplication and division
+ -	Addition and subtraction

To get around this, you have to use *parentheses* in the formula to indicate any math operations that have to go first. In this case, the formula should be:

= (A1 + A2 + A3 + A4 + A5) / 5

As you can see from Figure 5.7, this formula gives you the correct average for the numbers.

Figure 5.7

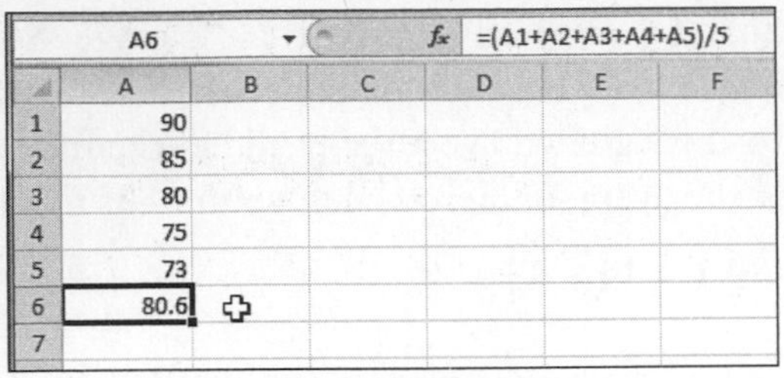

A6				f_x	=(A1+A2+A3+A4+A5)/5	
	A	B	C	D	E	F
1	90					
2	85					
3	80					
4	75					
5	73					
6	80.6					
7						

Using parentheses.

If you have the formula =9+5*2, you get a value of 19 because Excel multiplies 5*2 first and then adds 9. That is a completely different formula than =(9+5)*2, which gives you the result of 28.

You can have multiple, nested parentheses, too. For example, if you have ((9+5)/10)+6 then the 9+5 is evaluated first. That result is then divided by 10. Finally, the result is added to 6. If you select a block of cells, such as A1 to A5, you'll see that Excel gives you a quick glance at some of their statistics, including average, count, and sum on the Status bar.

The Least You Need to Know

- You can use Excel to perform basic math operations such as addition, subtraction, and multiplication.

- You can work with cell names or constant values such as numbers in your formulas.

- Be sure to remember the order of operations when creating your formulas. Multiplication and division are evaluated before addition and subtraction.

Chapter

6

Introduction to Functions

In This Chapter

- What is a function?
- Cell ranges
- SUM, AVERAGE, COUNT, MAX, and MIN functions
- AutoSum and Insert Function buttons

In Chapter 5, you learned how to create basic math calculations and formulas in Excel. In this chapter, you learn how to create functions that are much more powerful tools when working with data.

Performing Calculations Versus Functions

In Chapter 5, you learned how to calculate the average of a column of numbers by adding all the values and then dividing by the total number of items. Although this method works, a much easier way is to use a function.

You need to learn how to walk before you learn how to run, which is why you first learned the hard way to average numbers. Doing so shows you how to actually perform calculations and gives you a better appreciation for how functions work.

So what is a function? A *function* in Microsoft Excel is a special component that performs a specific task. That task might add a bunch of numbers, calculate a mortgage payment, or even tell you the current date. Functions are used to simplify complex or repetitive tasks.

NOTICE

You can think of a function as a little box. You dump in a bunch of values and shake the box, and then out pops a result. For example, the SUM function that you'll soon learn about adds a bunch of numbers for you.

Functions come in lots of different shapes and sizes. In this chapter, you learn a few of the more popular functions. Several other chapters cover the more advanced functions.

Why use functions? You saw that one way to add a column of numbers is to type in each cell, one at a time, separated by plus signs:

$$= A1 + A2 + A3 + A4$$

This works fine if you have 2, 3, or even 10 items to add. What if the column has 500 items? This method isn't very practical with that many numbers to add. That's when you want to use a function.

Using Cell Ranges in Function Calculations

To use most functions, however, you have to understand what a cell range is. In the previous example, if you're going to add 500 values, it's easiest to tell Excel to add everything from cell A1 down to A500. That specifies a range of cells you want to add.

In Excel, a *cell range* is a block of cells that can extend horizontally or vertically. You specify the range using its upper-left corner and its lower-right corner, separated by a colon. For example, Figure 6.1 shows the range A1:B6.

Figure 6.1

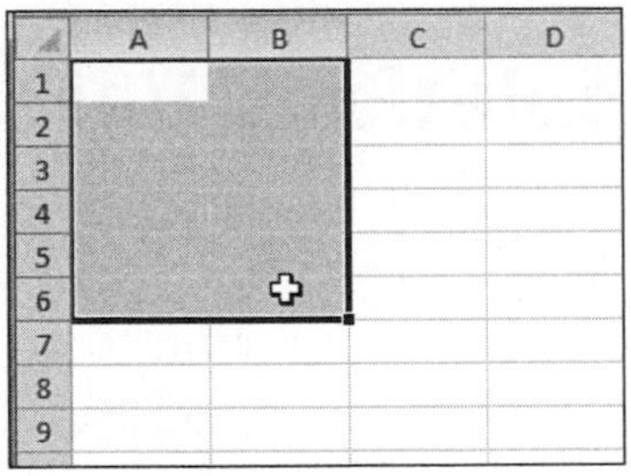

Range A1:B6.

Figure 6.2 shows the range B3:F3.

Figure 6.2

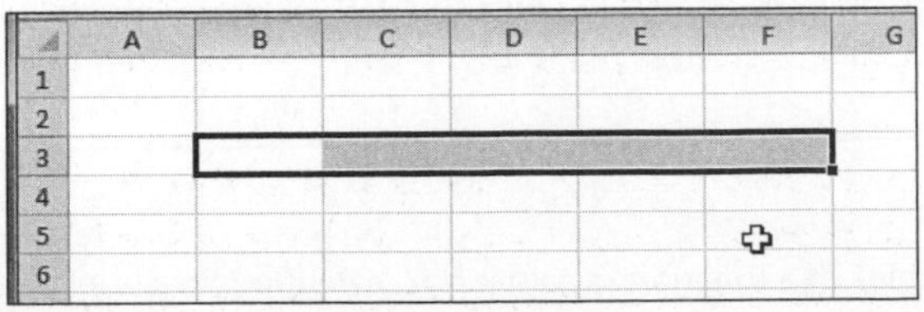

Range B3:F3.

You can reference an entire column as a range, such as B:B for column B. You can also reference an entire row, such as 5:5 for row 5.

SUM and AVERAGE Functions

Now that you know what functions are, why you want to use them, and what a cell range is, you can set up your first function. Start with a small sheet similar to the example in Chapter 5. Type four test scores into column A. In cell A5, type the following formula:

    =SUM(A1:A4)

Notice that you have to start with the equals sign. Remember, it's important that every formula or function begin with the equals sign. Type the name of your function (in this case, SUM), followed by an open parenthesis, your cell range, and then a close parenthesis (see Figure 6.3).

Figure 6.3

	SUM	▼	× ✓ *fx*	=SUM(A1:A4)	
	A	B	C	D	E
1	80				
2	65				
3	72				
4	89				
5	=SUM(A1:A4)				
6					

The SUM function.

Now press **Enter**. You should see the sum of all four of the values in cell A5.

TIP

Here's a shortcut you can use to avoid typing the cell range in your SUM formula. Start your function by typing this:

    =SUM(

After the open parenthesis, use your mouse to click and drag out the range. Excel automatically fills in the range for you. When you're done, press **Enter**. Excel automatically closes your parentheses, too. See how easy it is?

Now, the SUM function is great for adding test grades or other things. However, what if you want to average the test scores without doing it manually in a calculation? Click cell A5. You'll see the complete formula in the Formula bar. Highlight the word

SUM using the mouse and replace it with the word **AVERAGE**. Yes, you have to spell out the whole word; you cannot abbreviate it as AVE or AVG. (See Figure 6.4.)

Figure 6.4

SUM	▼	✕ ✓ ƒx	=AVERAGE(A1:A4)

	A	B	C	D	AVERAGE(number Returns the average
1	80				ƒx AVERAGE
2	65				ƒx AVERAGEA
3	72				ƒx AVERAGEIF
4	89				ƒx AVERAGEIFS
5	/ERAGE(A!				
6					

The AVERAGE function.

When you press Enter, you can see the average of these four test grades. Notice that the average function takes into consideration how many values are in your range. If you clear a cell, for example, it does not count as a zero. If you want to give the student a zero for a test grade, you need to manually type that 0 into the cell. If you delete the value from a cell, it will not be counted in the average. Only cells with actual values in them are averaged together.

NOTICE

You might have noticed when typing the words SUM or AVERAGE that a little drop-down box displays with other function names in it, like SUMIF, SUMIFS, AVERAGEIF, and so on. Excel tries to help by showing you function names that are similar to the one you're entering. If you want one of those other functions, click it. You learn more about these functions in later chapters.

You don't have to just SUM or AVERAGE a single column or row. Let's say that you have four test scores from three students, and you want to find the average of all those scores. You can use the AVERAGE function on all of them, as shown in Figure 6.5.

Figure 6.5

C5	▼	ƒx	=AVERAGE(A1:C4)

	A	B	C	D	E	F
1	80	87	67			
2	65	76	87			
3	54	56	76			
4	89	45	56			
5			69.83333			
6						

AVERAGE for a large range of cells.

COUNT, MAX, and MIN Functions

The other three functions that you will use on a regular basis are COUNT, MAX, and MIN. They're pretty self-explanatory. COUNT counts the number of numeric values in a range. It does not count text values (for that, you have to use COUNT's cousin, COUNTA, which you learn about later). MAX and MIN tell you the largest and smallest numeric value in a range, respectively.

These three functions work the same as SUM and AVERAGE. Just type =COUNT(A1:A4) in a cell, and you get the count of that range.

Figure 6.6 shows all five popular functions used in one sheet. I'll save this file as Book6.1. You will find it on the CD that came with the book, if you'd like to look at it.

Figure 6.6

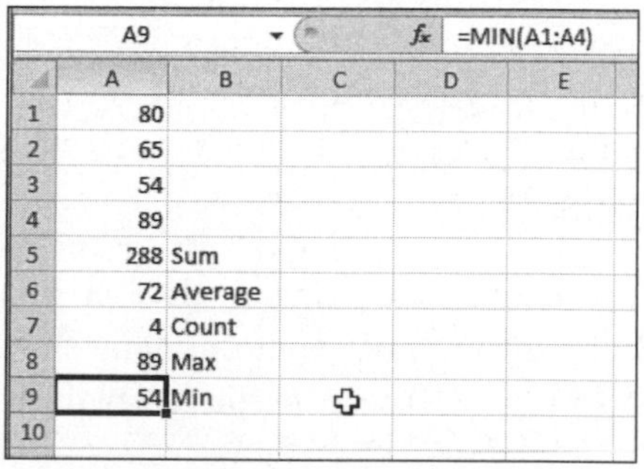

Popular functions.

The AutoSum Button

On the Ribbon in the Home tab under the Editing group is a button called *AutoSum*. This button quickly inserts one of these five popular functions into your sheet for you.

You can see the AutoSum button in Figure 6.7. Note that if your Ribbon is smaller, you might see only the symbol Σ on the button. That's the Greek letter sigma, and it's used to represent a summation function in mathematics.

Again, let's say that you have just the four test grades in cells A1 through A4, and you want to quickly add them. Click cell A5, which is where you want your function to go. Then click the **AutoSum** button. Voilà! Your function appears in cell A5.

Figure 6.7

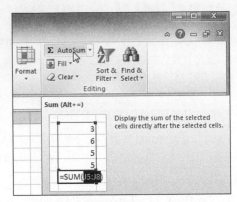

AutoSum button.

The AutoSum button defaults to the SUM function and tries to guess the range of cells you want. If the range is wrong, just click and drag the correct range with your mouse or type it in. Do double-check the range, however, because if you have a large or complex sheet, the AutoSum button can sometimes guess incorrectly. Press Enter when you're happy with the range.

If you want a function other than SUM, you can click on the tiny down arrow just to the right of the AutoSum button. That opens a menu showing Sum, Average, Count Numbers (which is the COUNT function you learned earlier), Max, and Min.

Using the Insert Function Button

On the Ribbon, click the **Formulas** tab, and then click the **Function Library** group. Future chapters spend a lot more time covering more of the hundreds of different functions in this group, but for now, find the **Insert Function** button.

The Insert Function button walks you through setting up a function in your sheet. For a simple function like SUM or AVERAGE, there's not much to do. However, some of the more complicated functions take multiple bits of information, and the Insert Function button can make setting them up a lot easier.

Next you see how the Insert Function button works with a simple SUM function.

If you have a function in A5 from the previous examples, delete it now. Click cell A5 and then click the **Insert Function** button.

The Insert Function dialog displays. If you're not sure of the name of the function you want to use, you can type your best guess in the top box, and Excel tries to identify what you mean.

For example, type **avg** to create an average. Then click the **Go** button. Excel searches its library of functions and creates a list of all the functions that have to do with creating averages. You'll see RANK.AVG, AVERAGEIF, and several others. Of course, the one that you want is AVERAGE. Click it and then click **OK**. (See Figure 6.8.)

Figure 6.8

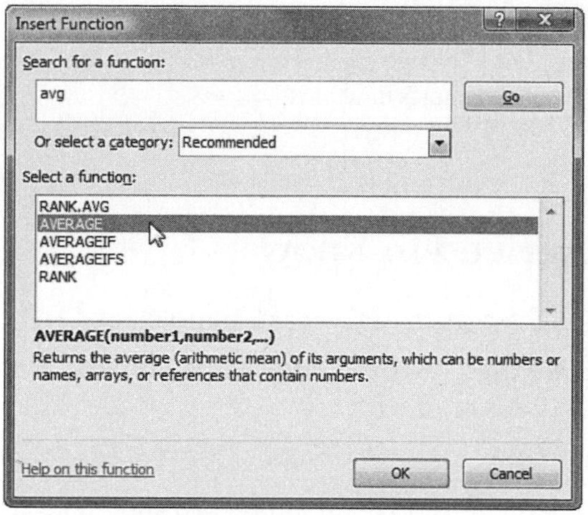

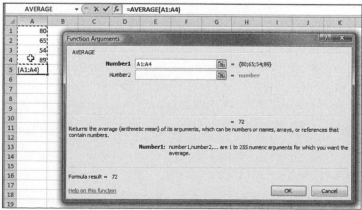

Search for a function by name.

The Function Arguments dialog displays. You can actually find the average of several different ranges using the AVERAGE function. For now, however, you are averaging only one simple range. Using your mouse, select cells A1 to A4; you can see that range display in the Number 1 box. (See Figure 6.9.)

Figure 6.9

Function arguments.

Some sample data and a formula result also show up in this dialog box. That gives you a preview of the final result. When you're satisfied, click **OK**. Excel fills in the function in cell A5 for you.

TIP

For simple functions like SUM and AVERAGE, it's much easier to type the functions by hand. Later, you'll see that the Insert Function button comes in handy when dealing with more complex functions.

The Least You Need to Know

- Functions enable you to easily make complex or repetitive calculations.
- Cell ranges are used for specifying a large number of contiguous cells in formulas.
- The five most popular functions are SUM, AVERAGE, MAX, MIN, and COUNT.
- The AutoSum and Insert Function buttons can make adding functions to your cells easier.

Manipulating Data

In This Chapter

- Moving data
- Cutting, copying, and pasting with the Clipboard
- Copying formulas
- AutoFill
- The Clipboard pane

Being able to manipulate data in Excel is very important. You will often need to move cells around, copy information to different locations, and even delete or shift whole columns. In this chapter, we examine all the ways in which you can manipulate data this way.

Moving Blocks of Cells

If you have a block of cells that you want to move from one location to another, the easiest way to accomplish this task is to follow these steps:

1. Select a range of cells using the mouse.

2. Move your mouse over the border of the selected cells. Your mouse turns into a pointer with a four-way arrow under it (see Figure 7.1).

3. Click and drag your mouse to move the block of cells to a different location (see Figure 7.2).

4. Your cells are moved (see Figure 7.3).

Figure 7.1

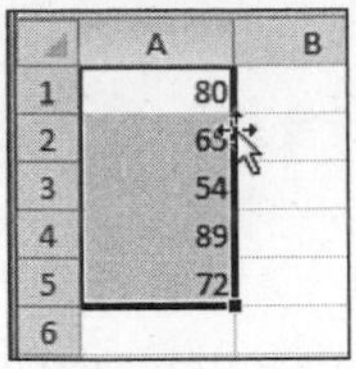

Moving cells, part 1.

Figure 7.2

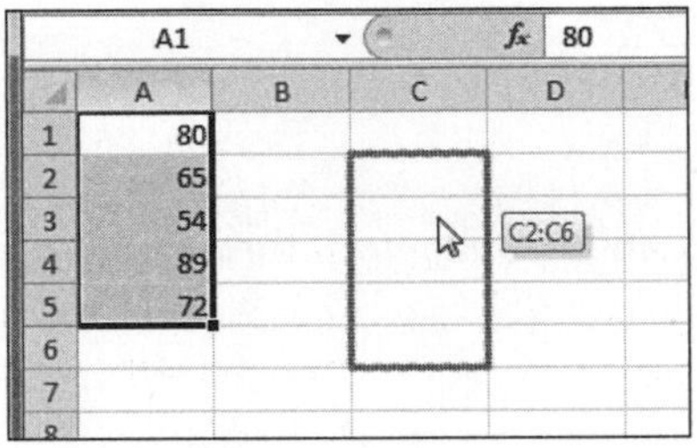

Moving cells, part 2.

Figure 7.3

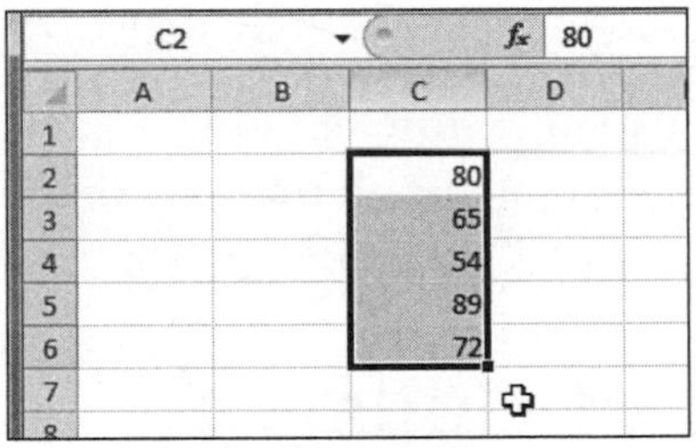

Moving cells, part 3.

> **TIP**
>
> If you hold down the Ctrl (Control) key while dragging a range of cells, you make a copy of the data in those cells.

Cutting, Copying, and Pasting Data

You can do more than just move cells. You might want to make a copy of those cells or copy just the values in them (when formulas are involved). In this case, it's essential to know how to work with the Microsoft Office *Clipboard*.

DEFINITION

The **Clipboard** is a special place in the computer's memory where you can temporarily store information. You can cut or copy data to the Clipboard and then paste it back in a different spot.

There's a difference between cutting and copying. When you *cut* data, it's removed from the original location when you *paste* it back into another place in the spreadsheet. However, when you just copy information, the original remains intact.

TIP

If cutting and copying are confusing, think about it as you might scissors and Silly Putty. Cutting and pasting is like using the scissors; once you cut with the scissors, the piece you cut off is removed from the original piece from the paper. Copying and pasting is like using Silly Putty. When you put Silly Putty over a newspaper, an image of the text is transferred to the Silly Putty. The original paper stays intact. You get an image without destroying it.

On the Ribbon on the Home tab is the Clipboard group. Copying data is easy using this group. Just select what you want to copy, whether it's a single cell or a range of hundreds of cells, and then click the **Copy** button in the Clipboard group (see Figure 7.4).

Figure 7.4

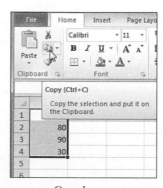

Copy button.

A blinking border surrounds the cells you copy. Think of these as the "dancing ants." Once you see the ants (see Figure 7.5) surrounding your cell(s), your data is on the Clipboard and ready to be copied (or cut).

Figure 7.5

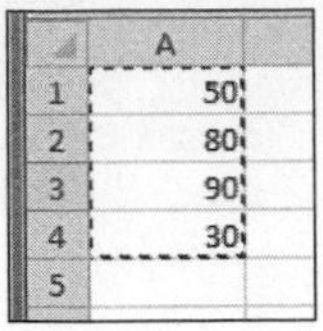

Cells copied to the Clipboard.

After your data is copied to the Clipboard, click where you want the data to go and then click the **Paste** button. You see the data in the copied cells display where you paste it.

Now you can see a complete copy of the data. The data that previously existed in cells A1:A4 is copied to C2:C5 (see Figure 7.6). If you had used the Cut button instead of the Copy button, the original data would have been removed from A1:A4.

Figure 7.6

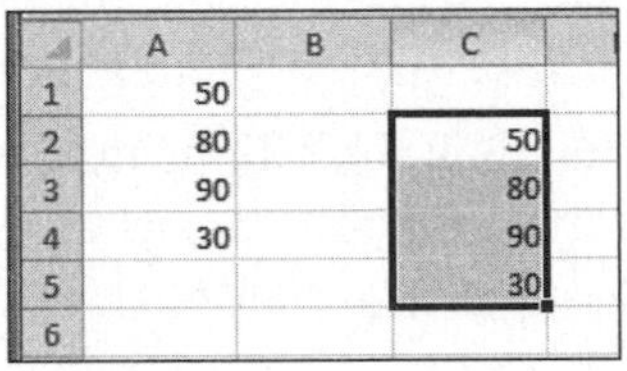

The original cells pasted into new cells.

Keyboard Shortcuts

You'll love keyboard shortcuts when they make your job easier. You can use Ctrl+X, Ctrl+C, and Ctrl+V to cut, copy, and paste, respectively. If you don't remember any other keyboard shortcuts, make it a point to remember these. Here's a great little memory trick: *C* stands for Copy, and the *X* looks like a pair of scissors, so Ctrl+X is for Cut. The *V* is right next to those other two keys, and it represents Paste.

They're included in Table 7.1 for easy reference.

Table 7.1   Cut, Copy, and Paste

Ctrl+X	Cut
Ctrl+C	Copy
Ctrl+V	Paste

If you want to make multiple copies of the same data, you just copy the data once to the Clipboard. You can then click Paste several times. Just click where you want the data to go, press Ctrl+V, press the arrow key to move to the next location, then press Ctrl+V again, and so on.

Copy and Paste Options

Some advanced options are available when using Copy and Paste. First, on the Copy button, you'll notice that the drop-down box next to it has the option Copy As Picture. This option creates an image or bitmap picture of the cells you have selected. You can then paste this image into other applications, like Microsoft Paint or even Microsoft Word, as a picture. You may not use this feature much, but it's handy when you need it.

Paste Options

After you've copied or cut any cells to the Clipboard, you can use a variety of options for pasting that data back into your sheet. You can find these options on the Paste button's drop-down menu (see Figure 7.7).

Figure 7.7

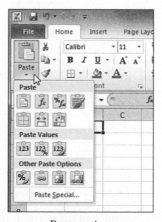

Paste options.

You'll also find a similar set of buttons when you've finished pasting. They display as a drop-down menu to the bottom right of the data you've pasted (see Figure 7.8).

Figure 7.8

Paste options after pasting.

These options may change based on the kind of data you've selected, but for normal cells, you'll generally see the following options:

- **Paste:** Pastes the contents of the original cell (whether data or a formula), along with any formatting, such as bold, colors, and so on.

- **Formulas:** Pastes the contents but no formatting.

- **Formulas and Number Formatting:** Pastes the contents and also number formatting (if you've changed the number of decimal places), but no other formatting (like colors).

- **Keep Source Formatting:** Keeps all the source formatting.

- **No Borders:** Pastes the contents but no cell borders.

- **Keep Source Column Width:** Pastes the contents and matches the destination column's width to that of the source column.

- **Transpose:** Transposes columns and rows. For example, if you have a single column of data, it's switched to a single row of data.

- **Values:** Pastes just the results of a formula, not the formula itself. For example, if you have a SUM function in a cell that calculates to 150 and you copy and paste its value, only the number 150 appears in the destination cell.

- **Values and Number Formatting:** Pastes values plus number formatting, but no other formatting (like colors).

- **Values and Source Formatting:** Pastes values plus all the source formatting.

- **Formatting:** Pastes *only* the source formatting, without any data. This option is handy if you have a column that's formatted a specific way (some red, some blue, some bold, for example) and want to copy just that format to a different range.

- **Paste Link:** Pastes the contents but creates a link to the original source data. If the source data changes, the destination cells change, too.

- **Picture:** Pastes the copied cells as an image.

- **Linked Picture:** Pastes an image and links it to the original source data.

- **Paste Special:** Opens a separate dialog box with a menu of different advanced options.

Keep in mind that you can select more than one option. If you copy and paste using Ctrl+V, for example, you can continue to pick options from the paste drop-down menu several times.

TIP

In addition to the Ribbon buttons for Cut, Copy, and Paste and the keyboard shortcuts, you can right-click almost anywhere and select to cut, copy, and paste data.

Copying and Pasting Formulas

Open the Sales Figures sample workbook file (included on your CD in the Chapter 7 folder) or re-create the simple spreadsheet shown in Figure 7.9.

Add a SUM function to cell B6 so you can see the total sales for all the reps for the month of January. (See Figure 7.9.) Here's the formula:

=SUM(B2:B5)

Figure 7.9

	A	B	C	D	E
1	Sales Rep	Jan	Feb	Mar	Apr
2	Chris	56	32	54	56
3	Alex	45	45	23	45
4	Jan	24	64	76	34
5	Pat	78	34	56	23
6	Total	=SUM(B2:B5)			
7					

Add a total row.

Now retype this function for column C as well. If you had several columns, such as 20 columns of data, you'd have a lot of typing. In this case, you can copy and paste the data. Copy cell B6 and paste it to C6.

Notice when you paste the data into cell C6 that Excel automatically updates the function's range for you. B2:B5 is automatically changed to C2:C5. This makes it easier for you to copy and paste functions that you want to be the same in multiple columns.

Using the AutoFill Feature

As incredibly easy as Excel makes copying and pasting formulas, it gets even better. You can use a great tool called *AutoFill* to instantly copy a formula across multiple columns or rows. Here's how it works:

1. Click the cell that has your formula. In this example, it's cell B6.

2. Move your mouse over the little black dot in the bottom-right corner of the cell. Your mouse pointer changes from a white plus to a black plus. (See Figure 7.10.)

3. Click and drag your mouse to the right, and select the entire range that you want the formula copied into (see Figure 7.11).

4. The formula is copied to all those cells, and the function ranges are updated for each column (see Figure 7.12).

Figure 7.10

	A	B	C	D	E
1	Sales Rep	Jan	Feb	Mar	Apr
2	Chris	56	32	54	56
3	Alex	45	45	23	45
4	Jan	24	64	76	34
5	Pat	78	34	56	23
6	Total	203			
7					

AutoFill 1.

Figure 7.11

	A	B	C	D	E	F
1	Sales Rep	Jan	Feb	Mar	Apr	
2	Chris	56	32	54	56	
3	Alex	45	45	23	45	
4	Jan	24	64	76	34	
5	Pat	78	34	56	23	
6	Total	203				
7						

Select the range.

Figure 7.12

	A	B	C	D	E	F
1	Sales Rep	Jan	Feb	Mar	Apr	
2	Chris	56	32	54	56	
3	Alex	45	45	23	45	
4	Jan	24	64	76	34	
5	Pat	78	34	56	23	
6	Total	203	175	209	158	
7						
8						

AutoFill the range.

For practice, calculate a total for each sales rep. Place a SUM function in cell F2 for the first sales rep, Chris. (See Figure 7.13.)

Figure 7.13

	A	B	C	D	E	F	G
1	Sales Rep	Jan	Feb	Mar	Apr	Total	
2	Chris	56	32	54	56	=SUM(B2:E2)	
3	Alex	45	45	23	45		
4	Jan	24	64	76	34		
5	Pat	78	34	56	23		
6	Total	203	175	209	158		
7							

Total for sales rep.

Now, using the AutoFill handle, copy that formula for rows 3 through 6 (see Figure 7.14).

Figure 7.14

	A	B	C	D	E	F	G
1	Sales Rep	Jan	Feb	Mar	Apr	Total	
2	Chris	56	32	54	56	198	
3	Alex	45	45	23	45	158	
4	Jan	24	64	76	34	198	
5	Pat	78	34	56	23	191	
6	Total	203	175	209	158	745	
7							
8							

Formula AutoFill.

NOTICE

Notice that a menu displays when you finish an AutoFill. This menu includes advanced options for copying the format only or for copying without the format when using AutoFill.

Want to have some fun with AutoFill? Go to a blank sheet in your workbook and type the word **January** into cell A1. Now use AutoFill to copy that cell to the right.

AutoFill knows the names of the months and days of the week (both spelled out and abbreviated). You can also use AutoFill to copy dates. Type **1/1/2010** in cell A3, so that AutoFill completes the entry. Notice that your dates are automatically incremented one day for each cell. (See Figure 7.15.)

Figure 7.15

	A	B	C	D	E	F	G
1	January	February	March	April	May	June	
2	Mon	Tue	Wed	Thu	Fri	Sat	
3	1/1/2010	1/2/2010	1/3/2010	1/4/2010	1/5/2010	1/6/2010	
4							
5							

AutoFill dates.

What about a series of dates? Let's say you want a list of just Mondays. You can use AutoFill to create series of dates or numbers. Follow these steps:

1. Type **6/7/2010** in cell A4.

2. Type **6/14/2010** in cell B4

3. Select both A4 and B4.

4. AutoFill to the right several cells.

Excel notices the pattern and creates a list of just Mondays. You can also do something similar with numbers. The key is to create enough of the pattern so that Excel can figure out what you're doing. If you want just odd numbers, for example, type **1** and **3**, and then let AutoFill complete the entry. (See Figure 7.16.)

Figure 7.16

	A	B	C	D	E	F	
1	January	February	March	April	May	June	
2	Mon	Tue	Wed	Thu	Fri	Sat	
3	1/1/2010	1/2/2010	1/3/2010	1/4/2010	1/5/2010	1/6/2010	
4	6/7/2010	6/14/2010	6/21/2010	6/28/2010	7/5/2010	7/12/2010	
5	1	3	5	7	9	11	
6							

AutoFill series.

You can also use the drop-down menu that displays after an AutoFill to create a series. If Excel sees something that it can make a series out of, it gives you the options for days, weekdays, months, years, and so on. You just need to AutoFill from one date to see these options.

Using the Clipboard Pane

Use the Clipboard pane if you want to copy multiple items and then be able to paste them at different locations. You can activate the Clipboard pane by clicking the dialog box launcher button for the Clipboard group on the Home tab on the Ribbon (see Figure 7.17). It's a tiny button in the bottom-right corner of the group.

Figure 7.17

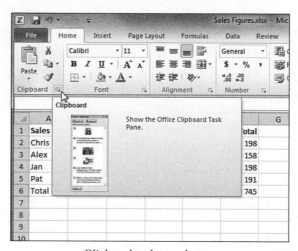

Clipboard task pane button.

Perhaps you want to copy both your list of sales reps and the months from your header row across the top of the sheet. Copy each to your Clipboard (select the cells and then press **Ctrl+C**); you'll see both in the Clipboard pane. (See Figure 7.18.)

Figure 7.18

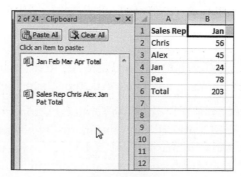

Clipboard pane.

Now go to a different sheet. You can paste each of these items at any location by clicking a cell and then clicking the item in the Clipboard pane. Alternatively, you can click the down-arrow drop-down next to the item and select **Paste**. (See Figure 7.19.)

Figure 7.19

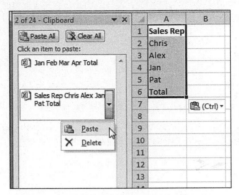

Paste an object from the Clipboard pane.

To remove an item from the Clipboard pane, select **Delete** from the drop-down menu.

Then click cell B3 and click the Months item in the Clipboard pane to paste your list of months there. (See Figure 7.20.)

Figure 7.20

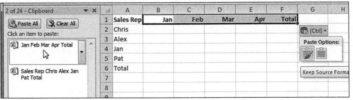

Paste another object from the Clipboard pane.

The Clipboard pane also has buttons for Paste All Items, which pastes everything that's in the Clipboard at once, and Clear All Items, which empties the Clipboard.

At the bottom of the Clipboard pane is an Option button that includes advanced features. You can show the Clipboard pane automatically whenever something is copied or cut. You can show the Clipboard when Ctrl+C (Copy) is pressed twice. You can collect items to the Clipboard without ever showing the pane. You can show or hide the Clipboard icon on the Windows taskbar. Finally, you can show the status near the taskbar when you perform a copy operation (you'll see a message that reads "Item 4 of 24 Collected").

The Least You Need to Know

- You can move data with the mouse by selecting the cells you want to move and then clicking and dragging the border of those cells.

- The Clipboard allows you to cut, copy, and paste one or multiple items. Copy leaves the original alone. Cut deletes the original.

- Remember the keyboard shortcuts for Cut, Copy, and Paste: Ctrl+X, Ctrl+C, and Ctrl+V, respectively.

- AutoFill is a great tool for quickly copying formulas or series of data across multiple rows or columns, updating your cell ranges automatically.

- The Clipboard pane allows you to collect multiple items and then paste them at different times or altogether.

Organizing Data

In This Chapter

- Basic sorting
- Custom sorting
- Find
- Replace

In this chapter, you learn how to organize data after you've built a spreadsheet. You learn how to sort your data in different ways and how to find data and then replace that data with something else.

A Simple Sort

Open the file Customers.xlsx, which is located on your CD in the Chapter 8 folder. This file contains an extended version of the customer list you created in Chapter 4. (See Figure 8.1.)

Figure 8.1

	A	B	C	D	E	F	G	H	I	J	K
1	First Name	Last Name	Address	City	State	Country	ZIP	Balance	Bathrooms	Discount	Customer Since
2	Joe	Smith	101 Park St	Hamburg	NY	US	14075	$1,500.00	0.5	50%	1/1/2009
3	Sue	Jones	298 Miller Ave	Toronto	ON	Canada	M4B 1B3	$50.45	1/2	25%	2/1/2010
4	Bill	Williams	28 Dennis Pkwy	Amherst	NY	US	14226-8272	-$25.00	3 1/2	33%	4/5/1998
5	Peter	Peterson	42 Hamton Ct	Portland	ME	US	04100	$6.20	2	10%	4/5/2010
6	Jim	Kirk	1701 Enterprise Dr	Riverside	IO	US	52327	$299.00	3	5%	3/22/1977
7	John	Picard	359 Wolf St	Barre	NY	US	14283	$9,182.00	2	25%	7/13/1986
8	Ben	Sisko	9 Bajor Ave	New Orleans	LA	US	70113	$800.00	5 1/2	15%	4/3/1990
9	Edward	Watson	42 Maple St	Buffalo	NY	US	14220	$90.00	3	10%	5/3/1990
10	Peter	Jones	34 Edmonds Place	Amherst	NY	US	14228	$0.00	1	4%	1/1/2002
11											

Sample customer data.

Notice that this data is in no particular order. Let's say you want to sort this list by the customer's last name. Here's how:

1. Click anywhere in column B.

2. On the Ribbon, click the **Home** tab.

3. In the Editing group, click the **Sort and Filter** button.

4. Click **Sort A to Z** to sort the list in ascending order (see Figure 8.2).

> **NOTICE**
>
> For text values, you see Sort A to Z. For numeric values, you see Smallest to Largest. For dates, you see Oldest to Newest. These are just different ways of indicating ascending or descending sorts.

Figure 8.2

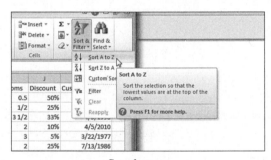

Sort buttons.

You can also click the Sort Z to A option to sort the data in descending order.

> **WARNING**
>
> Always double-check to make sure Excel sorted your data properly. If not, you can undo the sort at this point. If you wait until later, you might not be able to undo it.

Selecting Cells to Sort

Excel is smart when it comes to sorting. It realizes that you usually have a header row across the top of your data and a footer row at the bottom. It's usually pretty good about identifying those items.

However, Excel isn't perfect. Sometimes it doesn't realize that a row is the header or footer row and instead attempts to sort it as part of your data.

Consider the sheet in Figure 8.3.

Figure 8.3

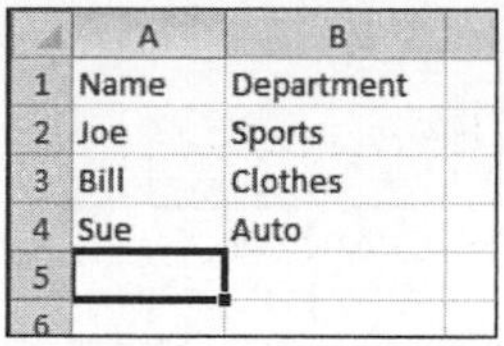

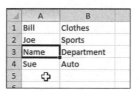

Sorting a small sheet.

If you click one of the columns and attempt to sort by that column, Excel sorts the column headers along with the data, as you can see in Figure 8.4. Notice that Name and Department are treated like regular data items.

Figure 8.4

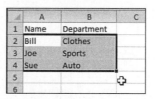

Sorting a small sheet.

To get around this problem, simply highlight the data that you want to sort, leaving the column headers (and potentially any column footers) out of the selection, as in Figure 8.5.

Figure 8.5

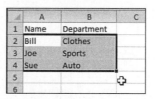

Basic sort.

As you can see here, I selected the cells from A2 through B4 and then clicked Sort and Filters > Sort A to Z. Excel sorted the data by the values in the first column—in this case, the person's name.

What if you have multiple columns and you want to sort by something other than the first column? Figure 8.6 shows a slightly more complicated sheet.

Figure 8.6

⊿	A	B	C	D
1	No	Name	Department	Supervisor
2	1	Bill	Clothes	Glen
3	2	Joe	Sports	Glen
4	3	Sue	Auto	Amy
5	4	Dave	Fishing	Amy
6	5	Ash	Housewares	Glen
7				✚
8				

Slightly more complex sort.

This time, you want to sort by the department, but you want to make sure that the column headers *and* the row headers (the numbers) aren't sorted. Here's how you do it:

1. Select the data you want to sort. In this example, this is B2:D6.

2. Press the **Tab** key. Notice that the white background from cell B2 moves to the right and is now in cell C2. This white cell determines which column the data is sorted on. (See Figure 8.7.)

3. Perform the sort by clicking **Sort and Filter > Sort A to Z**. The data is now sorted on that column.

TIP

Press **Tab** to move to the right. **Shift+Tab** moves to the left.

Figure 8.7

⊿	A	B	C	D
1	No	Name	Department	Supervisor
2	1	Sue	Auto	Amy
3	2	Bill	Clothes	Glen
4	3	Dave	Fishing	Amy
5	4	Ash	Housewares	Glen
6	5	Joe	Sports	Glen
7				

Sort by department.

If you have a large sheet that has multiple columns, you can select your data and then press Tab multiple times to select which column you want to sort by. Then when you're ready, perform your sort.

NOTICE

This technique goes back to the oldest versions of Excel, in which you *had* to select the data you wanted to sort. Those old versions didn't recognize the header row and always sorted it into the data. Furthermore, if you clicked on only one column, only *that* column was sorted, effectively scrambling the rest of your data. Excel has come a long way since then.

Sometimes you get an error message if you don't select enough data and Excel thinks you should select a wider range of cells. For example, if you select just B2 through B6 and try to sort it, Excel gives you the error message shown in Figure 8.8.

Figure 8.8

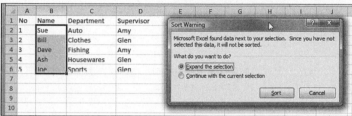

Sort error.

Excel says that it found data next to your selection and is asking whether you want to expand the selection to include all the rest of the data or just continue with the original selection. In this case, you should probably expand the selection; otherwise, you'll scramble the data (the names won't be properly matched with the departments or supervisors).

Custom Sorting

For performing a simple sort, the previous steps work fine. You'll probably be able to sort data that way 90 percent of the time. However, what if you want to sort based on multiple columns? For example, how would you go about sorting based on last name, then first name? In other words, if the last names are identical, Excel should sort by first name. This type of sort is a custom sort.

Let's go back to the Customer spreadsheet. Click anywhere in the region of data from A1 to K10 (basically, anywhere on this sheet where there's data, since it's all one nice data list). Now click **Sort and Filter > Custom Sort**.

The Sort dialog box opens and offers different options for sorting your data. Notice that Excel figured out that your sheet has nice column headers. The box My data has header is checked, and Excel didn't include row 1 in the selected range. If Excel was wrong and you previously selected the data that you wanted sorted, feel free to uncheck this box. For now, leave it checked.

Since you have data headers, Excel can figure out the name of each column by its header. You want to sort by last name and then first name, so select **Last Name** as the first column that you want to sort by. (See Figure 8.9.)

Figure 8.9

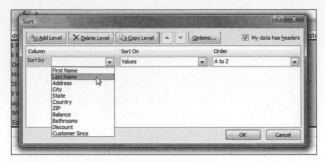

Sort by column.

Next, in the **Sort On** drop-down box, you can sort based on the value of the cell, the cell's (background) color, the font color, or the cell icon (see Figure 8.10). For now, stick with the cell's value.

Figure 8.10

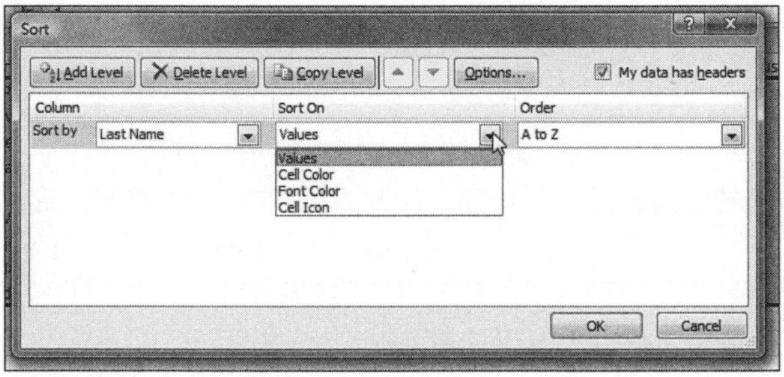

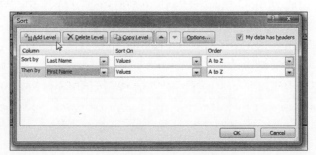

Sort On.

You also can select the sort order for this column. Do you want to sort it ascending or descending? Select **A to Z** for an ascending sort.

Now you have the first column set up for the sort. Let's add another one. Click the **Add Level** button. Set up the next item to sort on the First Name column. (See Figure 8.11.)

Figure 8.11

Another sort column.

When you're finished, click the **OK** button and notice that your sheet has been properly sorted by last name, then first name. You can see in Figure 8.12 that Peter Jones is listed before Sue Jones.

Figure 8.12

	A	B	C	D
1	First Name	Last Name	Address	City
2	Peter	Jones	34 Edmonds Place	Amherst
3	Sue	Jones	298 Miller Ave	Toronto
4	Jim	Kirk	1701 Enterprise Dr	Riverside
5	Peter	Peterson	42 Hamton Ct	Portland
6	John	Picard	359 Wolf St	Barre
7	Ben	Sisko	9 Bajor Ave	New Orleans
8	Joe	Smith	101 Park St	Hamburg
9	Edward	Watson	42 Maple St	Buffalo
10	Bill	Williams	28 Dennis Pkwy	Amherst
11				

Sort completed.

The Sort dialog box offers additional options. You can delete a sort level, copy a sort level, and move the sort levels up and down. For example, say you want to sort by first name before last name. You can click the arrow buttons to move the sorting levels.

The Options button enables you to perform a case-sensitive search in which upper- and lowercase matter. In this type of a sort, lowercase letters come before uppercase letters—for example, aa comes before AA. You can also change whether you're sorting top to bottom or left to right. The latter option is handy if you're sorting in rows instead of columns.

Sorting Based on Color

If you have the data in your sheet organized by color (perhaps all the overdue accounts are in red), then you can use the sort feature to group like colors together.

In Figure 8.13, the font color of several addresses has been changed. There are a couple of red items, a few green items, a black item, and a purple item. These may not be apparent in the figure since the printed book is in black and white, but trust me, it's colored.

If you want to group all the similarly colored addresses together, click the sheet data and then click **Sort and Filter > Custom Sort**. Choose the Address column to sort by. Sort on font color (not cell color—that's the background fill).

Figure 8.13

2	Jim	Kirk	1701 Enterprise Dr	Riverside
3	John	Picard	359 Wolf St	Barre
4	Ben	Sisko	9 Bajor Ave	New Orleans
5	Edward	Watson	42 Maple St	Buffalo
6	Bill	Williams	28 Dennis Pkwy	Amherst
7	Peter	Jones	34 Edmonds Place	Amherst
8	Joe	Smith	101 Park St	Hamburg
9	Sue	Jones	298 Miller Ave	Toronto
10	Peter	Peterson	42 Hamton Ct	Portland
11				
12			✛	

Colored addresses.

You can leave the Order property set to Automatic, to group all the colors together nicely, or you can decide which color goes on top (or bottom), as shown in Figure 8.14.

Figure 8.14

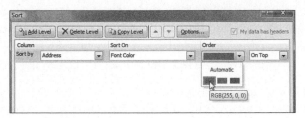

Sort by color.

If you then want to specify the next color, just add a new level, set the Address field, sort on font color, and then pick the next color. Personally, I usually use Automatic.

Finding Data

After a while, your spreadsheets are likely going to become very large, or someone else is going to give you a sheet with a few thousand rows in it. If you need to locate a specific bit of information fast, you can use Excel's Find feature.

Even though the sample sheet you've been working with in this chapter includes only nine customers, pretend that it has a lot more. The boss asks you to find Joe Smith's information. That's easy to do when you have only 9 records, but if you have 9,000 records, it's not so easy (especially if your data isn't sorted).

To find data, click anywhere on the sheet. Personally, I prefer to click cell A1 to make sure that my search starts at the top of the spreadsheet. Now, on the Home tab, in the Editing group, click **Find and Select > Find**.

In the box labeled Find What, type what you're looking for. In this case, type **Jones** and then click **Find All**. A list of all occurrences of this text displays in the bottom of the Find and Replace dialog box (see Figure 8.15).

Figure 8.15

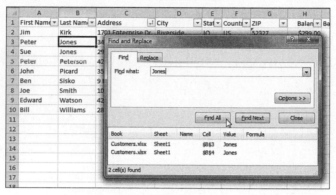

Find All.

Now you can click the items in this list individually to jump to the specific cell, or you can click the Find Next button to move to the next item. Of course, a lot of different options are available if you click the Options button.

- **Within:** Allows you to search the currently active sheet or the entire work-book file.

- **Search:** Changes whether Excel searches across by rows first and then down the columns or vice versa. The default is By Rows, which means that Excel searches across row 1, then row 2, and so on. If you change this to By Columns, Excel searches all the way down column A and then moves up to B1 and continues down column B.

- **Look In:** Determines whether you want to search the text of the formulas, the values in the cells (the results of the formulas), or the cell comments.

- **Match Case:** Checking this box instructs Excel to care about upper- and lowercase. A search for **Jones** will not reveal jones.

- **Match Entire Cell Contents:** Checking this box instructs Excel that the data in the cell must exactly match your search text. For example, a search for **Jones** will not find Jonestown.

Replace

You can also use the Find and Replace data to make changes to your sheet. For example, say that you want to find all customers who have a 10 percent discount rate and increase it to 11 percent. This is easy to do with Find and Replace.

Click the **Find and Select** button. This time, click **Replace**. Type **10%** in the Find What box. Type **11%** in the Replace With box. Click the **Find All** button to get a look at all the data you're replacing, before you commit to any changes. (See Figure 8.16.)

Figure 8.16

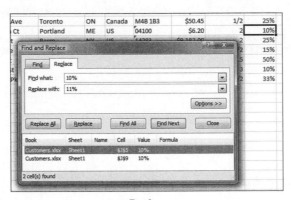

Replace.

Look over the list of cells and make sure it's correct. At this point, you can replace all the cell values with one click using the Replace All button, or you can manually step through them one at a time using the Replace button. Click **Replace All**.

You should see all the 10% values in your sheet replaced with 11%. If this is incorrect and you discover that something shouldn't have been changed, click the **Undo** button now or forever hold your peace. Don't discover an hour from now that you accidentally replaced a whole bunch of wrong information; you might not be able to undo it later.

TIP

If you want to search only within a specific range of cells, select those cells first before you click Find or Replace. Excel searches only inside your selected range of cells and leaves the rest of the sheet alone. This is handy if you have, for example, one or two specific columns of data you want to search in. Just select those columns first and then perform your Find operation.

You can also use the Find and Select button to select certain cells and objects for you. We haven't discussed what all these items are yet, but you can select all the cells that contain formulas by clicking the Formulas option from the Find & Select options.

The Least You Need to Know

- To sort data quickly, click the column you want to sort by and then click the **Sort** button.
- For a more advanced sort (such as sorting on multiple columns), click the **Custom Sort** button.
- You can use the Find and Replace feature to quickly locate and change data in your sheet.

Formatting

So far, we've focused on working with data. In Part 3, we focus on formatting sheets to make them look professional.

Chapter 10 is about fonts, colors, and borders. You learn how to change fonts, set foreground and background colors, and create borders around your cells.

In Chapter 11, we work more with rows and columns. You learn how to resize, insert, delete, hide, move, and manipulate rows and columns.

Chapter 12 covers cell alignment. You can see how to align text inside a cell, wrap text with multiple lines inside one cell, and change the vertical orientation of a cell. You can also see how to center text across multiple columns.

In Chapter 13, you learn about conditional formatting. This is a great tool for changing the look of cells based on the data in them. For example, you can make the high values appear green and the low values appear red.

Chapter 14 focuses on styles and themes. If you want to quickly reformat your entire sheet with a professional set of uniform colors and fonts, select a different style or theme.

We discuss page layout in Chapter 15. You learn about the different page views, page breaks, margins, orientation, paper size, and lots more.

In Chapter 16, we create custom headers and footers. If you want the same information to appear on the top or bottom of each page of your sheet, use a header or footer. You can add simple text, the page number, sheet name, and more information.

The File Tab and Backstage View

In This Chapter

- Excel's new File tab and Backstage View
- Creating a blank new workbook file
- Working with dozens of Excel templates
- Options for opening and saving workbook files in different formats
- Settings for printing your spreadsheets

You briefly learned about saving and opening your Excel workbook files in Chapter 2. In this chapter, you take a closer look at the Excel Backstage View, which is the fancy new name Microsoft has given to the File tab, formerly known as the Office Button, formerly the File menu. As you see in this chapter, the name has evolved over the years.

The File Tab

If you open Excel to a blank workbook and click the File tab, Excel Backstage View displays. By default, you start in the *Recent* section of the File menu. This enables you to see all the files you've worked on previously.

Figure 9.1 shows a lot of files. Notice the Customers and Sales Figures workbooks from previous chapters, in addition to some other miscellaneous files.

If you want to open a file, you simply click on it. As you can see, the most recently used files show up on the top of this list. You don't have to click File > Open and then browse (what may be) several files to find a workbook you recently worked on.

Figure 9.1

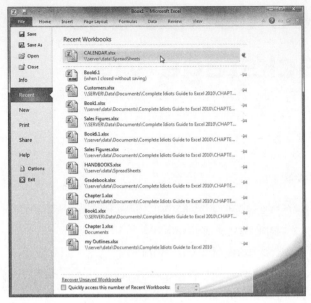

Backstage View.

TIP

Here's a neat tip. See the icons that look like push pins to the right of each file? If you click on an icon, you "pin" the file to the Recent menu and it stays there permanently, or until you "unpin" it. If you work with two or three workbooks on a regular basis, pinning them to the Recent file menu gives you quick access to them.

Creating a New Workbook File

If you want to create a new workbook file, click the **New** section of the **File** tab (see Figure 9.2).

You'll see a list of the available *templates* to create a new workbook from. A template is a starting block from which you can create your workbook. It may be empty or it may contain some data or formatting that someone else started for you. Some templates come directly from Microsoft and are installed with Excel. Other templates can be downloaded from Microsoft's website and may have been created by other users like you.

If you just want to create a new, blank workbook, click the **Blank Workbook** template. Next, click the **Create** button in the bottom-right corner of the window. Excel opens a blank new workbook that contains three blank worksheets.

Figure 9.2

The New section of the File menu.

TIP

You can also create a new, blank workbook by pressing Ctrl+N on your keyboard, which is quicker than opening the File tab.

Creating Workbooks with Templates

There are also a ton of different templates you can use to create workbooks. Click the Sample Templates icon (under New, Available Templates) to see the different templates Excel offers—everything from a Billing Statement (see Figure 9.3) template to a Loan Amortization template. Just click the template you want and then click the **Create** button to start working with one.

Figure 9.3

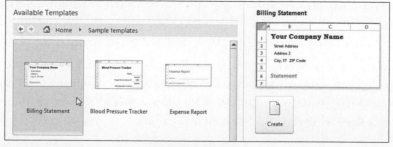

Sample templates.

Opening a template creates a new, blank document based on the template you choose. You are free to then customize it, add data, change formatting, save it, and print it—all without disturbing the original template file. For example, Figure 9.4 shows the Billing Statement template.

Figure 9.4

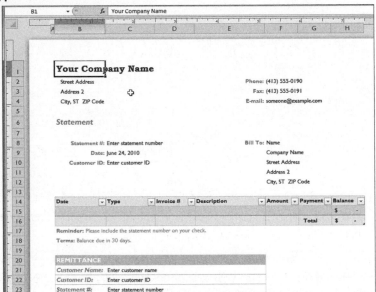

Billing Statement template.

If you have an active Internet connection, you can also browse templates that are available on Office.com, which is Microsoft's site that supports Excel and the other Microsoft Office programs. You can browse these templates right from inside of Excel; you don't actually have to load up your web browser.

You can browse different templates stored in folders, including templates for agendas, budgets, calendars, expense reports, faxes, and more. To see a template in a folder, just click that template.

Some template folders contain other folders. The Calendars folder, for example, includes different calendars for 2011, 2010, 2009, and so on. Open the 2011 calendars folder.

You should see the different calendars available (see Figure 9.5). Pick the one you like, and then click the **Download** button. The template is copied from Office.com right to your computer. You can then customize the calendar for your needs, edit it, change the formatting, and even print it.

Figure 9.5

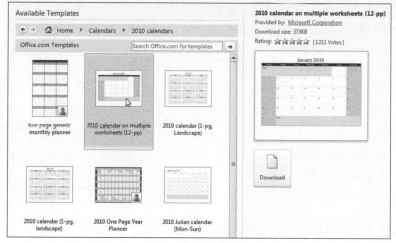

Calendars for 2010.

After you're done editing your calendar, if you go back into the File tab and click **New**, you'll see all the templates you've downloaded in the My Templates section. You don't have to keep downloading the same templates.

Many templates available on Office.com might not show up when you browse the file folders. You can perform a search for templates by typing your keywords into the search box. For example, you can search for a baseball score sheet by typing the word **baseball** into the search box and pressing **Enter**. Office.com then shows you the different baseball templates that are available (see Figure 9.6).

Figure 9.6

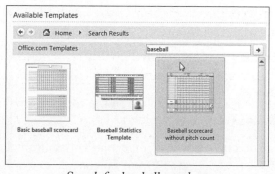

Search for baseball templates.

NOTICE

Keep in mind that Microsoft didn't create all the templates available. Many were uploaded by users just like you. You can see who created the template in the description, under the name; you'll see "provided by" followed by the user's name.

Opening a Workbook

If you want to open a workbook file and it's one you haven't used for a while, it won't show up on the Recent files list. In this case, click the **File** tab and then click **Open**. Excel displays the Open dialog menu, which enables you to browse your computer (or network folders) for any files you want.

In Figure 9.7, two files are available in the current folder: Sales Data 2009 and Sales Data 2010. Again, don't worry if you don't see the "XLSX" following your file names.

To open one of these files, just double-click it, or you can click the file once and then click the **Open** button.

Figure 9.7

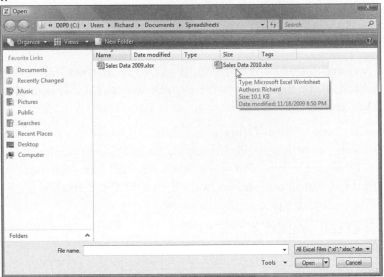

The File Open dialog box.

If you want to navigate to a different folder, you can either click the **Favorite Links** section to the left or click the address bar on the top of the Window to move around your hard drive or network folders.

Instead of clicking the **Open** button, you can select additional options by clicking the **down-arrow** button attached to the **Open** button.

NOTICE

The File Open dialog box is actually provided by Windows, so based on what version of Windows you have, your dialog box may appear slightly different than the one you see in Figure 9.7. Figure 9.7 is the one shown in Windows Vista.

Following are the options:

- **Open**—This opens the file normally; it's like double-clicking the file.

- **Open Read-Only**—This opens a copy of the file, but you're allowed just to read it. You cannot make changes and save over the file. However, you can save the file with a different file name.

- **Open as Copy**—This opens the file, but Excel makes a copy for you and automatically renames it.

- **Open in Browser**—This opens the file in your default web browser (such as Internet Explorer or Firefox). Obviously, this copy is read-only.

- **Open in Protected View**—You can use this mode to open Excel files that you're not sure are safe. Yes, bad people can do nasty things with Excel files (like creating harmful macro viruses). Protected View disables all these potentially harmful features and lets you look at the file.

- **Open and Repair**—If you get a message saying that one of your Excel files is corrupt, try this option. Excel opens the workbook file and attempts to repair it.

Normally, when you open a file, Excel shows you only Excel files, such as the normal workbook files you create in Excel. However, Excel can read and write other types of files, including text files, web pages, database files, and more.

Saving Your Workbook

When you have a workbook open, you can edit it, make any changes you want, and then save the workbook again. If you click the File tab, you'll see two options: Save or Save As.

- **Save**—This option saves your workbook with the same file name, overwriting the old file, if it exists. If you haven't specified a file name yet (that is, you have a brand new sheet that hasn't been saved yet), Excel prompts you for a file name.

- **Save As**—Use this option to specify a new file name for your workbook. This is handy for saving a copy of your current sheet, leaving the original intact. For example, this is handy if you're working with OctoberSales.xlsx and you want to make a few changes and then save it as NovemberSales.xlsx.

Saving to a Folder on Your Computer

Normally, in Windows Vista and in Windows 7, your files are stored in your personal Documents folder, located under your user name folder. For example, your documents are generally located here:

> C:\Users\Your Name\Documents

However, you might want to separate your files into different folders, to make them easier to find. For example, you might save your Word documents in a Word Documents folder, save your Excel files in a Spreadsheets folder, and so on.

When you click **File > Save As**, the Save As dialog box displays. Here the default location for saving a file is the Documents folder. If you want to create a new subfolder underneath this folder, just click the **New Folder** button (see Figure 9.8).

After you click the **New Folder** button, you see that Windows creates the folder for you and allows you to immediately type in a name for it (see Figure 9.8). Now, I already have a Spreadsheets folder, as you can see. So perhaps I'll create another folder underneath that for all my Sales Data workbooks.

After you type in the folder name **Sales Data** and press **Enter**, you move into that folder and you can then save your workbook. Change the file name, if you want to, and then click **Save**. I'll call my sheet Sales Data 2010.xlsx.

Figure 9.8

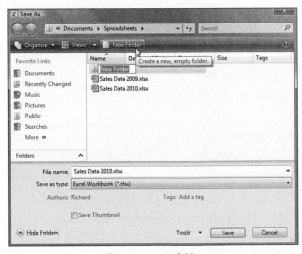

Create a new folder.

Saving in a Different File Format

You can save your workbooks in other file formats. This is sometimes handy if you need to share data with people who don't have Excel or perhaps have an older version of Excel. Version 2007 introduced a new format for Excel files. If you need to send your workbooks to people who are using Excel 2003 or earlier, you'll need to save your workbook accordingly.

NOTICE

If you need to give a copy of your workbook to an Excel 2003 (or earlier) user, always save your workbook in the default Excel 2010 file format first, and *then* save a copy of your workbook for 2003 users. This is because certain features aren't available in the older file format, and you may lose them.

To save your workbook in a different file format, click **File > Save As** and then open the **Save As Type** drop-down menu (see Figure 9.9). Normally you would save your Excel 2010 file as an "Excel Workbook," which has an XLSX file extension. If you need to give the workbook to an Excel 2003 user, select the **Excel 97-2003 Workbook** format that has the old XLS extension.

Figure 9.9

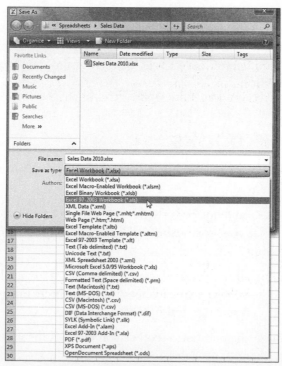

Save As Type.

You can see a lot of other file formats listed on the drop-down menu (see Figure 9.9). For the most part, you don't need to worry about a lot of them. The only ones you'll likely use are these:

- **Excel Workbook (XLSX).** The default Excel 2010 format.

- **Excel 97-2003 Workbook (XLS).** The format for older versions of Excel.

- **Excel Macro-Enabled Workbook (XLSM).** If you do any work with recording macros (an advanced feature, kind of like programming) you have to save your workbook in this format.

- **Web Page (HTM).** This stores your Excel file in a format that can be viewed in a web browser. You will probably lose some formatting, however. It's not perfect, but it gets the job done.

- **Text (TXT).** This is a plain text file that almost every computer can read. You will lose all of your formatting (colors, fonts, and so on) with text, but this file format is the best when you don't know what kind of program the recipient uses to view spreadsheet data, and you have to send him or her your information.

- **Portable Document Format (PDF).** This is the long-time standard of "portable" documents on the web. Adobe created this format many years ago, and the PDF reader is freely available from their website. Use this format if you want to retain as much of your formatting as possible to show a document to someone who doesn't have Excel. Keep in mind, however, that they will not be able to edit it.

Printing Workbooks

When it's time to print your workbook on paper, click the **File** tab and then click **Print**. The Print menu displays.

The first thing you should notice is the large *preview* of your sheet to the right. Excel tries to show you what your spreadsheet will look like when you print it, as close as it can to the actual thing.

In the middle column of the window, you can see a large Print button. Press this when you are ready to send the spreadsheet to the printer. But before you do, you can change some additional settings and options.

First, you can change the number of copies you print. This is straightforward. If you want three copies, change this value to 3.

You should also see a drop-down box to select which printer you want to print to. If you have more than one printer on your computer, or if you are connected to any network printers, you should be able to select from all of them here.

NOTICE

A link under the printer selection drop-down reads Printer Options. This opens up the Printer Settings dialog box that is specific to your printer. Here you can change whatever options your particular printer might have available (duplexing, colors, multipage printing, and so on). Since each printer is different, check your printer documentation for specifics.

In the Settings area, you'll find a drop-down box that reads Print Active Sheets. This generally means that only the current sheet you were on before you clicked Print will be printed, but it is possible to select multiple sheets by holding down the Ctrl key and clicking on each sheet tab you want to print.

The other settings for this option include printing the entire workbook (every sheet) or printing the current selection. You can select a range of cells and then choose this option to print only those cells. This is handy if you have a huge sheet and you want to print only a small portion of it.

Next, you have two boxes where you can choose to print a range of pages. For example, if you want to print pages 3 to 7 in a large workbook, you can specify those pages here. Below that are options to print on one side or both sides of the page (you'll have to refeed the paper into the printer, of course).

You also have an option to collate the pages. If you choose to collate the pages, Excel prints pages 1, 2, and 3 in order for how many copies you specify. If you turn off collation, you'll get all your copies of page 1, followed by all your copies of page 2, and so on. This is faster but makes you manually collate the pages.

Next, you'll see an option to print the sheet in portrait or landscape orientation (tall or wide, respectively) followed by an option for the paper size. The default paper size is 8.5 by 11 inches (standard letter). You can select from legal, statement, executive, and a variety of other paper sizes. You will also see an option box here to change the margins of the printed page, but you'll see a different way to do this in Chapter 15.

You will also see a Print Scaling drop-down menu. This enables you to increase or decrease the size of the printed page. It does not affect the size of the actual sheet itself—just how big it prints on the page. The Fit Sheet on One Page option is great if you have a large sheet that you want to squeeze into one page. You can scale the printout to fit all the columns on one page or all the rows on one page.

There's also a link here to access the Page Setup dialog box. This option likely is familiar to you if you used previous versions of Excel. You'll learn more about this menu in Chapter 15.

After you've specified all your desired options, click the **Print** button to send your spreadsheet to the printer. If you don't want to actually print now, click one of the other tabs on the Ribbon (like the **Home** tab) or click on the **File** tab again to close Backstage View.

Notice now, however, that you see dotted lines on your worksheet (see Figure 9.10). This is because Excel knows the dimensions of your printed page. These are guidelines to help you when laying out your page, to show you where all the automatic page breaks are. Again, you'll learn how to manually adjust these page breaks in Chapter 15.

Figure 9.10

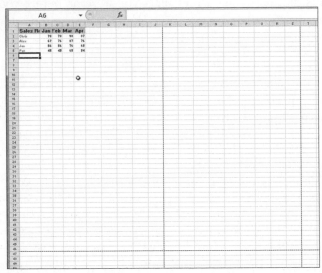

Print page break guides.

The Least You Need to Know

- Excel 2010's new File tab is where you go to save, open, or print your files.
- The quickest and easiest way to create a blank new workbook file is to press Ctrl+N.
- You can choose from dozens, if not hundreds, of free templates on Office.com. You can get calendars, fax cover sheets, and lots more.
- You can open and save your Excel files in different formats by using the Save As Type option box. You can access most print options under the File tab/ Backstage View.

Fonts, Colors, and Borders

In This Chapter

- Changing the look of your text
- Bold, italics, and underline
- Working with foreground and background colors
- Adding borders to your cells

In Chapter 2, you learned some simple formatting techniques to make your sheets look good. You learned how to align data to the right side of a cell, how to make the text of a cell bold, and a few other simple formatting tricks. In this chapter, you spend more time learning how to make your spreadsheets look professional.

Why is this important? In addition to just storing and analyzing data, Excel is a powerful tool for conveying a message with your data and helping others to review and understand trends in your data. The more pleasing your spreadsheet is to the eye, the easier it is for the user to comprehend. This is especially true when you get to charts and graphs later—for now, just making your spreadsheet look attractive can go a long way.

The Font Group

Most of the cell-formatting capabilities in Excel are on the Ribbon's Home tab. First, let's look at the Font group. This group has many different tools available to change the look and feel of the fonts, colors, borders, and other attributes of our cells.

To get started open the Customers.XLSX workbook that you built in previous chapters (you'll find a copy of it in the folder for this chapter as well).

Changing Font Faces

A *font* is simply unique type and set of lettering. Some people use the word *style* to define a type, as in a unique style of lettering, but the term *style* refers to something completely different in Excel, as you learn later (in Chapter 14). It's easier to show you what the different fonts are than try to explain them in detail.

In the Customers workbook, click the row header for the first row (right on the number 1). This highlights the entire first row so that you can make a change to every cell in the row (see Figure 10.1).

Figure 10.1

	A	B	C	D
	First Name	Last Name	Address	City
2	Bill	Williams	28 Dennis Pkwy	Amherst
3	Peter	Jones	34 Edmonds Place	Amherst
4	Peter	Peterson	42 Hamton Ct	Portland

A1   fx   First Name

Selecting a row.

Now that you have the row selected, find the Font drop-down box in the Font group on the Home tab. The default setting is Calibri—that's the name of the font face.

When you open this box, you'll see dozens of available different fonts. As you move your mouse over them, notice that you see a preview (called Live Preview) of what the new font will look like in your spreadsheet behind the drop-down box. This is a nice feature—before Office 2007, you had to select the font first to see the changes.

Figure 10.2

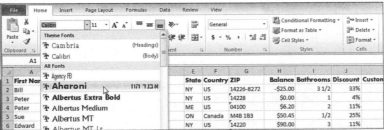

Font preview.

When you find a font that you like, go ahead and click it (see Figure 10.2). Excel commits the changes to your sheet, and the font faces change for all the cells in the first row. In Figure 10.3, the font choice is Arial Black.

Figure 10.3

	A	B	C	D
1	**First Nam**	**Last Nam**	**Address**	**City**
2	Bill	Williams	28 Dennis Pkwy	Amherst
3	Peter	Jones	34 Edmonds Place	Amherst

Changing the font to Arial Black.

Notice that some of the column labels are cut off because they're too wide to fit in the cell at its current width. You have two options at this point. You can either reduce the size of the text or make the column wider. You learn about changing column widths in Chapter 11. Here you learn how to make the text smaller.

Changing Font Sizes

Again, select the entire first row. Next to the Font drop-down box, you'll see a drop-down box to change the font size. The default setting is 11. Change it to 9, to allow all the labels to fit inside their cells.

You can change the font size to pretty much anything you want. You can select values from 8 to 72 by clicking on them in the drop-down box. You can also type in any value you want. For example, you won't see 13 on the list, so if you want 13 points for your font, type it in the Font Size box.

Two buttons next to the Font Size drop-down box increase and decrease the font size one step at a time. Just click these buttons repeatedly to visually increase or decrease the font size in steps.

Bold, Italics, Underline

Below the Font drop-down box are the familiar Bold, Italics, and Underline buttons. As I mentioned in Chapter 2, these buttons are toggle switches; you can click them on or off. Bold makes the font thicker. Italics leans the font to the right a bit. Underline places a single or double underline beneath the text (click the down arrow for the double-underline option).

Excel handles format changes in an interesting way. Let's say you have some bold items, such as the ones in Figure 10.4.

As you can see, cells A5, A8, B6, B7, and C8 are bold. They're in no particular order. Select all the cells from A4 to C10, and then click the **Bold** button. You might *expect* that Excel would unbold these cells and bold the rest of them, effectively reversing the Bold setting of each cell.

Figure 10.4

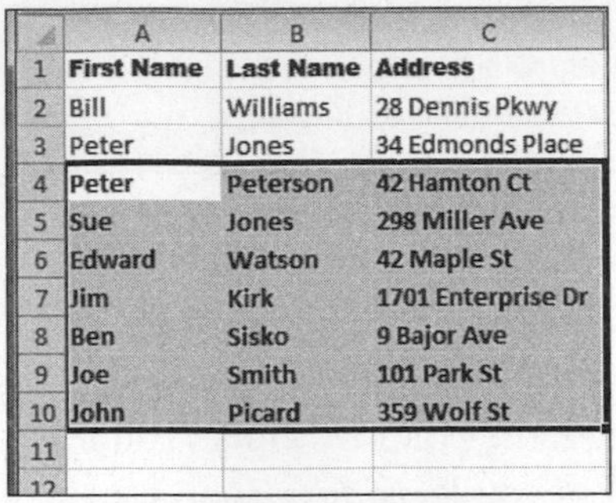

	A	B	C
1	First Name	Last Name	Address
2	Bill	Williams	28 Dennis Pkwy
3	Peter	Jones	34 Edmonds Place
4	Peter	Peterson	42 Hamton Ct
5	Sue	Jones	298 Miller Ave
6	Edward	Watson	42 Maple St
7	Jim	Kirk	1701 Enterprise Dr
8	Ben	Sisko	9 Bajor Ave
9	Joe	Smith	101 Park St
10	John	Picard	359 Wolf St
11			
12			

Several bolded items.

But that's not what happens. Excel instead looks at the first cell in A4. It applies the formatting change to A4 (which, in this case, makes it bold) and then makes all the rest of the cells in this range look like A4. (See Figure 10.5.)

Figure 10.5

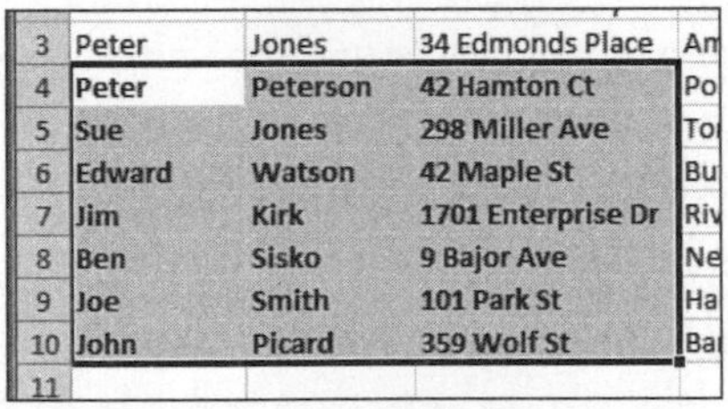

3	Peter	Jones	34 Edmonds Place	An
4	Peter	Peterson	42 Hamton Ct	Po
5	Sue	Jones	298 Miller Ave	To
6	Edward	Watson	42 Maple St	Bu
7	Jim	Kirk	1701 Enterprise Dr	Riv
8	Ben	Sisko	9 Bajor Ave	Ne
9	Joe	Smith	101 Park St	Ha
10	John	Picard	359 Wolf St	Ba
11				

Format changes to a range.

Keep in mind that, whenever you want to apply a formatting change to a whole range of cells, the first cell is the "key" cell—it controls how the format is applied to the rest of the cells in the range.

Reverse that bold again by clicking the **Bold** button. Notice that now *all* the items in this range are unbolded. Why? Because the formatting change applies to A4, and then the rest of the cells are made to look like A4.

Changing Fonts

You can change the color of a font. The following sections show you how.

Changing Font Color

If you want to change the color of your cell, you can work with two different kinds of colors: the foreground (or Font) color and the background (or Fill) color. Let's look at the Font color first.

Let's say you want to color all the customers who have a balance over $1,000 in red. Select cells H9 and H10, and then click the **Font Color** button (see Figure 10.6).

Figure 10.6

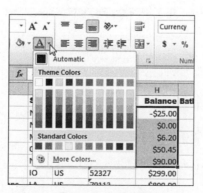

Changing the font color.

Now, what if you don't want red? What if you want to change the customers who have balances of less than $100 to green? Select cells H2 through H6 and, instead of clicking the Font Color button (the A), click the **down arrow** to the right of it. A color palette displays (see Figure 10.7).

You can pick from any of the colors on this palette to change the color of the current font. The default setting is Automatic, at the top of the palette; this is usually black.

Figure 10.7

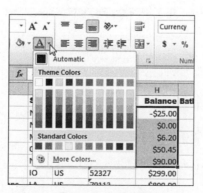

Font color palette.

If you want more control over the color you pick, click the **More Colors** button at the bottom of this drop-down menu. This opens the Colors dialog box. On the

Standard tab, you'll see a large color wheel that gives you more color selections, plus black and white and a wide variety of grays (see Figure 10.8).

Figure 10.8

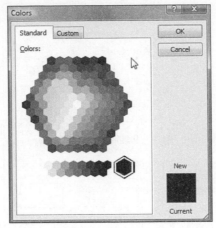

Standard color wheel.

If you *really* want to go crazy with color, click the **Custom** tab. You'll see the complete spectrum you can pick from. Click anywhere on the color map to pick a base color. You can then slide the brightness level up and down to get an exact color. You can also see (or type in) the exact RBG (red, blue, green) or HSL (hue, saturation, luminosity) numbers associated with that color. When you've picked your color, click **OK** (see Figure 10.9).

Figure 10.9

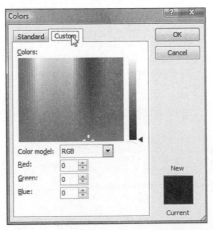

Custom colors.

Notice now that your new color is in the bar under the A on the Font Color button. To use this color again, click the button. The last color that you use is always on the button, and you'll see it in the Recent Colors section if you click the drop-down arrow again.

Fill Colors

Now that you know how to change the Font color, you'll find the Fill color easy to use. The Fill color changes the background of a cell, not the text in it. For example, imagine that you want to give customers with balances of more than $1,000 a yellow background to go with their red font color. Select cells H9 and H10 again and then click the **Fill Color** button (see Figure 10.10).

Figure 10.10

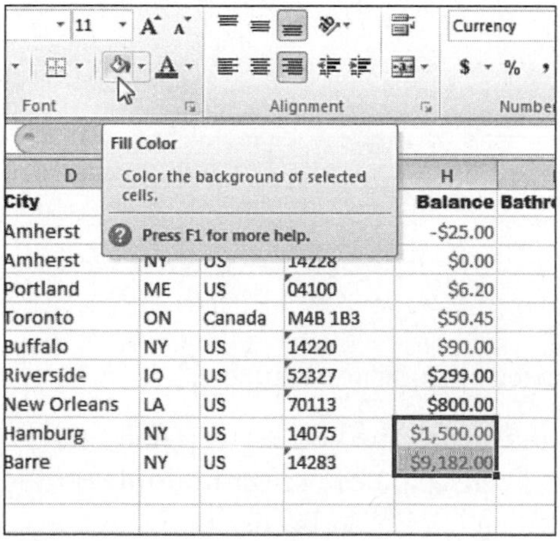

Fill colors.

Changing the fill color from yellow to something else works exactly the same way as changing the font color. Just click the down arrow next to the button for the color palette and advanced options.

Borders

You can add borders around cells that will show up both on the screen and when you print your spreadsheet. The Border button is just to the left of the Fill Color button (see Figure 10.11).

Figure 10.11

Border button.

The default setting is Bottom Border, which puts a solid bottom border around the selected cells. If you select a group of cells, the border is on the bottom edge of that entire group of cells, not within each individual cell in the range.

You can see an example of this in Figure 10.12. The bottom border is great for your column header row, for example. I selected cells A1 to K1 and then clicked the Bottom Border button.

Figure 10.12

	C	D	E	F	G	H	I	J	K
1	Address	City	State	Country	ZIP	Balance	Bathrooms	Discount	Customer Since
2	28 Dennis Pkwy	Amherst	NY	US	14226-8272	-$25.00	3 1/2	33%	4/5/1998
3	34 Edmonds Place	Amherst	NY	US	14228	$0.00	1	4%	1/1/2002
4	42 Hamton Ct	Portland	ME	US	04100	$6.20	2	11%	4/5/2010

Bottom Border.

Several additional border options are available.

The first four options give you the bottom, top, left, and right borders of the currently selected range of cells. You can select multiple options. For example, you can click Left Border and then click Top Border to make both of those borders visible.

The No Border option removes all the visible borders from the selected range of cells. All Borders turns on every border line for every cell in the entire range. This option is great for showing a mini table on my sheet, such as the Sales Rep table I added in Figure 10.13.

This table explains what the sales rep codes mean. It basically shows the abbreviation followed by the rep's name. The entire range of cells (J13:K16) has a border around it.

The Outside Borders option turns on just the outside border of a range of cells, but none of the inside borders. The Thick Box Border option does the same thing, but it makes the border size extra thick. Notice how this looks with the mini table in Figure 10.13.

Figure 10.13

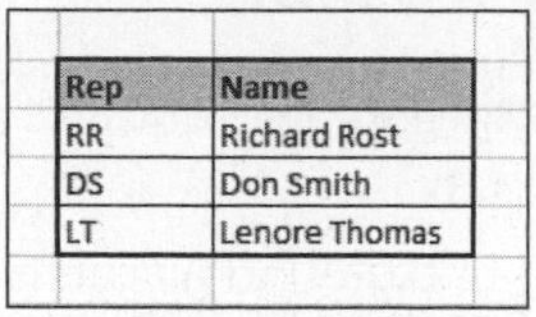

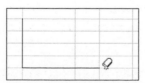

Thick Box Border.

You can see additional options for a bottom double border, a thick bottom border, and so on. These create exactly the borders you expect them to.

In the Draw Borders area of the menu is an option that says Draw Border. If you select this option, your mouse pointer changes into a pencil. You can then click and drag on your spreadsheet to draw borders by hand.

Click and release on a specific cell border to highlight just that border. Click and drag across several cells in a straight line to highlight all those borders. Finally, click and drag a square to highlight the outside borders of a range of cells.

TIP

If you hold down the Ctrl key while clicking and dragging, you create an All Borders effect inside the range of cells you select. Likewise, if you hold down the Shift key, you switch to the Erase Borders tool.

If you decide that you've make a mistake with your borders, just click the **Erase Borders** tool. This turns your mouse pointer into an eraser that you can use to click and drag over your borders to clean them up. (See Figure 10.14.)

Figure 10.14

Eraser tool.

Also on the Borders drop-down menu are options to change the line color and line style. This makes it possible for you to create, for example, a blue dotted-line border or a thick red border. You can use your imagination to create some fun combinations.

The Least You Need to Know

- You can easily change the font face and size of your text using the Font group on the Ribbon's Home tab.
- Adjusting the text and background fill colors makes your spreadsheet more readable.
- Use borders to give your spreadsheets a more professional look and feel.

Rows and Columns

In This Chapter

- Manipulating the rows and columns in your spreadsheets
- Automatically resizing columns to fit the data in them
- Inserting and deleting rows and columns
- Hiding information from prying eyes
- Using the Ribbon to work with rows and columns

So far, you've learned how to format the data inside cells. In this chapter, you look at how to format the rows and columns that make up your spreadsheets.

Resizing a Row or Column

Open the Customers spreadsheet that you worked on in previous chapters. You can find a copy of it on the CD in this chapter's folder.

One of the customers, Bill Williams, has moved. His new address is 1234 Longknecker Blvd, Apt 32a. As you can see from Figure 11.1, when you enter this into the address cell, C2, it's too big to fit.

Figure 11.1

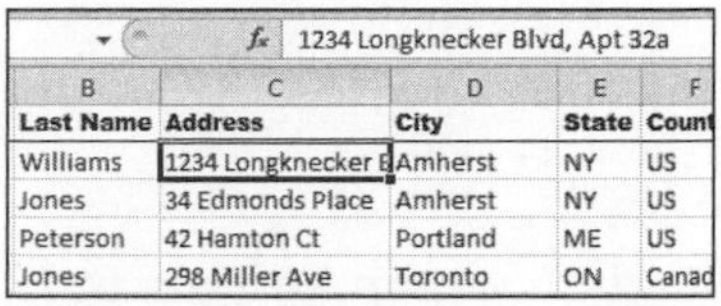

The data is too long for the cell.

In a previous chapter, when this happened, you simply reduced the font size so the data fit inside the cell. What if you don't want to reduce the font size because it's the size you want it? There's a better way to handle this problem: make the column wider. Here's how you do it:

1. Move your mouse over the line to the right side of the column header. It changes to a double arrow. (See Figure 11.2.)

2. Click and drag to the right or left to resize the column as wide or as narrow as you'd like.

Figure 11.2

Font		⌐	Alignment		⌐	Nui

| ▼ | ⌐ | | f_x | 1234 Longknecker Blvd, Apt 32a | | |

		C		⊕	D	E
lame	Address				City	State
ms	1234 Longknecker Blvd, Apt 32a			Amherst		NY
	34 Edmonds Place			Amherst		NY
on	42 Hamton Ct			Portland		ME

Resizing columns.

TIP

If you double-click on the border between two column headers while you have the double arrow, Excel automatically resizes the column perfectly to fit whatever data is in it.

You might notice that some of your cells have nothing #### symbols in them, such as the ones shown in Figure 11.3. This is simply because the data is too large to fit inside those cells and you need to make the column wider. This often happens with numeric data.

Figure 11.3

	H	I	
	alance	Bathrooms	Di
272	#####	3 1/2	
	$0.00	1	
	$6.20	2	
	#####	1/2	
	#####	3	
	#####	3	

A column that is too narrow.

If you like control and you want to be able to specify the *exact* width of your column, right-click the column header and then select the **Column Width** option (see Figure 11.4).

Figure 11.4

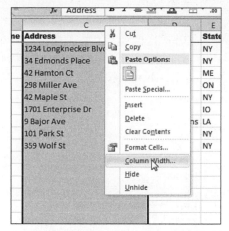

Manually adjusting a column width.

You can then type in a number for the column's width. This number is roughly the number of characters that the column can hold, but it isn't exact because different fonts and font sizes can affect this number.

Everything mentioned in this chapter applies equally to rows and columns. This means that you can click and drag or double-click to resize the height of a row by eye, or you can right-click and select **Row Height** to type a manual height (although this is in font points, not characters).

Resizing Multiple Rows or Columns

If you want to resize multiple columns (or rows) so that they're all the same width, follow these steps:

1. Move your mouse over the middle of the first column header you want to resize, as in Figure 11.5. It doesn't have to be the *exact* middle, but don't click the edges of it.

2. Click and drag to the right or left to select multiple columns.

3. Release the mouse button. Multiple columns are now highlighted.

4. Move to the edge of any column header until you get the double arrow for resizing.

5. Click and drag to resize the column. When you release the mouse button this time, *all* the columns you selected are resized to the exact same width. (See Figure 11.6.)

Figure 11.5

	A ↓	B	C	
1	First Name	Last Name	Address	Ci
2	Bill	Williams	1234 Longknecker Blvd, Apt 32a	Ar
3	Peter	Jones	34 Edmonds Place	Ar
4	Peter	Peterson	42 Hamton Ct	Po
5	Sue	Jones	298 Miller Ave	To

Selecting multiple columns.

Figure 11.6

A1 ▼ ⬤ *fx* First Na

	A	B	C	
1	First Name	Last Name	Address	City
2	Bill	Williams	1234 Longkn	Amb
3	Peter	Jones	34 Edmonds	Amb
4	Peter	Peterson	42 Hamton C	Port
5	Sue	Jones	298 Miller Av	Torc

Resizing multiple columns.

NOTICE

If you select multiple columns and then double-click to resize any of the columns, they're all resized to fit the data inside each column. This is the best way to make all your columns fit their data exactly.

Yes, these tricks also work for resizing rows. You can select multiple rows and then click and drag or double-click to resize all the rows together.

Deleting a Row or Column

If you want to erase data from a column, simply select the column by clicking the column header and then press the **Delete** key on your keyboard. This is called "clearing" the column's contents. It erases only the data from the column; it does not delete the column itself. (See Figure 11.7.)

Figure 11.7

C1 ▼ ⬤ *fx*

	A	B	C ↓	D	
1	First Name	Last Name		City	S
2	Bill	Williams		Amherst	N
3	Peter	Jones		Amherst	N
4	Peter	Peterson		Portland	N
5	Sue	Jones		Toronto	C
6	Edward	Watson		Buffalo	N

Clearing a column.

Instead of clearing the contents of a column, sometimes you want to delete the column and remove it completely from the spreadsheet. To do that, right-click the column header and select **Delete** from the pop-up menu.

Now the entire column is gone. This is especially handy if you want to remove formatting such as colors or borders that might have been in that column. Sometimes you can delete the data but you still have to delete all the formatting; deleting the column removes it completely from the sheet.

TIP

You can also delete individual cells or ranges of cells. If you right-click a cell or range of cells, you also see a Delete option. If you select Delete, you are asked whether you want to shift the cells left or up (to fill in the hole left by the deleted cells) or whether you want to delete the entire row or column. I seldom use this feature, but it's available.

Of course, you can select multiple columns and delete them all at once. These techniques also apply equally to rows.

Inserting a Row or Column

Sometimes you want to insert a column between two other columns. Let's say you want to add a Middle Initial column between First Name and Last Name. Here's how to insert a column:

1. Click to select the column you want to insert in front of. For this example, click to highlight the Last Name column.

2. Right-click the column and select **Insert**.

A new, blank column is inserted into your sheet at the desired location. Also notice that some of the formatting from the surrounding columns is in place in that new column. For example, the bottom border and font from the header row has been copied into this column.

TIP

Here's a neat trick: want to insert three columns? Select three columns first, starting at the location you want to insert in front of, and then right-click and select **Insert**. You'll see three columns inserted at that spot.

You can insert rows the same way you insert columns.

Hiding Rows or Columns

Sometimes you need to hide a column. Perhaps you have a spreadsheet that contains sensitive information and you don't want the casual observer to see it. Or perhaps you have financial calculations and you don't need to see every single column—you need to see just the finished result. All that extra data can clutter up your screen.

You can easily hide columns by right-clicking the column's header and selecting **Hide**.

After you select Hide, you'll see the column disappear. The astute observer will notice a gap in the sequence of letters (this example skips from H to J). Also notice in Figure 11.8 that the column header border is a bit thicker in that spot. That's to let you know that there's a hidden column at that point.

Figure 11.8

	H	J	
y	ZIP	Bathrooms	Di
	14226-8272	3 1/2	
	14228	1	
	04100	2	
a	M4B 1B3	1/2	

Hidden column.

When you hide a column, Excel effectively makes the width of the column zero. Another way to hide the column is to manually shrink the column width yourself by clicking and dragging—that's basically the same as selecting the Hide option.

To unhide the column, you have two options. The first way is to select the two columns that border the hidden column and then right-click and select **Unhide**. This brings the column back to the land of the visible.

The second way to unhide the column is to move your mouse over that border. To do this, you have to come at it from the *right* side. Notice that your mouse pointer changes to a double arrow, but it's slightly different from the normal resizing double arrow. This arrow has two thin vertical lines in the middle instead of one thick one. When you see the double arrow, you can click and drag to the right, to give your column some width and effectively unhide it.

> **WARNING**
>
> Keep in mind that this method of hiding your rows and columns is not a surefire way of keeping people from viewing your data because they can always unhide your columns.

Moving a Row or Column

If you want to reorganize your columns, you have a couple options. The easiest method is to simply cut and paste the columns.

1. First, select the column(s) you want to move.

2. Right-click them and select **Cut**. Notice the selection box around those cells (what I like to call the "dancing ants").

3. Right-click the column that you want to move the selected columns in front of.

4. Select **Insert Cut Cells**. This effectively moves your columns to this new location. (You can also do the same thing with rows.)

The second way you can move a column is a little trickier, but after you get the hang of it, it's a piece of cake.

1. Click to select the column you want to move.

2. Move your mouse anywhere over the thick selection border that surrounds the data in the column so that you have a four-way arrow, as in Figure 11.9. You can use the top, left, or right sides—it doesn't matter.

Figure 11.9

Move range arrows.

3. Now, if you just click and drag to move the column, you will replace the column you drop the selection on. This is generally not what you want to do. Instead, right-click and drag the column. When you drop it, you get a menu. Select **Shift Right and Move**. That shifts the rest of the columns to the right and moves your column.

Ribbon Buttons

Buttons on the Ribbon can replicate a lot of the row- and column-related features you've used so far in this chapter. Some people prefer the right-click context menus, but you might like the Ribbon buttons, so we show you both methods.

You can find these buttons on the Home tab in the Cells group. You'll see buttons labeled Insert, Delete, and Format.

Clicking the Insert button inserts a blank cell at the current location and then pushes everything else in that column down one row. If you don't want this behavior, click the down arrow next to Insert to get these options:

- Insert Cells gives you the option of shifting the rest of the cells right or down, or inserting a whole row or column.

- Insert Sheet Rows inserts an entire row above the current row.

- Insert Sheet Columns inserts an entire column to the left of the current column.

- Insert Sheet inserts a whole new worksheet in front of the current sheet.

The Delete button and its related options work almost the exact same way as the Insert button, except to delete cells, rows, columns, and sheets.

On the Format button, you can see options to change the row height and column width (including AutoFit, which we talked about earlier, when Excel automatically adjusts the size of a row or column based on its content).

You'll also notice options to hide or unhide rows or columns, rename, move or copy sheets, and lots more. Generally, these commands are available on the Ribbon menus because some people prefer to use the keyboard to access them. Without a mouse to click and drag a column width, for example, you would press Alt, H, I, C to insert a column.

The Least You Need to Know

- You can use the right-click menus or the Ribbon to insert or delete rows and columns.
- Double-click the right edge of a column header to have Excel AutoFit the column to the data.
- Hide columns simply by dragging their width to zero (or right-click and click Hide).
- Use the Ribbon commands to insert and delete rows and columns almost as easily as with the mouse.

Cell Alignment

In This Chapter

- Controlling the exact alignment of text inside a cell
- Displaying column headers diagonally at any angle
- Merging multiple cells and centering sheet headers on top of the page

You learned a little about cell alignment back in Chapter 2. You saw how to horizontally align text left or right inside a cell. In this chapter, you learn a lot more about how to control the positioning of your text in a cell or in multiple cells. Cell alignment involves a lot more than just left and right.

Left, Right, and Centered Text

First, open the Delivery Log sample file on the CD that came with the book in the Chapter 12 folder.

You learned about left and right alignment in Chapter 2. Dates always line up to the right of cells. Select all of column A, and then, on the Ribbon, on the Home tab, in the Alignment group, click the **Align Left** button. (See Figure 12.1.)

Figure 12.1

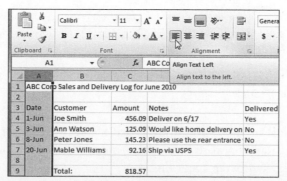

Aligning dates left.

Next, although the sale amounts are all lined up to the right of the column, the word "Amount" is not. Select all of Column C and then click the **Align Right** button, which is in the same group as the Align Left button.

Now center the delivery column by selecting all of column E and then clicking the **Center Text** button, which is right between the Align Left and Align Right buttons.

Wrapping Text

Take a look at the Notes in column D. If you click cell D6, you can see that the amount of visible information in that cell is small compared to the actual text that displays in the Formula bar.

You could just make this column wider, but doing so won't always help you. If you have hundreds of characters in that cell, you can't keep widening the column forever. And if you need to print the sheet, you don't want a superwide column.

You need to force whatever text is in that cell to *wrap* to a second line and then make the row higher. However, just making the row higher won't fix the problem because the text will still try to spill over to the next column. This is what the Wrap Text button is for. It "wraps" the text around to multiple lines in the same cell.

Select column D and then click the **Wrap Text** button in the Alignment group (see Figure 12.2).

Figure 12.2

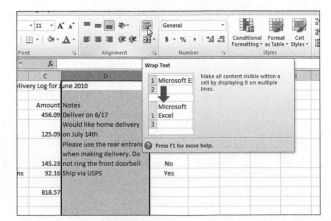

Wrapping text.

You can see that all the notes that were typed for each customer wrap inside each respective cell, just as in a word processor. You can make the column wider or narrower, and the text will wrap accordingly.

NOTICE

If you make your column wider, you may have to adjust the row height manually to avoid having some empty space in the row. Likewise, if you make the column narrower, you might find some of your text chopped off. An easy fix is to just select the column again, click the **Wrap Text** button to turn it off, and then click it on again. This automatically resizes all of your row heights.

Top, Middle, and Bottom Alignment

If you have cells that wrap to multiple lines, you might find that the adjacent cells in the same row line up to the bottom of their cells. You can easily change this by clicking the **Top Align** button, which is also in the Alignment group (see Figure 12.4).

Whenever you are working with a sheet that has wrapped text, you can select the whole sheet and then click the **Top Align** button. This way, you don't have to keep dealing with this issue.

You can use the Bottom Align or Center buttons in a similar manner. This is a matter of personal preference. Do whatever you think looks best for your spreadsheet.

To select the whole sheet, click the box where the row and column headers meet (see Figure 12.3).

Figure 12.3

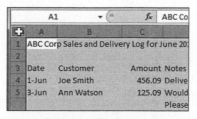

Selecting all of a sheet.

TIP

You can also press Ctrl+A on your keyboard to select all the cells in your sheet.

Click the **Top Align** button. All the cells in the sheet have a top-vertical alignment. Notice in Figure 12.4 that all of row 6 is top-aligned.

Figure 12.4

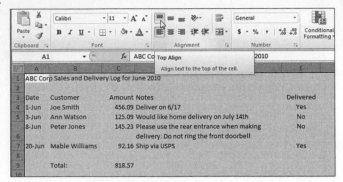

Top-aligning cells in a worksheet.

Notice that you can also find Middle Align and Bottom Align buttons right next to the Top Align button. They function similarly, giving you a middle and bottom vertical alignment for the text in your cells.

Orientation Angle

Let's have some fun with the column header labels by changing their angle of orientation. Select cells A3:E3 and apply some formatting by changing the font to Tahoma, making it a little bit bigger (12pt), changing the foreground color to blue, and changing the fill color to light yellow. You will have to widen the columns to fit the larger labels (see Figure 12.5).

Figure 12.5

	A	B	C	D	E	
1	ABC Corp Sales and Delivery Log for June 2010					
2						
3	**Date**	**Customer**	**Amount**	**Notes**	**Delivered**	
4	1-Jun	Joe Smith	456.09	Deliver on 6/17	Yes	
5	3-Jun	Ann Watson	125.09	Would like home delivery on July 14th	No	

Column header labels.

With A3:E3 still highlighted, click the **Orientation** button. You can select from a wide variety of angles to rotate your text; they're all self-explanatory. Have fun experimenting. Start by picking **Angle Counterclockwise** (as shown in Figure 12.6).

Figure 12.6

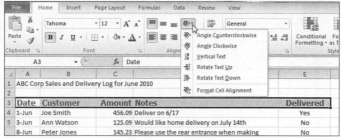

Angle Counterclockwise.

After the text is rotated, on the Home tab, in the Alignment group, click the **Bottom Align** button (see Figure 12.7). This will line all of the text up nicely on its left side (which is really the bottom of the cell).

Figure 12.7

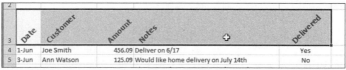

Bottom Align.

The Format Cells: Alignment Dialog Box

If you decide that you don't like an angle or any of the preset angles, you can change the exact angle of your text by clicking the **Format Cell Alignment** option at the bottom of the Orientation menu. Alternatively, you can click the **Format Cells: Alignment** dialog box launcher, which is the button in the bottom-right corner of the Alignment group area.

The Format Cells: Alignment dialog box has several alignment options. The first thing you'll probably notice is the Orientation box, in the upper-right corner. You can manually type in a number of degrees for your angle.

Otherwise, you can click and drag the Text marker to any angle you want, from 90 to –90 degrees. Optionally, if you want the text to be stacked vertically, you can click that option as well. This will display the letters one on top of the other, vertically. In Figure 12.8, it's set to 20 degrees.

Figure 12.8

Orientation is set to 20 degrees.

As you can see in Figure 12.9, the angle of the slope is gentler now.

Figure 12.9

The result of the orientation change.

Also in that Format Cells dialog box, you find options for the horizontal and vertical alignment of cells. Following are the options for horizontal alignment:

- **General**—The default cell alignment. Text aligns left. Numbers align to the right.

- **Left**—Aligns cell contents to the left. Text continues to the cell to the right unless that cell has a value, in which case, the text is truncated.

- **Center**—Aligns cell contents to the center of the cell. Text spills over to both sides of the cell. If one of those sides has a value, it is truncated.

- **Right**—Aligns cell contents to the right. Text spills to the left unless that cell is full, in which case it's truncated.

- **Fill**—Fills just the current cell with text unless you also format the cells to the right of this cell with the Fill format. If you do this, the text spills over into the formatted cells. You can fill as many cells as you want with the text from one cell.

- **Justify**—For cells that have a lot of text, gives you a "newspaper" look in which the text is justified to the left and right sides of the cell and spacing is added between words. You have to have more than one line of text to notice the effect, of course.

- **Center Across Selection**—Centers text over multiple columns.

- **Distributed**—Spreads out the text in a cell to fill the whole cell, changing the spacing between words to fit the text evenly.

You'll find similar formatting options for vertical alignment. You have seen Top, Center, and Bottom alignments on the Ribbon. The Justify option spreads out multiple lines of text (increasing the line spacing between them) if the row height is larger than it should be to fit the text.

Distributed does the same thing. The only real difference emerges if you have vertically stacked text (because you changed the orientation angle). If you have only one word, for example, Justify aligns it to the top of the cell, whereas Distributed centers it vertically. Otherwise, both options basically do the same thing.

Figure 12.10

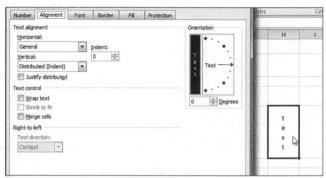

Vertically aligning text.

The Center Across Selection Options

One of the neatest effects in text alignment involves the Center Across Selection options. These options are great for sheet headers that you want to go across the entire page. Notice that the sample sheet has a sheet header in cell A1. To center these headers across the entire top of the page (at least, columns A through E), follow these steps:

1. Place the text you want to use for a header in the leftmost cell of the range you want to span. This sheet already has text in cell A1.

2. Starting with A1, select all the cells from A1 to the end of the span, which is E1.

3. Open up the **Format Cells** dialog box. Go to the **Alignment** tab. In the Text alignment section, open up the **Horizontal** drop-down box. Click the **Center Across Selection** option.

This centers the text among the selected cells (A1:E1). Note that even though it looks like the text has moved, it's still in cell A1.

It can be confusing having random text just floating in the middle of your spreadsheet. This is why there is also another, slightly different technique called Merge and Center.

Merge and Center

Click **Undo** once to remove Center Across Cells, placing the header back to the left in A1. Repeat the same steps for 1 and 2, but this time, instead of clicking the Center Across Cells option, click the **Merge and Center** button on the Ribbon (see Figure 12.11).

Figure 12.11

Merge and Center.

Now your text looks the same as it did before (centered across that range of cells). However, this time, the cells are *merged* and can be treated as *one* cell (see Figure 12.12).

NOTICE

Usually you Merge and Center only text labels, but if you do Merge and Center values, this cell is still A1 for the purposes of formulas.

Also, you can remove the Merge and Center effect by simply clicking the Merge and Center button again, after clicking on the merged cells.

You'll also see a Merge Cells option in the same drop-down menu. This merges the cells without applying the Center format.

Now you can click this one cell to edit it, change formats, apply colors, and more. Figure 12.12 shows the header. Also note that the original row 2 has been deleted.

Figure 12.12

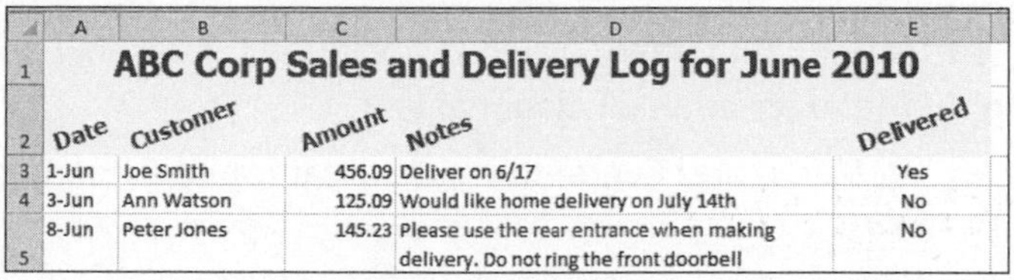

	A	B	C	D	E
1	ABC Corp Sales and Delivery Log for June 2010				
2	Date	Customer	Amount	Notes	Delivered
3	1-Jun	Joe Smith	456.09	Deliver on 6/17	Yes
4	3-Jun	Ann Watson	125.09	Would like home delivery on July 14th	No
5	8-Jun	Peter Jones	145.23	Please use the rear entrance when making delivery. Do not ring the front doorbell	No

Updated sheet header.

Indenting

Some of the buttons on the Ribbon increase and decrease the indent inside a cell. You won't likely use these buttons often; they're used to increase (or decrease) the margin between the text and the left border of the cell (see Figure 12.13). These are the Increase Indent and Decrease Indent buttons in the Alignment group of the Home tab.

Figure 12.13

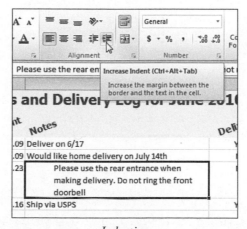

Indenting.

You can also find the option to indent text in a cell on the Format Cells: Alignment dialog box. You'll see a little box with a number on it labeled "Indent." The default value is 0. You can adjust it accordingly.

The Least You Need to Know

- You can use the Ribbon for most cell alignment tasks, including left, right, center, top, and bottom.
- The Format Cells: Alignment dialog box includes additional options, such as changing the exact angle of diagonal text.
- You can use Merge and Center to create great-looking headers for the top of your sheets.

Conditional Formatting

In This Chapter

- Changing the format of a cell based on the value in that cell
- Adding data bars, color sets, and icons to cells based on their values
- Managing, editing, and creating your own formatting rules

Conditional formatting allows you to change the format that is applied to a cell based on its value or other conditions. You can make seriously overdue invoices show up in red. You can flag all your New York customers with a yellow background. You can create different data bars and icons to appear in cells to illustrate values.

Conditional formatting is a fun way to make your sheets look professional, and to make specific information stand out based on criteria that you specify.

Conditional Formatting

Open up the Customers workbook from the Chapter 13 folder on your CD. The following sections use this workbook to show you what conditional formatting is about.

Highlight Cell Rules

The first and easiest type of conditional formatting simply highlights a cell that meets certain criteria that you specify. For example, let's say that you want all the customers who have a balance of $500 or more to show up in red text. Here's how you do it:

1. Select the cell or cells to which you want to apply conditional formatting. In this case, select all of column H, which has the balance information on customers.

2. On the Ribbon, on the Home tab, in the Styles group, click **Conditional Formatting > Highlight Cells Rules > Greater Than** (see Figure 13.1).

Figure 13.1

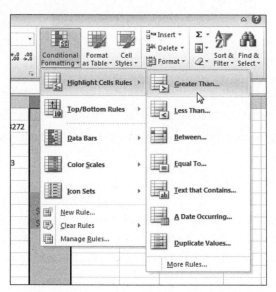

Greater Than conditional formatting option.

3. Type in the amount you want to use as the minimum value that gets formatted—in this case, $500. Notice the Live Preview of your data in the background as soon as you change this value.

4. Select a format for this text. You can pick from the list of available options (in the right drop-down menu) or choose **Custom Format** to make your own. For now, select **Light Red Fill with Dark Red Text**. Click **OK**.

The three values in column H that are over $500 are now formatted in red font. If you change any of the values in this column, the format automatically adjusts. The conditional formatting is now part of the cells in the entire column (see Figure 13.2).

Figure 13.2

	H	
	Balance	Ba
8272	-$25.00	
	$0.00	
	$6.20	
B3	$50.45	
	$90.00	
	$299.00	
	$800.00	
	$1,500.00	
	$9,182.00	

Conditional formatting in use.

NOTICE

The header label Balance has also been filled in red. That's because the header cell was part of our original range. To remove the formatting from that cell, just click cell H1 and then click **Conditional Formatting > Clear Rules > From Selected Cells**.

Let's say you want to make any customers with a balance of less than $50 show up in green. Repeat the previous steps, but this time, select **Less Than** instead of Greater Than as the rule. Then type **$50** and pick the **Green Fill with Dark Green Text** format.

Notice that all the rows higher than 10 are now also green. This is because Excel treats blank cells as having values less than zero. You'll see how to deal with formatting blank cells later in this chapter.

Variable Criteria

You aren't limited to just typing a number for the conditions. Let's say that you want to be able to make the high and low values something the user can set on the sheet without having to know how to work with conditional formatting.

First, clear the conditional formatting from this sheet by clicking **Conditional Formatting > Clear Rules > From Entire Sheet**.

Next, create a mini table to specify the maximum and minimum values. In Figure 13.3, this table is in cells A13:B14.

Figure 13.3

	A	B	
9	Joe	Smith	101
10	John	Picard	359
11			
12			
13	Max:	$1,000.00	
14	Min:	$500.00	
15			
16			
17			

Criteria table.

Now you can use these values for the conditional formatting. Instead of typing the actual values, however, you give Excel the location of the cells. Here's how:

1. Select column H again.

2. Click **Conditional Formatting > Highlight Cells Rules > Greater Than**.

3. This time, instead of typing a value, click the box just to the right of the amount (see Figure 13.4). Notice that the dialog box shrinks.

Figure 13.4

Selection box, expanded.

4. Now click the cell that holds the value you want to use. In this example, click B13. Notice that "=$B$13" is now in the amount box (see Figure 13.5).

Figure 13.5

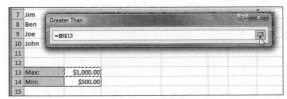

Selection box, collapsed.

5. Click the same button next to the amount again. The dialog box expands to its normal size.

6. Choose a format. Choose **red** again. Click **OK**.

NOTICE

Don't worry about the dollar signs that display in cell $B$13. That's called an *absolute reference,* and you'll learn what that means in Chapter 22.

Now you'll see that the conditional format has taken place; however, this time, if you change the value in B13, the format automatically updates for all the cells in column H. You can repeat the same steps for the minimum value.

In addition to greater than/less than logic, the Highlight Cells Rules enable you to highlight cells based on the following:

- **Between**—Highlights cells whose values fall between two criteria.

- **Equal**—Highlights cells that are exactly equal to a value.

- **Text That Contains**—Highlights cells that contain a specific value. This is great for highlighting all of your customers from "NY," for example.

- **A Date Occurring**—Highlights dates that occur within a common set of dates, such as yesterday, tomorrow, last week, and so on. If you want to use static dates, such as 1/1/2010, you can use the Greater Than, Less Than, or Between rules.

- **Duplicate Values**—Highlights any values in your range that are duplicates of other values in that range. You can also set it for unique values.

Top-Bottom Rules

In addition to checking specific criteria, you can use conditional formatting to compare data to itself. For example, let's say that you have a list of sales reps with their monthly sales figures. You want to know the top and bottom performers.

Open the Sales Data 2010 spreadsheet from the Chapter 13 folder on your CD.

Because our sheet has 16 points of data (4 sales reps and 4 months), let's find the top 3 values in our sales data. This enables you to visually point out which sales reps have the highest sales and in which months those sales occurred. Follow these steps:

1. Select the range B2:E5.

2. Click **Conditional Formatting > Top Bottom Rules > Top 10 Items**.

3. Change the number on the left (the criteria) to 3.

4. Change the format on the right to whatever you think looks good, such as **"Green Fill with Dark Green Text."** Click **OK** (see Figure 13.6).

Figure 13.6

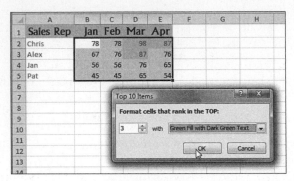

Top 3 values.

Now you can clearly see the top three performers. You can use this technique to see the Top X items in any set of data.

You also see options for the Bottom X items and the Top or Bottom X percent of items. If you want to see the top 5 percent of items, select the "Top 10%" option and then change the percentage to 5.

Finally, you can also select Above or Below Average. Excel calculates the average value of your set of data and then highlights all the items that are above or below that value, depending on which option you choose.

Data Bars

In addition to changing the color of a cell based on its value, conditional formatting can add simple graphics to a cell. One type of graphic is called a *Data Bar*.

> **DEFINITION**
>
> A **Data Bar** allows you to visualize trends in data by creating a color horizontal bar across the back of a cell, the size of which is proportional to the value of that cell with regards to the rest of the values in that column. In a nutshell, a Data Bar is a mini bar chart displayed behind the data in a column.

On the sales data sheet, let's add a total for each sales rep in column F. Total up the sales for each rep with a SUM function in column F. (See Figure 13.7.) In cell F2, for example, you would say:

=SUM(B2:E2)

Figure 13.7

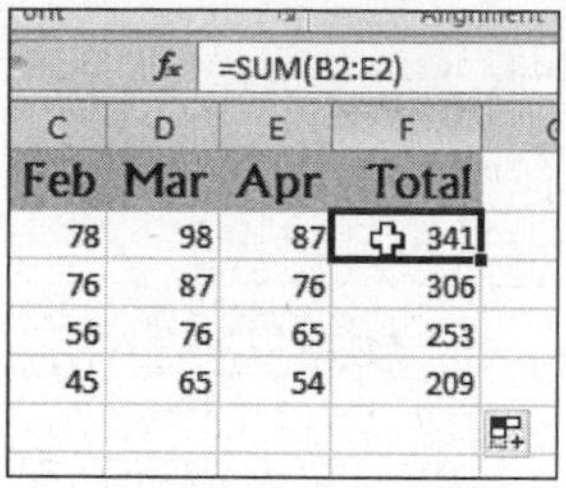

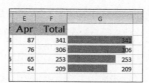

	C	D	E	F	
fx	=SUM(B2:E2)				
	Feb	Mar	Apr	Total	
	78	98	87	341	
	76	87	76	306	
	56	76	65	253	
	45	65	54	209	

Add SUM of sales.

Now select cells F2:F5 and click **Conditional Formatting > Data Bars**. Now pick either one of the solid bars or gradient fills. Notice the data bars in the cells—you might want to make the column wider to see them better (see Figure 13.8).

Figure 13.8

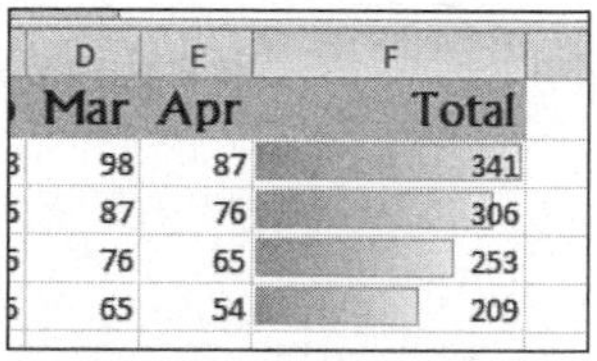

D	E	F
Mar	Apr	Total
98	87	341
87	76	306
76	65	253
65	54	209

Data bars.

Here's a neat trick. You can use data bars instead of adding a chart to your sheets. Remove the current data bars by clicking on the **Undo** button, and then try this:

1. In cell G2, type the formula: **=F2**

2. AutoFill the formula down the column. This essentially makes the values in column G the same as in column F. If you don't remember how to use AutoFill, review Chapter 7.

3. Add data bars to column G (Conditional Formatting > Data Bars). Your sheet should now look like Figure 13.9.

Figure 13.9

E	F	G
Apr	Total	
87	341	341
76	306	306
65	253	253
54	209	209

Added data bars.

4. Select the range G2:G5 and click **Conditional Formatting > Manage Rules**.

5. Click the Data Bar rule and then click **Edit Rule** (see Figure 13.10).

Figure 13.10

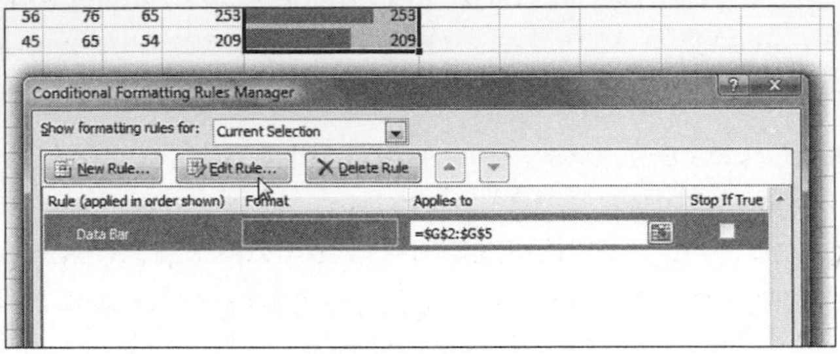

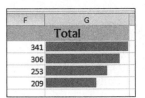

Edit Rule.

6. Click the box that reads **"Show Bar Only"** and then click **OK** twice.

7. Select cells F1 and G1, and then click **Merge and Center**.

As you can see in Figure 13.11, you have a nice set of data bars that are almost as good as embedding a chart in your sheet (which you learn all about in Chapter 20).

Figure 13.11

	F	G
		Total
	341	
	306	
	253	
	209	

Finished data bars.

Color Scales

Like data bars, color scales enable you to visually see the differences in your data by comparing data points to the rest of the data points in a range.

Try this:

1. Select the range B2:E5.

2. Click **Conditional Formatting > Color Scales > Green–Yellow–Red Color Scale**.

All the cells in the range have colors based on their values relative to the other values in the range. Low values are red; higher values are progressively more yellow and then green.

You can pick from several different available color schemes. If you really want a custom look to your sheet, you can make your own color scale by clicking **Conditional Formatting > Color Scales > More Rules**.

Now you can specify whether you want a two-color or three-color scale (see Figure 13.12). You can also pick the colors, and the minimum and maximum values—which you can leave as the lowest and highest values in the range, or specify set values. If you're grading tests, for example, you might want to set the maximum value to 100.

> **WARNING**
>
> When picking colors, don't make them too dark; otherwise, you won't be able to read the foreground text.

Figure 13.12

Edit the Rule Description:		
Format all cells based on their values:		
Format Style: 2-Color Scale ▾		
	Minimum	Maximum
Type:	Lowest Value ▾	Highest Value ▾
Value:	(Lowest value)	(Highest value)
Color:	▾	▾
Preview:		
	OK	Cancel

Editing Color Scale rule.

Icon Sets

The last graphical indicator you can use with conditional formatting is the icon set. This displays a simple icon graphic that changes based on the values in your cells. For example:

1. Select F2:F5.

2. Click **Conditional Formatting > Icon Sets > 3 Arrows (Colored)**.

Notice in Figure 13.13 the different-colored arrows displaying in the cell with your values. The highest values have green arrows pointing up. The medium values have yellow arrows pointing to the side. The lowest values have red arrows pointing down.

Figure 13.13

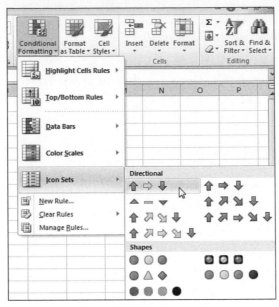

Icon sets.

If you don't like those icons, click **More Rules** to choose from a bunch of different icon sets. You can pick arrows, triangles, circles, bars, and more. You can also change the individual icons (see Figure 13.14).

Figure 13.14

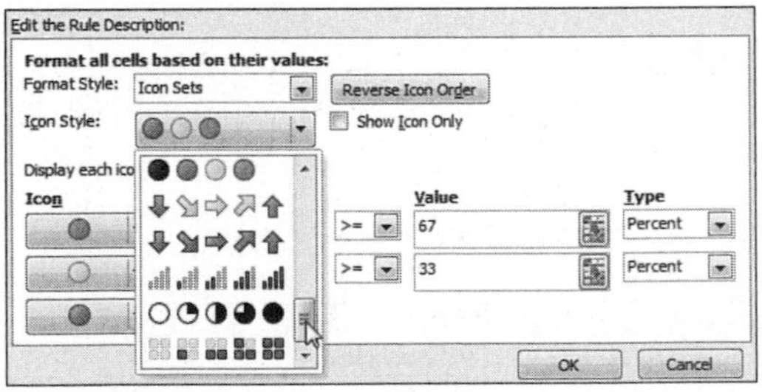

Icon styles.

You can also change the values that determine when to change icons (see Figure 13.15). For example, the five data bars' icon style changes values at 20, 40, 60, and 80 percent.

Figure 13.15

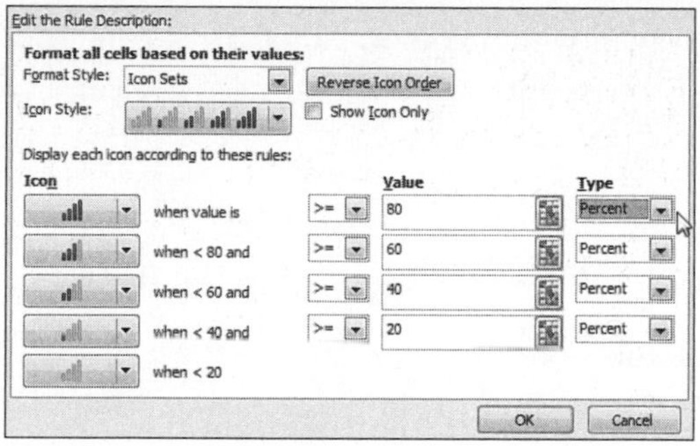

Changing icon values.

Managing Rules

After you have all of these rules in place, you need a way to manage them. Just click **Conditional Formatting > Manage Rules**. This will allow you to add new rules, edit existing rules, or delete any rules you no longer want (see Figure 13.16).

Normally, you'll see only the rules in the currently selected region. To see all the rules on the entire sheet, click the drop-down box next to Show Formatting Rules For and pick **This Worksheet**.

Figure 13.16

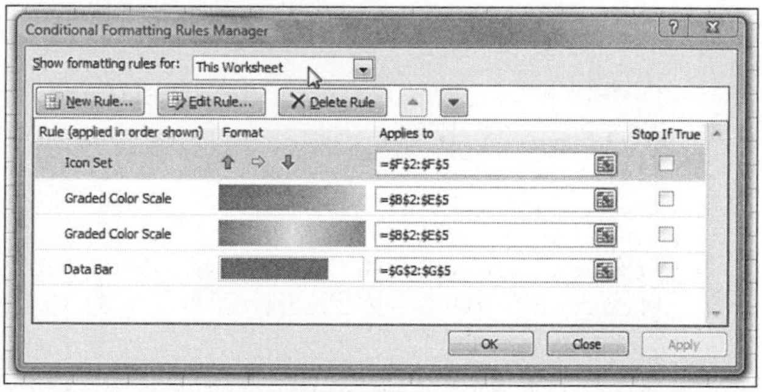

Managing rules.

Here, you'll see a list of all the rules on the worksheet in the order in which they are applied. The only time the order makes a difference is if you have a conflicting set of rules for the same range of cells. You can move the order in which they're applied by clicking the rule and then clicking the **Move Up** or **Move Down** buttons.

To edit a rule, click the **Edit Rule** button. Likewise, to delete a rule, there is a **Delete Rule** button.

You can also come here to create a new rule from scratch by clicking the **New Rule** button. This is the way in which you would create a rule to do something that you cannot do with the Ribbon buttons. For example, you can create a rule to highlight blank cells in red.

1. Select the range B2:E5.

2. Click **Conditional Formatting > Manage Rules**.

3. Click **New Rule**.

4. Click **Format Only Cells That Contain**.

5. Under the Format Only Cells With section, select **Blanks** from the drop-down menu (see Figure 13.17).

6. Click the **Format** button.

7. Click the **Fill** tab.

8. Click the bright red color box. Click **OK** three times.

Figure 13.17

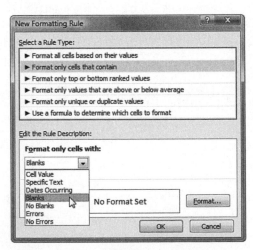

Blanks.

Now delete a value from your range of cells. The cell should turn bright red. This indicates that you are missing a value from that cell.

You can also use this technique to show cells that have error messages in them. Instead of showing blanks, just pick the "Errors" option. Now, any cells that have Excel error messages in them (such as the dreaded Divide By Zero error) will be formatted accordingly.

The Least You Need to Know

- You can use Highlight Cells rules to change the foreground and background color of cells based on their values.
- Data bars, color sets, and icon sets are a good way to graphically display data on your sheets without the need for charts.
- You can create highly customizable Conditional Formatting rules using the Manage Rules feature.

Styles and Themes

In This Chapter

- Applying a consistent look and feel to your spreadsheets
- Using the Format Painter to copy formats (only) from cell to cell
- Working with styles to make updating the look of a sheet easy
- Using themes to create professional, consistent-looking spreadsheets

You can make your spreadsheets look a lot more uniform and professional by properly utilizing styles and themes. A *style* is a packaged set of formatting that you can apply to a cell. A style can consist of a set font, alignment, borders, fill color, format, and more. Groups of styles are then packaged together into a *theme* to give your spreadsheets a uniform look. Styles and themes make editing and updating your sheets a breeze.

Formatting Without Styles

Before we take a look at using styles, let's see an example of when maintaining a consistent look and feel for spreadsheets is important. Open the Gradebook sample spreadsheet, which is located in the Chapter 14 folder on the CD (see Figure 14.1).

The gradebook consists of test and quiz scores from several students. To make this sheet easier to read, you can apply some formatting. Give the header row a light blue background and bold the font. Then set the quiz grades apart from the test grades by making the background for the tests a light orange and the quizzes a light green.

Figure 14.1

	A	B	C	D	E	F	G	H	I
1	Student	Test 1	Test 2	Quiz 1	Test 3	Test 4	Quiz 2	Final	Average
2	Joe	98	97	56	87	85	76	97	85
3	Mike	87	86	45	98	74	65	93	78
4	Sue	76	75	43	76	74	54	87	69
5	Pat	56	64	54	65	87	43	85	65
6	Bill	54	53	76	87	76	76	83	72
7	Bob	54	42	65	63	75	76	72	64
8	Dave	76	34	45	74	74	65	63	62
9	Average	72	64	55	79	78	65	83	71
10									

Gradebook sample spreadsheet.

Use a red background on the final exam grades and make the font bold. Finally, set all the averages to aqua and bold. Now the sheet is a little easier to read. You can clearly tell the tests apart from the quizzes, final exam grades, and averages. (See Figure 14.2.)

Figure 14.2

	A	B	C	D	E	F	G	H	I
1	Student	Test 1	Test 2	Quiz 1	Test 3	Test 4	Quiz 2	Final	Average
2	Joe	98	97	56	87	85	76	97	85
3	Mike	87	86	45	98	74	65	93	78
4	Sue	76	75	43	76	74	54	87	69
5	Pat	56	64	54	65	87	43	85	65
6	Bill	54	53	76	87	76	76	83	72
7	Bob	54	42	65	63	75	76	72	64
8	Dave	76	34	45	74	74	65	63	62
9	Average	72	64	55	79	78	65	83	71
10									

The gradebook formatted.

Now, let's say you want to add a Test 5 to the sheet. You'd need to insert it before the Final Exam grade. Right-click the column header for column H and select **Insert**. This inserts a blank new column. Now type the data for Test 5 (see Figure 14.3).

Figure 14.3

	E	F	G	H	I
	Test 3	Test 4	Quiz 2	Test 5	Final
	87	85	76	88	97
	98	74	65	77	93
	76	74	54	66	87
	65	87	43	55	85
	87	76	76	44	83
	63	75	76	33	72
	74	74	65	0	63
	79	78	65	52	83

Test 5 has been added.

Normally, the column is formatted based on the column to the left of it—in this case, that's Quiz 2. So column H has a green background. You could manually format the column, or, if you wanted to automatically copy the format from one of the other test columns onto this one, you could use the Format Painter.

Format Painter

The Format Painter enables you to copy and paste just the format of one cell to another, without copying the data.

Using the Format Painter is easy. Just click the cell (or select the range) that has the format you want to copy. For example, in the Gradepoint spreadsheet, select F2:F8.

Next, on the Home tab, in the Clipboard group, click the **Format Painter** icon (see Figure 14.4).

Figure 14.4

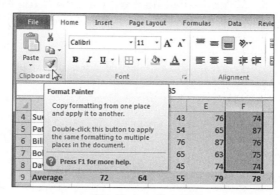

The Format Painter.

Notice that your icon changes to a plus with a paintbrush. Select the cell (or range) where you want to "paste" the format. In this case, select H2:H8. This pastes the format from the first range of cells into the second range.

> **TIP**
>
> If you want to copy the format to multiple locations, double-click the **Format Painter** icon. It stays on, enabling you to paste the format in several places. Click the **Format Painter** again to turn it off (or press **Escape**).

This was a simple edit to make because you are working with a small sheet. But what if you had 500 students and 20 tests to format? You can see how a more complex sheet requires a better approach. The Format Painter is nice, but it's good for small-scale operations.

When you have a humongous sheet with thousands of rows and dozens of columns, and the boss wants you to change all the test values to dark green, that could take quite a while to do. If you want full control over the formatting of your sheets, you'll benefit greatly from learning how to work with styles.

Close the Gradepoint sheet without saving any of your changes. Reopen the copy that has no formatting from the CD, and let's start over.

Applying Styles

Styles provide a specific look and feel to sections of sheets. For example, you can find a style for the header row. Select A1:I1, and then, on the Home tab, in the Styles group, click the **Cell Styles** box.

Several styles display on a menu. The styles have names like Normal, Bad, Good, Neutral, Calculation, Warning Text, Accent1, and so on. You can ignore the names at this point and just focus on the look and feel of each style.

Pick a style you want to use for the header row (see Figure 14.5). Notice as you move your mouse over each style that you can see a Live Preview of what that style would look like in your sheet behind the drop-down menu.

Figure 14.5

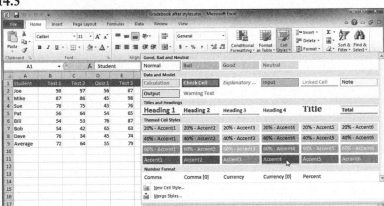

Apply a style.

Select **Accent4** for the header row. Click it and notice the purple background with white text color. Very nice.

Now let's select all the test grades and apply a different style to them. You can select multiple *noncontiguous* ranges of cells by selecting the first range, holding down the **Ctrl** key, and then selecting additional ranges. This enables you to select as many different ranges of cells as you want that might not be next to each other.

Select all the test grades and apply the 20% Accent2 style, which is black text on a light red background. (See Figure 14.6.)

Figure 14.6

	A	B	C	D	E	F	G	H	I
1	Student	Test 1	Test 2	Quiz 1	Test 3	Test 4	Quiz 2	Final	Average
2	Joe	98	97	56	87	85	76	97	85
3	Mike	87	86	45	98	74	65	93	78
4	Sue	76	75	43	76	74	54	87	69
5	Pat	56	64	54	65	87	43	85	65
6	Bill	54	53	76	87	76	76	83	72
7	Bob	54	42	65	63	75	76	72	64
8	Dave	76	34	45	74	74	65	63	62
9	Average	72	64	55	79	78	65	83	71
10									
11									

Style the test grades.

Apply the 20% Accent5 style to the quiz grades, the 60% Accent2 style to the final exam, and the Accent1 style to the averages.

Modifying Styles

Now here's the real beauty of using styles. Let's say you want to make a change. Instead of light red, you want all the test grades to have a light green background. Well, there's no sense in selecting everything again and changing all the styles, or even using the Format Painter. Instead, you can modify the style that you already specified for the test grades. Here's how you do it:

1. Click any *one* cell that has the style you want to modify. Click F4.

2. Click the **Cell Styles** drop-down box. You'll see that the style currently applied to that cell is highlighted.

3. Right-click that style and select **Modify**.

4. A dialog box displays asking you to specify the components of this style. You can choose the number format, alignment, font, border, fill, and so on. The style shown in Figure 14.7 (20% Accent2) is just made up of a font and fill color. Stick with that for now.

5. Click the **Format** button in the upper-right corner of the Style dialog box.

6. The Format Cells dialog box displays. Click the **Font** tab and select whichever font you want. You can also change the font color here. Make it a dark green, and then leave the rest of the font information alone.

7. Click the **Fill** tab and select a background color. Select **light green**. You can also choose from different fill effects, patterns, and more.

8. Click **OK** twice.

Now that you're back to the spreadsheet, notice that *all* of the cells that had the Test style applied to them have been changed to the new specification. This is the power of styles. If you set up your sheet right in the first place and assign everything to a style, all you have to do is change the style itself, and the whole sheet is updated. Formatting changes are now easy, and you can update whole sheets with just a few clicks.

Creating Your Own Styles

If you want to create your own styles, it's not hard. Here's how you do it.

1. Modify a single cell (or range of cells) with the format you want to have in your new Style, or just pick an existing cell that has the format you like. For example, click one of the Test cells you currently have, such as F4.

2. Click **Cell Styles > New Style** (see Figure 14.7).

3. Type a name for the new style: **Test Style**.

4. Choose the elements this style will include. Don't worry about the number format, alignment, border, or protection. Check those boxes off. Just worry about the font and fill for your style.

5. Click the **Format** button and change the font and fill colors accordingly, just as you did previously. Make this one Tahoma, 12pt, dark blue, with a yellow fill color, just to set it apart from everything else.

Figure 14.7

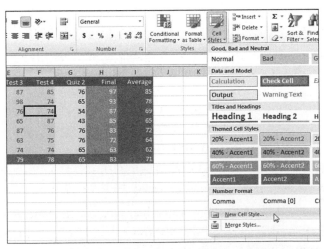

Create a new style.

6. Click **OK**. Now, nothing appears to happen on your sheet, but that's because you haven't applied the style to anything yet. Select all the Test grades again and apply the new Style you just made (see Figure 14.8).

Figure 14.8

	A	B	C	D	E	F	G	H	I
1	Student	Test 1	Test 2	Quiz 1	Test 3	Test 4	Quiz 2	Final	Average
2	Joe	98	97	56	87	85	76	97	85
3	Mike	87	86	45	98	74	65	93	78
4	Sue	76	75	43	76	74	54	87	69
5	Pat	56	64	54	65	87	43	85	65
6	Bill	54	53	76	87	76	76	83	72
7	Bob	54	42	65	63	75	76	72	64
8	Dave	76	34	45	74	74	65	63	62
9	Average	72	64	55	79	78	65	83	71

Sheet with new Test style.

Want to change that new style even more? You can right-click it to modify it, delete it, or even duplicate it to create another, similar style (like one for quizzes).

If you have custom (or modified) styles in a different Excel workbook that you want to use in this workbook, just open that other workbook and then click **Cell Styles > Merge Styles**; you'll then be able to import those styles into this workbook.

Using Themes

As you learned at the beginning of the chapter, styles can be grouped into bundles called *themes*.

DEFINITION

A **theme** is a collection of colors, fonts, and effects that are designed to give your spreadsheets a professional and consistent look and feel.

Moreover, the built-in themes are used in most of the popular Office 2010 applications (like Word, Excel, and PowerPoint), so you can give all your Office documents, spreadsheets, and presentations a consistent look and feel.

You can find the different themes on the Ribbon on the Page Layout tab. The Themes group is on the far left. Click the big **Themes** drop-down menu.

The default theme is Office. All the styles that come with the Office theme have a particular look and feel in terms of colors, fonts, and effects. You can get a preview for all the different themes that are available by hovering your mouse over them.

Pick a different theme for the sheet, such as Black Tie. Click the theme you want to apply, and notice all the changes to the fonts and colors in your sheet.

NOTICE

Effects change the properties of drawing objects like pictures and graphics, which you learn about in upcoming chapters.

Notice that, once you change the theme, most of the colors and fonts in your sheet change. The exception is the Test style you created earlier. Since this is a custom style, the changes to the theme don't affect these cells.

Go back to the Home tab and click the **Cell Styles** drop-down menu again. Notice how all the styles have the same names, but they've been updated for this theme. (See Figure 14.9.)

Figure 14.9

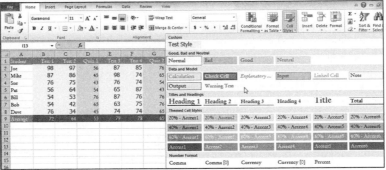

New styles for the new theme.

For the purposes of further instruction, replace the custom Test styles in these cells with the 40% Accent6 style, just so the sheets look good and use the standard style sets.

Modifying Themes

Themes are made up of sets of colors, fonts, and effects. You can actually pick and choose from these different sets to customize your own themes. For example, let's say you like the fonts in this Black Tie theme, but you don't like the color scheme. Click the **Colors** drop-down menu in the Themes group and select a different color scheme.

You can customize the colors further. At the bottom of the Colors drop-down menu, you'll see Customize New Theme Colors. Take some time to experiment with this menu—you can create your own color set for use in your themes. (See Figure 14.10.)

Figure 14.10

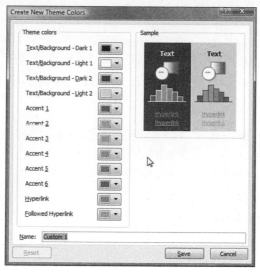

Create new theme colors.

You can do the same thing with Fonts. Once you have the colors set for your theme, click the **Fonts** drop-down menu and change to another predefined set of Fonts, or create your own. Each font set consists of a heading font (which is usually thicker) and a body font.

Finally, you have the effects. Again, these are used for drawing objects that you'll learn about later in Part 4. You'll see subtle differences in the colorations, shading, shadows, and so on. Choose an effect that you like. (Note that you cannot customize these.)

When you have the colors, fonts, and effects that you like all specified, you can save your creation as your own custom theme. Just click **Themes > Save Current Theme** and specify a file name; your theme then is saved. You will see it in the Custom section on top of the Theme menu in the future, or you can click **Browse for Themes** to load it back.

The Least You Need to Know

- You can use the Format Painter to copy a simple format from cell to cell, but this is good only for simple edits.
- Use Styles to make mass formatting edits easy.
- Themes control the overall look and feel of your document, including colors, fonts, and effects.

Page Layout

In This Chapter

- Learn how to view your spreadsheet in different ways with page views
- Tell Excel where you want your printed pages to end with page breaks
- Manage the way your printouts look with Page Setup

Most of the features in Excel that have to do with formatting your printed page can be found on the Page Layout tab. These features include groups dealing with page setup, options for scaling the output to size, and sheet options.

Open the Gradebook spreadsheet from the Chapter 15 folder on your CD. Notice that this sheet is much larger than the previous gradebook sheets. It has additional students and test/quiz grades, so the sheet fills more than one page.

Page Views

Before delving into the different page-layout features, it's important to understand how to switch the page views in Excel. In the bottom-right corner of the Excel window, just to the left of the Zoom controls, you see three little buttons that change the way Excel displays your sheet. You can use these buttons to switch among Normal, Page Layout, and Page Break Preview views.

As with most features in Excel, you'll also find the equivalents of these buttons on the Ribbon, on the View tab, in the Workbook Views group (see Figure 15.1).

Figure 15.1

View buttons on the Ribbon.

Normal view is the default view. Excel starts up in this view. You can see your formatting, but you might not see page breaks—where data flows over onto the next page.

Page Layout view shows you what your spreadsheet looks like when you print it (see Figure 15.2). This is close to a Print Preview.

Figure 15.2

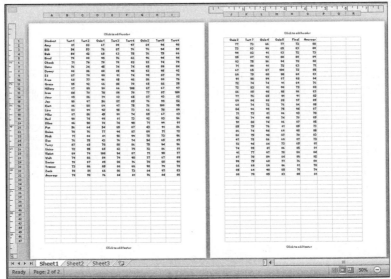

Page Layout view.

TIP

Use the Zoom bar to zoom out so you can see more of your sheet. If you want to be able to view two or three pages at a time, you can zoom out to 50 percent or so, depending on the size of your monitor.

After you click Page Layout view and then return to Normal view, Excel has an idea where your page breaks are going to be. Dotted lines show up even in Normal view, pointing out the page breaks (see Figure 15.3). This is only a rough approximation.

Figure 15.3

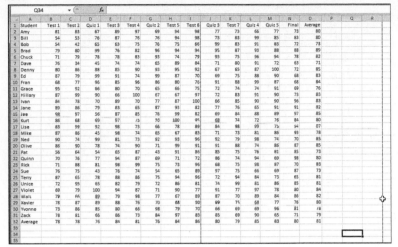

Page breaks visible in Normal view.

Page Breaks

If you want full control over where your page breaks appear, you can manually set them by clicking **Page Break** view. In Figure 15.4, the two pages are a little uneven; the first page contains more data.

Figure 15.4

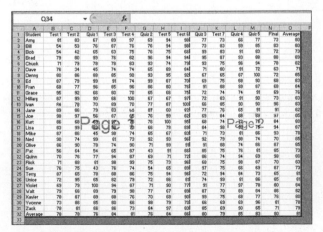

Page Break view with an uneven page spread.

To balance the pages a little bit, just click and drag the blue dotted line between pages 1 and 2 over to the left a few columns. This produces a more even spread of the data over both pages. (See Figure 15.5.)

Figure 15.5

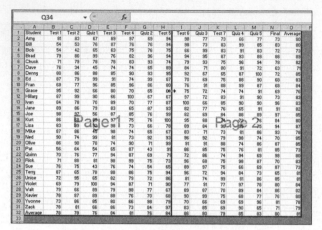

Page Break view with balanced page spread.

Notice now, however, that the line is no longer dotted. This indicates that it's a manual page break that you created. Dotted lines indicate where Excel figures the page break should be.

If you decide that you no longer want the manual page breaks, you can click **Page Layout > Breaks > Reset All Page Breaks** to clear all of them. To remove just one break, click just to the right of that page break on the sheet and click **Page Layout > Breaks > Remove Page Break**.

TIP

If you want to manually insert a page break but you don't want to use the Page Break view, you can also click **Page Layout > Breaks > Insert Page Break**.

When you click an individual cell, Excel inserts a horizontal and vertical page break above and to the left of that cell. So if you click E5, you get a vertical page break to the left of column E and a horizontal page break above row 5. In essence, page 1 then becomes A1:D4.

If you just want to insert a horizontal page break, select an entire column first. For example, if you click the header for column E and click **Insert Page Break**, then page 1 consists of columns A through D. Likewise, it works this same way for rows.

The Page Setup Group

The Page Setup group contains options for changing your page margins, the orientation of the page (portrait or landscape), the page size, and more.

Margins

In the Page Setup group, the first button is Margins. This button lets you choose from three standard margin configurations (normal, wide, and narrow). Notice that when you change your margins, the page breaks automatically recalculate to take this new setting into effect (unless you've added manual page breaks).

You can also set your own margins by clicking the **Custom Margins** option. This opens the Page Setup dialog box on the Margins tab (see Figure 15.6).

Here you specify the exact margin sizes (in inches) for the top, left, bottom, and right margins. You can also set how far the header and footer are from the top and bottom of the page, respectively.

This dialog menu also has options to center the spreadsheet on the page horizontally and vertically. These options center the sheet without resizing the page.

Figure 15.6

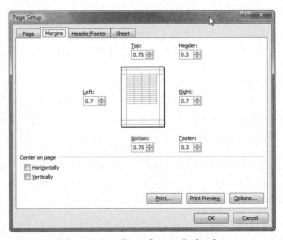

Margins on Page Setup dialog box.

Orientation

The Orientation button is pretty straight-forward. You can use this option to change between portrait (vertical) and landscape (horizontal) modes.

The sample gradebook that we're working on, for example, might look better in landscape mode, because it's wider than it is tall. (See Figure 15.7.)

Figure 15.7

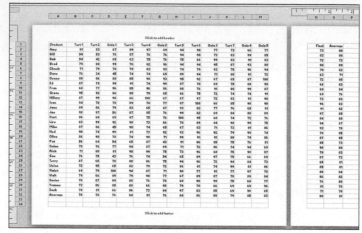

Landscape mode.

TIP

If you have columns that don't fit on one page, you could manually adjust the page break, or you could use the Scale to Fit option discussed in the next section.

Paper Size

The Paper Size button enables you to change the size of the paper that your sheet will print on. The popular options are at the top: letter, legal, statement, and so on.

If you switch to legal-size paper, you have enough room for extra columns to fit on the page. (See Figure 15.8.)

Figure 15.8

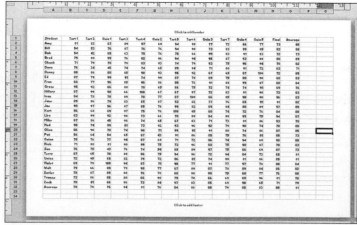

Legal size.

But you don't want legal paper here, so switch back to the letter option, which is the default.

Click the **More Paper Sizes** option at the bottom of the Paper Size button to go to the Page tab of the Page Setup dialog box (see Figure 15.9).

Figure 15.9

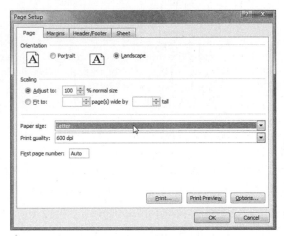

Page Setup dialog box.

Here you see the complete list of paper sizes that Excel supports. You also see a Print Quality drop-down box. This enables you to print in a higher or lower resolution on your printer. Higher resolutions produce better-looking printouts. Lower resolutions are faster and can save ink.

You also see an option to set the first page number. If you want to start the page numbering at a higher number than 1, you can set that here. This is handy, for example, if you are including some full-page Excel printouts inside a larger report that you've made up in some other program (like Microsoft Word) and you want to specify the page numbers.

Print Area

The Print Area button enables you to specify which area of the sheet you want to print. This is handy if you have information on your sheet that you don't want to include in the printout.

For example, let's say that you want the grades and averages to appear on the printout, but you don't want the students' names to be included.

1. Select the range of cells you want to be printed. In the example, it is B2:O32.

2. Click **Print Area > Set Print Area**. This defines the region as printable. The rest of the sheet will not print.

3. To verify your setting, click **File > Print** for a print preview.

NOTICE

See the dashed lines around the printable region that you selected? If you switch to Page Break Preview, you can easily change this region by clicking and dragging on the solid blue edge border that surrounds the sheet.

Notice in Figure 15.10 that we've dragged the left border over one column to exclude Test 1 from printing as well.

You can click **Print Area > Add to Print Area** to add ranges to your printable area, although Excel doesn't arrange them very well when you print them.

Click **Print Area > Clear Print Area** to return the sheet to its default state, which makes the entire sheet printable.

Figure 15.10

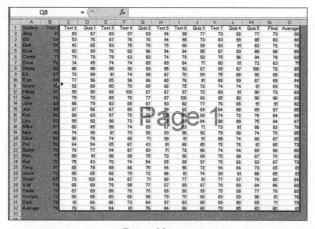

Printable area.

Background

The Background button enables you to select a graphic file from your computer to use as a background for your spreadsheet. You can use this feature to add a watermark behind your sheet.

Print Titles

The Print Titles button is handy if you want to have a row or column repeat at the left or top of each page, respectively. For example, we formatted the gradebook in Figure 15.11 to have two columns on page 2 without including student names for each of the grades.

Figure 15.11

Student	Test 1	Test 2	Quiz 1	Test 3	Test 4	Quiz 2	Test 5	Test 6	Quiz 3	Test 7	Quiz 4	Quiz 5	Final	Average
Amy	81	83	67	89	97	69	94	98	77	73	66	77	73	80
Bill	54	53	76	87	76	76	94	98	73	83	99	85	83	80
Bob	54	42	65	63	75	76	75	66	99	83	91	83	72	73
Brad	79	80	99	76	82	96	94	94	95	87	93	88	88	89
Chuck	71	79	78	78	83	93	74	79	93	75	96	94	78	82
Dave	76	34	45	74	74	65	89	84	71	80	91	72	63	71
Denny	80	86	88	85	90	93	95	92	67	65	87	100	72	85
Ed	87	79	99	91	74	99	87	70	69	75	88	90	68	83
Fran	68	77	96	85	96	86	80	76	91	88	99	87	68	84
Grace	95	92	66	80	70	65	66	75	72	74	74	91	69	76
Hillary	87	99	90	66	100	67	67	97	72	83	91	90	73	83
Ivan	84	78	70	89	70	77	87	100	66	85	90	90	96	83
Jane	89	86	79	83	65	87	93	82	77	76	65	91	91	82
Joe	98	97	56	87	85	76	99	82	69	84	88	89	97	85
Kurt	86	68	69	97	75	76	100	95	68	74	72	76	84	80
Lisa	83	99	92	98	73	66	78	89	84	98	99	75	94	87
Mike	87	86	45	98	74	65	67	83	71	73	81	86	93	78
Ned	90	74	99	81	73	92	93	96	92	79	98	74	70	85
Olive	86	90	78	74	90	71	99	91	91	88	74	86	87	85
Pat	56	64	54	65	87	43	91	86	85	75	76	81	85	73
Quinn	70	76	77	94	87	69	71	72	86	74	94	69	98	80
Rick	71	88	81	98	99	75	73	96	68	75	98	87	70	83
Sue	76	75	43	76	74	54	65	89	97	75	66	69	87	73
Terry	87	65	78	88	86	75	94	96	72	94	84	73	65	81
Unice	72	95	65	82	79	72	86	81	74	99	81	86	85	81
Violet	69	79	100	94	87	71	90	77	91	77	97	78	80	84
Walt	79	66	89	79	98	77	67	89	87	70	89	84	86	82
Xavier	78	87	89	88	76	70	68	90	99	75	68	77	76	80
Yvonne	73	86	85	80	66	98	79	70	66	69	69	96	81	78
Zack	78	81	66	86	73	84	97	83	85	69	90	65	71	79
Average	78	78	76	84	81	76	84	86	80	79	85	83	80	81

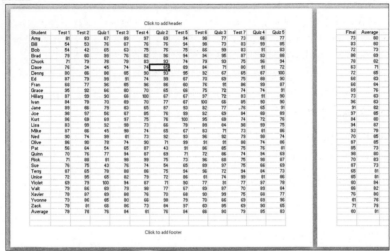

Print Titles button.

The Print Titles feature tells Excel to repeat the list of student names on each page of the printout. Here's how it works:

1. Click the **Print Titles** button.
2. The Page Setup dialog box displays on the Sheet tab. Click the little cell selection button on the right side of the box next to "Columns to repeat at left" (see Figure 15.12).

Figure 15.12

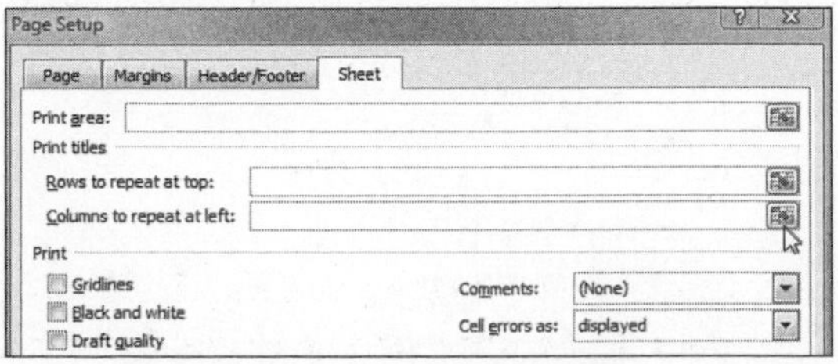

"Columns to repeat at left" option.

3. The Page Setup dialog box shrinks so you can select the column(s) you want to repeat. Click the header for column A.

4. $A:$A displays in the Page Setup box. This is a range reference meaning "columns A through A" which is Excel's shorthand way of saying "just column A." Now click the little cell selector button again to the right to expand the Page Setup dialog box (see Figure 15.13).

5. Click **OK**.

Figure 15.13

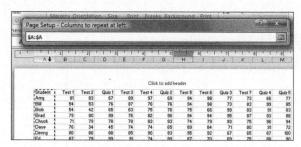

Page Setup dialog box in expanded view.

Notice that the Student column appears on the left of page 2 as well as page 1. It will repeat on the left side of every column. You can also make more than just one column repeat.

The process is exactly the same for row headers—just use the "Rows to repeat at top" option instead. Yes, you can have both rows and columns repeat on each page.

Scale to Fit Commands

The Scale to Fit commands are nice if you want to change the size of the content to fit the number of pages that you want. For example, the sample gradebook is currently two pages wide by one page tall. You can use the Scale to Fit Width feature to squeeze that sheet down to 1×1. (See Figure 15.14.)

Figure 15.14

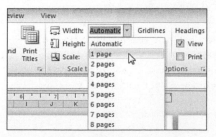

Scale to Fit set to 1×1.

Notice that the width of your sheet has been scaled down to fit on exactly one page. The height is still "automatic," so it could grow in that direction. But, of course, you can change that setting, too.

WARNING

The Scale to Fit feature will not *expand* your sheet to fill more pages—only shrink it down to fit fewer pages.

However, you can use the Scale Percentage setting to increase or decrease the size of your printed page. By changing the percentage to 150 percent, you'll see that the same sheet now takes up four printed pages. This makes everything larger on the printed page. (See Figure 15.15.)

Figure 15.15

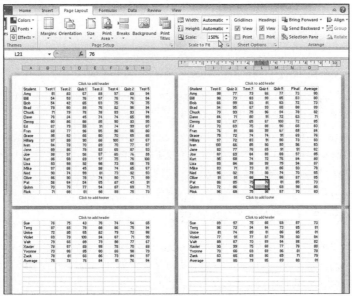

Scale Percentage set at 150 percent.

NOTICE

Don't confuse the scale percentage with the zoom. Changing the scale of your sheet actually makes the printed material larger on the page, whereas the zoom ratio just changes how large it appears on the screen for your benefit. Zoom doesn't actually change the printout.

Sheet Options

The Sheet Options group includes check boxes that control whether you see gridlines and headings, and whether those items print.

Gridlines are the thin lines between the cells. Gridlines just separate the individual cells on your spreadsheet. Normally you see gridlines onscreen, but they don't print on the page. You can change this behavior with the check boxes. For example, you might want to see gridlines on the printed page. This keeps you from having to add cell borders everywhere. Again, this is just a matter of personal preference.

You can do something similar for the row and column headings. Those are the labels that say "A, B, C," across the tops of the columns, and "1, 2, 3," down the rows. If you actually want these labels to print on the page, you can check the Print box below Headings.

The Least You Need to Know

- You can view your sheets in different ways with the Page Views buttons.
- Insert manual page breaks or use Page Break view to tell Excel exactly how large each printed page should be.
- Control your margins, orientation, paper size, and more from the Page Setup options.
- Use the Scale to Fit feature to force your spreadsheet to shrink to exactly the number of pages you want.

Headers and Footers

In This Chapter

- Adding headers to the top of each page and adding footers to the bottom of each page
- Selecting from standard Excel headers and footers
- Adding dynamic information, such as page numbers, to your headers and footers with element codes

A header repeats at the top of each printed page, and a footer repeats at the bottom of each page. You can create customized headers and footers in Excel, or you can select from some of the standard, popular headers and footers that are available. In this chapter, you will learn how to create your own headers and footers.

Adding Headers and Footers

Open the sample Gradebook file in the Chapter 16 folder on your CD. If you're working in Normal view, click the Ribbon's **Insert** tab and then click **Header and Footer**.

Excel switches to Page Layout view and places you in Header and Footer edit mode. The Header and Footer Tools, Design tab on the Ribbon displays.

> **TIP**
>
> If you find it easier, you can switch to Page Layout view and then click in the area at the top of the page that says "Click to add header."

You can see three sections for each header (left, middle, right) and another three sections at the bottom of each page for the footer. You can click on any of these sections and begin entering text. For example, type **Math 101** in the center header section (see Figure 16.1).

Figure 16.1

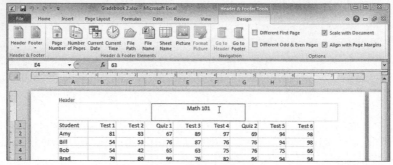

Inserting header text.

If you want to add any formatting to this text, you can. Just select the text, click the **Home** tab, and then apply any formatting you like (font, size, color, and so on).

NOTICE

You might notice that a mini toolbar pops up whenever you select text in Excel. This is a popular feature in Microsoft Word that is also available in Excel. After selecting text, just move your mouse up and to the right, and you can select from a limited list of popular formatting functions, such as options to change the font, the font size, and the color of the text.

Any text that you enter in the left header section is left aligned, and any text in the right section is aligned to the right. (See Figure 16.2.)

Figure 16.2

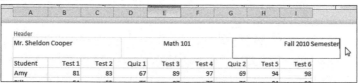

Header alignment.

If you perform a print preview of your sheet, you can see what the header and footer look like. Note that they appear on each page in your printout.

If at any time you decide to go back to Normal view to work on your sheet, don't worry; your header and footer will still be there. You can see (or edit) them at any time by switching back to Page Layout view.

Selecting Headers and Footers

You can do more with headers and footers than just place static text in them. You can also add dynamic text to display information about your sheets, such as the date and time they were printed, the current page number, and more. To select a standard page header, just click the Header drop-down item on the Header and Footer Tools, Design tab.

You see different headers to choose from (see Figure 16.3). The first one, labeled "(none)," is just a plain, blank header. The second item, "Page 1," places the current page number in the center header section.

Figure 16.3

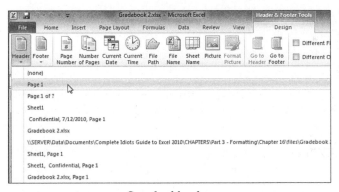

Standard headers.

Feel free to experiment with the different standard headers and footers. Keep in mind, however, that the standard headers replace any headers that you have in your sheet already. Old header information is erased.

If you insert the "Page 1" header and then click the center header section, you see some strange text there: it says, "Page &[Page]" instead (see Figure 16.4). This is a special design code that Excel uses to place the current page number in that location.

Figure 16.4

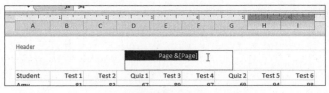

Header codes.

Header and Footer Codes

You can use these header and footer codes to add more information to the header/footer sections. You can also mix the codes with your own text. Look at the Header and Footer Tools, Design tab. Notice the Header and Footer Elements group. These buttons represent different codes you can insert into your headers and footers.

For example, if you want to create a header that says "Page 1 of 3," start by adding the Page Number code to your header. It then says "Page &[Page]," just like in Figure 16.4.

Click just after (to the right of) that header code, press the spacebar, and then type the word **of** and press the spacebar again. Then click the **Number of Pages** element button. Your header now says "Page &[Page] of &[Pages]" and looks like Figure 16.5.

Figure 16.5

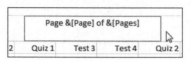

Number of pages.

If you perform a print preview right now, you should see "Page 1 of 2" at the top of your document. (See Figure 16.6.)

Figure 16.6

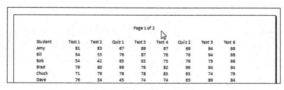

Header print preview.

You can use several different header/footer elements, as shown in Table 16.1.

You can insert whatever text you want into your header and footer sections. You can mix and match codes, use multiple lines, and so on. The only thing you have to remember is that if you want to insert an actual ampersand sign (for example, "Smith & Jones Inc."), you have to type two ampersands ("Smith && Jones, Inc."), because Excel uses that ampersand sign to signal the start of an element code.

Table 16.1   Page Header and Footer Element Codes

Button	Code	Inserts ...
Page Number	&[Page]	Current page number.
Number of Pages	&[Pages]	Total number of pages in sheet.
Current Date	&[Date]	Current date.
Current Time	&[Time]	Current time.
File Path	&[Path]&[File]	Full path and file name of the current sheet (you can manually delete the File part, if you want).
File Name	&[File]	File name of the current sheet.
Sheet Name	&[Tab]	Name of the current worksheet.
Picture	none	A picture. Great for small images, like a company logo.

Header and Footer Options

Finally, there is an options section on the Header and Footer Tools, Design tab (see Figure 16.7). The first option enables you to specify a different header for the first page. This is great if you want to include a descriptive cover page for your printouts, or perhaps you want to put the header and footer only on the first page. Check this box if you want to enable this option.

Figure 16.7

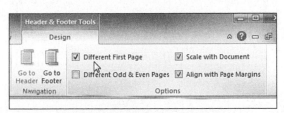

Header and Footer options.

Next, you can select whether you want to have a different header and footer for odd and even pages. Use this option if you're printing on both sides of the paper and you want to "mirror" your pages. For example, on odd pages you might want to have the page number on the right side, and on even pages you might want it on the left side.

There's also an option to "scale with document," which basically means that the size of the header/footer grows or shrinks if the Scale to Fit option is used to make the sheet larger or smaller. You learned about Scale to Fit in Chapter 15.

Finally, "align with page margins" causes the left and right header sections to align with whatever you set the left and right page margins to be. If you turn off this option, Excel uses its predefined margins for the header/footer sections.

Header and Footer Tips

If you want to create a multiline header, you can find that the header section bumps into the top of your spreadsheet. Look at the example in Figure 16.8. This is an example of a three-line header. The text has run into the first couple rows of the sheet.

Figure 16.8

Gradebook 2.xlsx				Page 1 of 2					11:14 PM
Student	Test 1	Test 2	Quiz 1	Test 3	Test 4	Quiz 2	Test 5	Test 6 This is my header section	
Amy	81	83	67	89	97	69	94 This is more of my header section	98	
Bill	54	53	76	87	76	76	94	98	
Bob	54	42	65	63	75	76	75	66	
Brad	70	80	90	76	83	95	94	94	

Large header section.

To fix this, either you can change the margin settings so that the top margin is low enough to fall below the header section or you can move the top of the header section closer to the edge of the page—or both.

You learned about changing the margin settings in Chapter 15. You can click the **Page Layout** tab and then click **Margins**, but here's a quick trick to adjust the size of the top margin (see Figure 16.9). In Page Layout view, move your mouse over the vertical ruler bar that displays on the left side of your screen. Position it just to the left of the Row 1 header, and you'll see a double arrow display. Click and drag here to adjust the top margin.

Figure 16.9

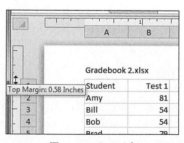

Top margin trick.

Now you can see the corrected margin settings to accommodate the larger header (see Figure 16.10).

Figure 16.10

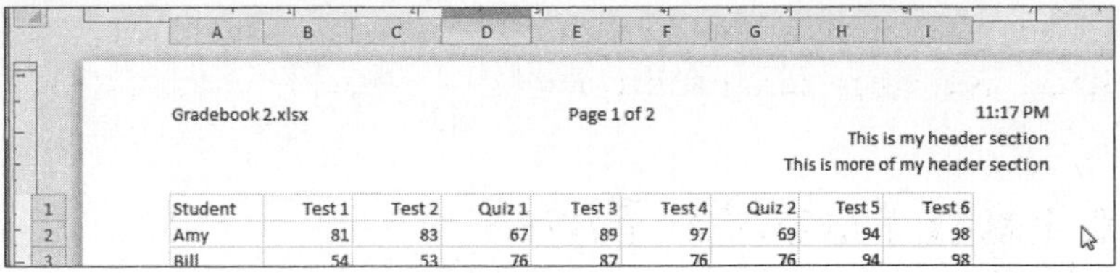

Top margin adjusted.

The Least You Need to Know

- You can switch to Page Layout view to quickly type a header or footer for your spreadsheet.
- Select from any of the predefined standard headers and footers in Excel.
- Use the buttons on the Header and Footer Tools, Design tab to quickly insert element codes, or type your own.

Illustrations

You can insert many items into a spreadsheet, and we cover them in this part.

In Chapter 17, you learn about pictures and how to manipulate them. You find out how to insert a picture into your sheet and how to move, resize, stretch, crop, and rotate your pictures. We also cover some of Excel's new picture-enhancement features. For example, you can now apply color corrections and artistic effects right inside Excel.

Chapter 18 covers ClipArt and shapes. Chapter 19 covers SmartArt and screenshots.

In Chapter 20, you study one of the most popular features in Excel: charts and graphs. You learn how to create column and pie charts, and you look at many of the different chart layouts, styles, and options.

Chapter 21 covers most of the other types of objects that you can insert into a spreadsheet, including text boxes, WordArt, signature lines, equations, symbols, hyperlinks, and a new feature in Excel 2010: Sparklines.

Pictures

In This Chapter

- Adding professionalism to your spreadsheets with pictures
- Learning how to manipulate and control images in your sheets
- Exploring artistic effects, picture styles, and a lot more

Excel is about more than just numbers and text. You can insert pictures to make your spreadsheets more visually appealing, to convey additional information, and to give your work a more professional appearance.

Inserting a Picture

Open the sample Gradebook file from your CD in the Chapter 17 folder. This is a shortened version of the Gradebook file you've worked with in previous chapters.

You'll find a picture in the Chapter 17 folder called ABC University. This is the logo for our fictional school. You will insert this logo into your spreadsheet so that when the grades are printed, it appears on the sheet.

You can insert a picture into your sheets in many ways. The easiest is to click the **Insert** tab of the Ribbon and select **Picture**.

You see the Insert Picture dialog box, a standard Windows browsing dialog box. You can browse to any folder on your computer, network, or CD/DVD drives. Browse to the Chapter 17 folder on the CD and pick the ABC University logo file. Then click **Insert**.

Excel inserts the picture into your sheet (see Figure 17.1). We look at these options soon, but for now, let's see how you can work with this picture.

Figure 17.1

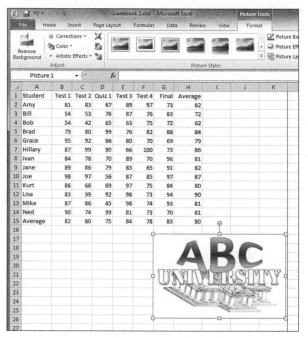

Picture inserted.

Manipulating a Picture

To move the picture around on the sheet, first select the picture. The boxes and circles around it (on the corners and edges) and the appearance of the Picture Tools tab indicate that you have selected the picture (see Figure 17.2).

When the picture is selected, move your mouse pointer anywhere over the middle of the picture (not over the edge). The mouse turns into a four-way arrow. Now click and drag to move the picture anywhere you'd like.

TIP

To get a good feel for how the final printed page will look with your pictures, it's best to work in Page Layout view. However, if you still want to work in Normal view, click **Page Layout** (or Print Preview) once and then go back to Normal view so you can see the dotted lines indicating where the page break will be.

Figure 17.2

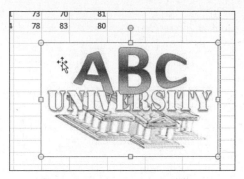

Four-way arrow to move picture.

Move the picture into the upper-right corner of the sheet. Notice that this obstructs some of the data. In this case, you want to make the logo a little smaller so that it fits in the corner.

To resize a picture, first make sure it's selected. Then move your mouse over any of its four corners. Your pointer turns into a two-way arrow (see Figure 17.3).

Figure 17.3

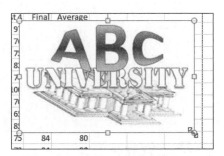

Two-way arrow to resize the picture.

Click and drag to resize the picture. You can make it any size you like so that it fits in the space you want. (See Figure 17.4.)

Figure 17.4

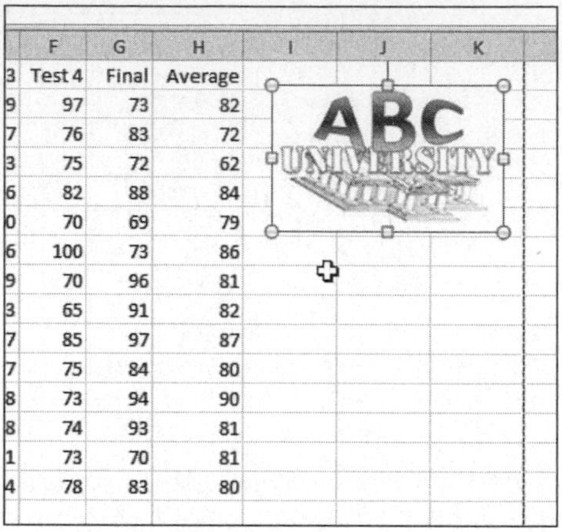

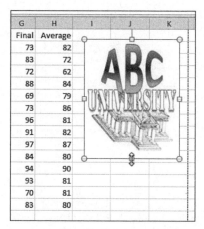

	F	G	H	I	J	K
3	Test 4	Final	Average			
9	97	73	82			
7	76	83	72			
3	75	72	62			
6	82	88	84			
0	70	69	79			
6	100	73	86			
9	70	96	81			
3	65	91	82			
7	85	97	87			
7	75	84	80			
8	73	94	90			
8	74	93	81			
1	73	70	81			
4	78	83	80			

Resized picture.

You can also click the boxes in the middle of the sides of the picture. This enables you to stretch the picture in one dimension (width or height). (See Figure 17.5.)

Figure 17.5

G	H	I	J	K
Final	Average			
73	82			
83	72			
72	62			
88	84			
69	79			
73	86			
96	81			
91	82			
97	87			
84	80			
94	90			
93	81			
70	81			
83	80			

Stretched picture.

To rotate the picture, click and drag the green dot over the top, middle of the picture (see Figure 17.6). You can rotate the image to any angle.

TIP

Hold down the **Shift** key while you rotate the picture to force it to stay in 15-degree angle increments.

Figure 17.6

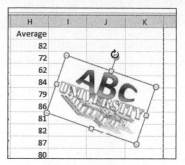

Rotate picture.

You can delete a picture simply by making sure that it's selected and pressing **Delete**. If you want multiple copies of the same picture on your sheet, you can copy and paste using the Clipboard buttons or keyboard commands (Ctrl+C to copy, Ctrl+V to paste).

Working with Multiple Pictures

Insert the School Building picture (located in the Chapter 17 folder) into your sheet (see Figure 17.7).

Figure 17.7

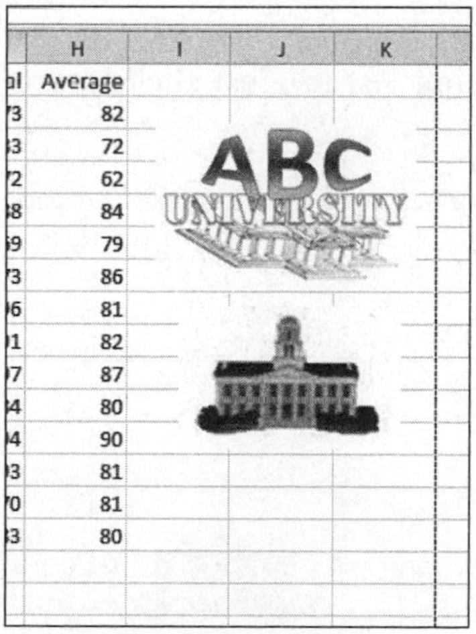

School Building picture.

Now that you have two images on your spreadsheet, it might be convenient to group them together. This way, if you move one of them, the other one stays with it.

You can select multiple pictures by clicking the first one, holding down the Ctrl key, and then clicking the second one (and a third, fourth, and so on, if you so desire).

After you select the pictures, you can perform operations that will affect both of them. For example, you can group them together.

On the Picture Tools, Format tab, is an Arrange group. This group contains the same controls that are available on the Page Layout tab's Arrange group.

Click the **Group** drop-down box, and select **Group** to group the two pictures together (see Figure 17.8). If you click and drag to move them, or try to resize them, they behave as one object.

Figure 17.8

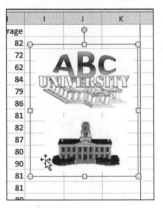

Grouped objects.

If you don't like the grouping feature, just click **Group > Ungroup** to break them apart.

If one picture overlaps another, you can control which is on top and which is on the bottom. In Figure 17.9, the picture of the school building is on top of the ABC logo.

Figure 17.9

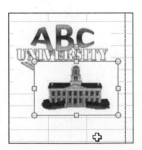

Overlapping objects.

To change the order of the pictures, click the school building picture and then select **Send Backward > Send To Back**. This sends the selected object to the back of the "stack" of objects. (See Figure 17.10.)

You can think of all the objects (pictures, charts, shapes, and so on) that you can place on your spreadsheet as drawings on sheets of paper. These sheets of paper make up the drawing layer. Each object is like a picture drawn on a transparency paper that sits on that drawing layer. You can move these objects up and down as you see fit to arrange them.

Figure 17.10

School building now behind logo.

The Send to Back command sends the current object to the back (bottom) of the stack of drawing objects. The Send Backward command moves the object down one level. Likewise, you can use Bring to Front and Bring Forward commands as needed.

If you want to see a list of the drawing objects on your sheet, you can turn on the Selection pane by clicking on the button of the same name in the Arrange group of the Picture Tools > Format tab (see Figure 17.11).

Figure 17.11

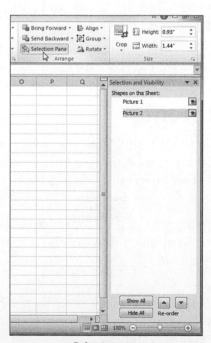

Selection pane.

Next to each item, you see a picture that looks like a eyeball. Click the eyeball to hide the object. This is handy if you don't want to delete the object, but you don't want to see it right now.

Show All and Hide All buttons are located on the bottom of the pane, as well as up and down arrows to move selected objects up or down in the drawing layer stack.

> **TIP**
>
> You can click the top of the Selection pane and drag it to "undock" it from the side of your window. This makes it a free-floating box.

Several alignment features are available for your objects. Let's say you want to make sure that both of your pictures are lined up evenly on the left side. Just select them both as you did previously, and then select **Align > Align Left**.

Both pictures are now nicely lined up at the left side. Options also are available to center, right-align, and align to the top, middle, or bottom vertically.

Distribute Horizontally and Vertically are available only if you select three or more items. It makes the spacing between those items even.

Also notice the Snap to Grid option. This option tries to keep all your pictures and other objects lined up nicely to a hidden "grid" that sits on top of your spreadsheet. Turn off this option (or hold down the Alt key while dragging) if you want exact control over the placement of your objects.

Finally, a Rotate option gives you commands to rotate and flip your objects. Click the **More Rotation Options** menu item for even more control.

Picture Adjustments

One of the best upgrades to Office 2007 was the enhancement of the picture tools. Microsoft continued improving upon them in Office 2010. You'll also notice a great deal of adjustments and other effects that you can add to pictures on the Picture Tools, Format tab.

To start, in the Adjust group are Corrections, which enable you to sharpen or soften the image (add or remove hard edges). You can also adjust the brightness or contrast of the picture. (See Figure 17.12.)

Figure 17.12

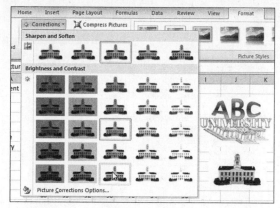

Adjust corrections.

The Color command enables you to change the color saturation (how much or little color is in the picture), adjust the color tone, and recolor the image with a different overall hue.

NOTICE

A whole book can be written on the different image adjustments and effects that Office 2010 offers. This chapter's goal is to show you the basics of what's available. Take some time and play with these different settings to experiment and have fun.

Located on the Color menu, the Set Transparent Color command enables you to pick one color in the picture as the transparent "background" color. This is handy if, for example, you import a picture that has a green background. You can use this tool to click the green background and make it transparent.

In Office 2010, Microsoft added some Adobe Photoshop–like filter effects called Artistic Effects. You'll find options such as Blur, Paint Strokes, Photocopy, and more. (See Figure 17.13.)

Figure 17.13

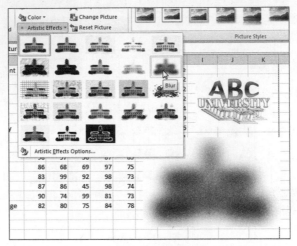

Artistic Effects.

Find an effect that you like, but it's not quite perfect? Click **Artistic Effects Options,** and you'll see that almost every effect has a set of variables you can change (see Figure 17.14). For example, if you want only a little of the Blur effect, change the Radius setting to 2 or 3.

Figure 17.14

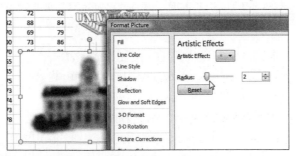

Artistic Effects options.

Compress Pictures causes Excel to apply file compression to the images in your sheet. If you add a few very complex or large image files to your sheet, they can cause the size of your workbook file to skyrocket. Click the **Compress Pictures** button to reduce the file size of your images without losing much quality.

The Change Picture option enables you to change the picture in the current object (replace the picture with something else). It's easier than reinserting a new image and deleting the current one. Plus, you'll keep the current size and location.

Finally, the Reset Picture button forces the image to revert to its initial state and remove all the filters and other adjustments that you might have placed on it.

Picture Styles

The Picture Styles feature helps you easily transform an ordinary picture with special effects—and make it look like you spent hours editing it. With just one click, you can give your picture a cool border, 3D look, shadow, and so on.

Select **Picture Styles** on the Picture Tools, Format tab. Depending on the size of your Ribbon, you can choose from several visible styles. Click your picture and then choose a style. Remember, you can hover your mouse over a style to get a preview. (See Figure 17.15.)

Figure 17.15

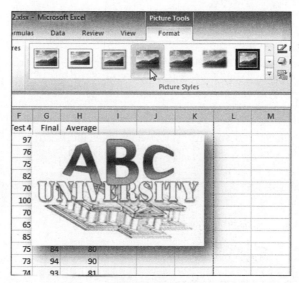

Picture Styles.

The style in Figure 17.15, for example, adds a cool shadow to the background of the picture. Several preset styles are available. Click the **down-arrow** button next to the Picture Styles presets.

This opens the full menu of preset Picture Styles that you can choose from (see Figure 17.16).

Figure 17.16

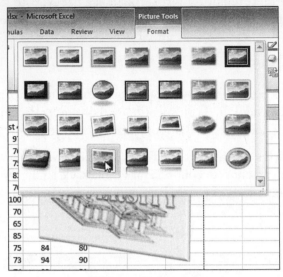

All Picture Styles presets.

After you select a preset that's close to what you want, you have even more options for you to change. You can tweak the picture border, effects, and layout.

On the Picture Border drop-down menu, you can change the border (outline) color, the weight (thickness), and the line style (dashes). (See Figure 17.17.)

Figure 17.17

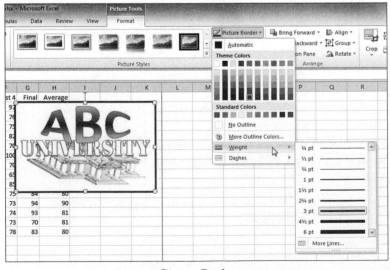

Picture Border.

On the Picture Effects menu are several different effects you can choose from: shadows, reflections, glows, and so on. You can pick from the preset options here or click the Options menu item at the bottom for even greater control. Figure 17.18 shows the Shadow options.

Figure 17.18

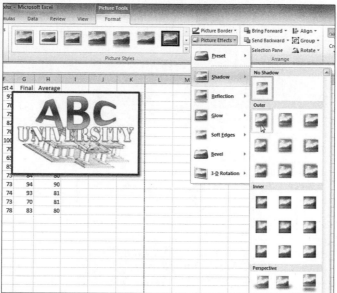

Shadow options.

If you like one of the shadows but want to make it larger, click the **More Shadows** item at the bottom of the menu for additional options, such as color, transparency, size, blur, distance, and so on. (See Figure 17.19.)

Figure 17.19

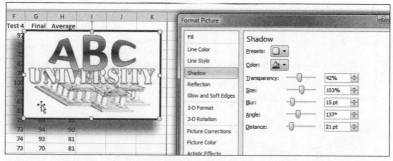

More Shadows options.

Cropping Pictures

To "crop" a picture is to select only a portion of it, removing unwanted areas. For example, if you have a picture of someone but there are other people around him that you don't want to see, you can crop them out. If you want to crop your image, you use the Crop tool. Click your image and then click the **Crop** button.

Notice small black lines in the corners and edges of your picture. Click and drag any of these to crop the picture in that direction. (See Figure 17.20.)

Figure 17.20

Crop a picture.

When you're finished, simply click off the image, and Excel crops it for you. You can also have some fun with cropping. For example, one option enables you to crop your image in a shape. If you just love your university, the one in Figure 17.21 is for you.

Figure 17.21

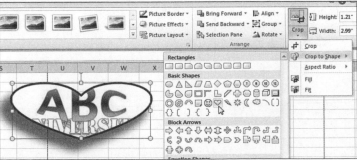

Crop to shape.

Format Picture Dialog Box

You've seen pieces of this dialog box before, but if you open the Format Picture dialog box, you see several different formatting options. As a reminder, you can open this dialog box by clicking any of the dialog box launcher buttons on the Ribbon. This tab has them on the Picture Styles and Size groups.

After you click this button, the Format Picture dialog box opens. There are many, many options for formatting pictures in this dialog box. This chapter will only cover a small portion of them. If you do a lot of work with images in Excel, you should take some time to explore them all. Once you learn the basics, you shouldn't have any problems figuring out the rest on your own.

Some of these options are available on the Ribbon. Some are extensions of Ribbon buttons that give you more flexibility and control over your formatting.

The Least You Need to Know

- Inserting pictures into Excel adds visual appeal to your spreadsheets.
- You can move, resize, and rotate pictures quickly and intuitively with your mouse.
- Use the Arrange commands to group and arrange multiple images.
- Office 2010's Artistic Effects tools make your images look professional without the need for additional image-editing software.

ClipArt and Shapes

In This Chapter

- Selecting ClipArt from Microsoft Office or the web to insert into your spreadsheets
- Using the Clip Organizer to keep all your ClipArt neatly ordered
- Creating shapes with text, basic flowcharts, and more

In Chapter 17, you learned how to insert pictures into your spreadsheets. You can use more graphical objects with Excel, including ClipArt, shapes, SmartArt, screenshots, charts, and more. In this chapter, you take a look at ClipArt and shapes.

ClipArt

Want to include images in your spreadsheet, but you don't have any of your own? That's what ClipArt is for. It's a collection of photos, illustrations, videos, and even audio clips that you can use in your Excel sheets.

To begin using ClipArt, click the Ribbon's **Insert** tab. In the Illustrations group, you'll find ClipArt.

This opens the ClipArt pane on the right side of your window. Search for a picture of a computer to include in the spreadsheet. Type in the word **computer** in the search box, and click the **Go** button. Microsoft Office ClipArt samples appear (see Figure 18.1).

Figure 18.1

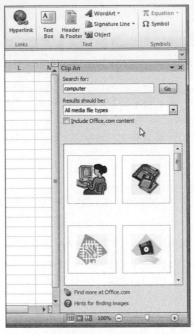

Search for ClipArt.

Scroll through the list of images to see the different ClipArt that is available. To access more ClipArt online, click **Include Office.com content** for your search. Excel also shows ClipArt from Microsoft's website.

TIP

You can limit the types of ClipArt that appear by changing the options in the "Results should be" drop-down box. You can pick from photographs, illustrations, video, and audio selections.

When you find a piece of ClipArt, you can insert it into your sheet simply by clicking it.

Notice that the image has now been inserted into the sheet in the upper-left corner. Click and drag to move it just like a picture. Use the green dot on top to rotate it, just like a picture. The Picture Tools, Format tab appears so that you can use many of the same picture tools on ClipArt.

Because of the wide variety of color options, you can make any ClipArt match the palette or theme of your spreadsheet by recoloring it (see Figure 18.2).

Figure 18.2

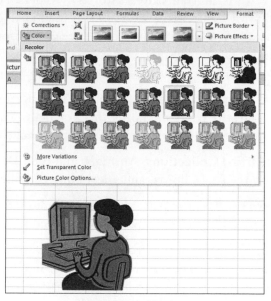

Recoloring ClipArt.

In addition to inserting ClipArt into your sheet, the ClipArt pane gives you some options. If you hold your mouse over a piece of ClipArt, you see a drop-down arrow appear on the right side of it.

On this option menu, you see Insert, which is the same as clicking on the ClipArt. There is also a Copy option that copies the ClipArt to your Clipboard (so that you can paste it later) but doesn't insert it directly into your sheet.

Clip Organizer

Notice the options to delete the current clip from your Clip Organizer. Select this option to permanently remove the ClipArt from your system. Options also enable you to copy the selected piece of ClipArt to a different collection, move it to a different collection, edit the ClipArt's keywords, and preview the ClipArt.

What is the Clip Organizer, anyway? It is a program that comes with Office 2010 that helps you keep all your ClipArt organized.

NOTICE

Unlike previous versions of Excel, you can't access the Clip Organizer directly from inside Excel 2010. You'll find a shortcut to it in your Office 2010 program folder. Click your Windows **Start** button and then click **All Programs, Microsoft Office** to see the Office 2010 Clip Organizer.

The Clip Organizer keeps all your ClipArt stored in folders. For example, you have your own collection (My Collection), which starts out empty. Then there are the Office Collections and Web Collections. The Office Collection includes all the ClipArt that's installed on your system, which came with Office 2010. The Web Collection goes to Microsoft's Office.com website to gather more ClipArt.

This is where those "copy to collection" and "move to collection" options come in handy. If you find a favorite piece of ClipArt that you plan to use over and over, copy it from the Office or Web Collections to your own personal collection.

For example, click **Office Collections**, **Animals**, and then **Domestic**. Open the drop-down menu on the cow ClipArt, and select **copy to collection**.

Now select the **Favorites** folder to place this piece of ClipArt in. Select the **New** button on the bottom of this menu to create your own collections and folders.

If you click the Edit Keywords option, you get the Keywords dialog box, where you can control what keywords trigger a search for this piece of ClipArt (see Figure 18.3). Notice that the cow is triggered on searches for animals, cattle, cows, dairies, and so on. You can add, modify, or delete the keywords here.

Figure 18.3

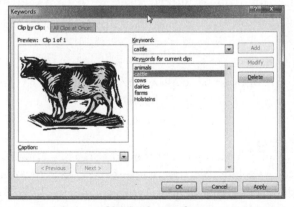

ClipArt keywords.

TIP

With the Clip Organizer, you can click and drag pieces of ClipArt from it directly into your Office applications. When working with several images, you can open the Clip Organizer side by side with Word and Excel, and click and drag the ClipArt over.

Shapes

You can use shapes to add a lot of visual pizzazz to your spreadsheets. Excel offers simple shapes (such as squares, circles, lines, and triangles) as well as more complex options (such as block arrows, flowchart symbols, stars, banners, callouts, and so on). (See Figure 18.4.)

Figure 18.4

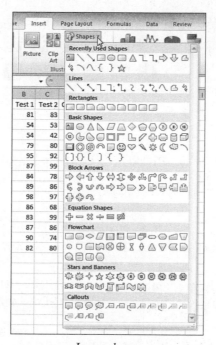

Insert shapes.

Let's start with a simple rectangle. On the Ribbon, click **Insert**, **Shapes**. Under the Rectangles section, select the first rectangle shape. (Notice the nine different styles of rectangles available, each with different types of corners. We'll keep it simple for now.)

As soon as you click the rectangle shape, your mouse pointer changes to a simple crosshairs pointer. Click and drag your spreadsheet to create the rectangle. When you're finished, release the mouse button.

Notice that a new tab has appeared on the Ribbon: the Drawing Tools, Format tab. Use this tab to format the objects that you draw in Excel, such as shapes.

In Shape Styles, you can change what your shape looks like. Choose from any of the preselected styles in the gallery, or adjust the shape's fill (background color), outline, and effects manually. Start with the gallery, select a style, and then adjust the details from there. (See Figure 18.5.)

Figure 18.5

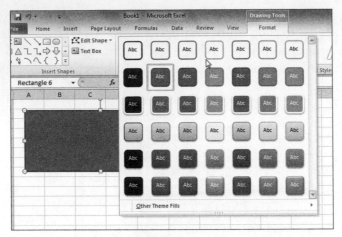

Shape styles.

After you created your shape, fill it with a solid color, or select a picture, *gradient*, or texture as a background for it.

DEFINITION

A **gradient** fill is where one color slowly dissolves into another color.

You can choose from the gradient fill options available, which are mostly simple two-color fades, or you can access more options by clicking **More Gradients** (see Figure 18.6).

In the Format Shape dialog box, on the Fill group Gradient Fill is selected. The Gradient Fill options were automatically set for us by the initial shape style that we picked earlier.

Figure 18.6

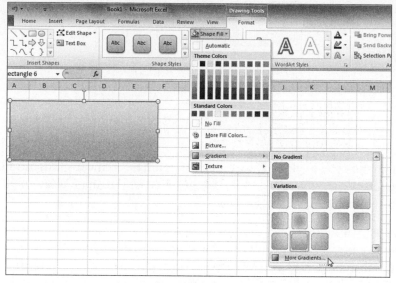

Shape fill gradients.

You can change the type of gradient from linear (straight across from one color to another) to radial (out in concentric circles from a center point), rectangular, or path. (See Figure 18.7.)

Figure 18.7

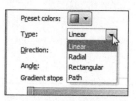

Shape fill gradients type.

The Direction variable is based on what kind of gradient type you select. For example, if you are working with a linear gradient, you'll see options such as up, down, left, and right. If you have a radial or rectangular type, you can radiate out from the center or any of the corners. (See Figure 18.8.)

Figure 18.8

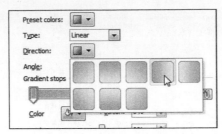

Shape fill gradients direction.

You can change the angle of the gradient if you have a linear gradient. For example, if you choose Linear Down for your direction type, the angle is set to 90 degrees. You can tweak the angle, if necessary.

Next, we set the colors. The Gradient Stops bar shows you the two colors in your gradient at opposite ends of the bar. (See Figure 18.9.) If you click one of these endpoints, the color, position, brightness, and transparency options are all set for that color. The left endpoint shown in Figure 18.9, for example, is a light blue, which shows up as grey in your book.

Figure 18.9

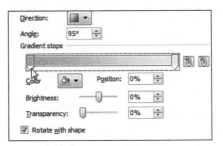

Shape fill gradient stops.

To change the color, click the color drop-down box.

To change the color of the other side of the gradient, click the other endpoint. Notice that the options are reset for that color. (See Figure 18.10.) The right endpoint is currently white; change it to yellow.

NOTICE

You can also change the brightness and transparency of each individual color. This allows some of the data from the sheet behind the shape to show through.

Figure 18.10

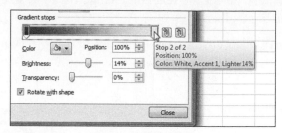

Change other color.

The Rotate with Shape option indicates that the colors rotate if you rotate the angle of the shape itself. Otherwise, the colors stay as they are, and only the outline of the shape moves.

You can easily add a third or fourth color in your gradient. Notice the two buttons to the right of the Gradient Stops bar. Click the **Add Gradient Stop** button to add a new stop. Notice that it's placed between the other two. (See Figure 18.11.)

Figure 18.11

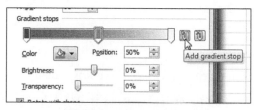

Add Gradient Stop button.

Of course, now you can change all of the colors and other options with this gradient as well. In fact, using three gradients, it's possible to start with blue, have white in the middle, and end with blue again. The sky's the limit.

In addition to gradient fills, you can choose from several different styles of textured fills: marble, granite, paper bag, water droplets, and so on.

NOTICE

After you select a texture fill, the Picture Tools tab becomes active. You can use these picture options (like color corrections) on your fills as well.

In the WordArt Styles group, you can change the style of the text inside your shape. Just right-click your shape and select **Edit Text** from the menu (sometimes it shows up as Add Text).

Now type in some text. Select the text and change the font, size, color, and so on, in the Quick Formatting toolbar.

After sizing the text, choose from one of the options in the WordArt Styles gallery (see Figure 18.12).

Figure 18.12

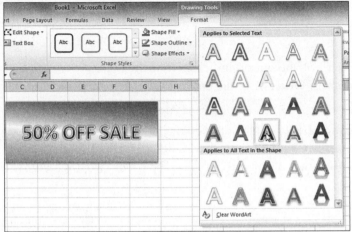

WordArt styles.

And, of course, you can manually tweak the color, border, and fill like objects.

Some of the shapes have additional slider controls when you add them to your sheet. For example, find the Smiley Face shape under the Basic Shapes group (see Figure 18.13). Notice the yellow diamond near the mouth. You can click and drag that diamond to go from a smile to a frown.

Figure 18.13

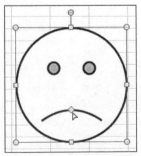

Smiley face to a frown.

On the block arrows, for example, you might find two such diamonds. One changes the size of the arrowhead, and the other changes the width of the arrow's tail. Adjust each according to your needs.

Many of the different shapes have similar adjusting diamonds. You can manipulate them accordingly. There are several shape options and effects. It's up to you to experiment with them and have fun.

You can even use shapes to create your own flowcharts, complete with connecting arrows. Add a couple of the flowchart shapes (or any shapes, for that matter) to your sheet, and insert text if you'd like.

Now select an arrow or line from the Shapes tool. When you move over the first shape, notice that red dots appear on all four sides of the shape (see Figure 18.14). Click one of those dots.

Figure 18.14

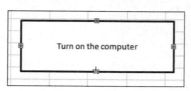

Flowchart connectors.

Next, click and drag to another shape. When you move over that shape, you can also see red dots. Click any of those dots to "connect" the two shapes with the line.

Move either of the shapes, and notice that the line moves with it. The two shapes are now connected by that line. Of course, you can click on the line and either delete it or just detach it from either shape by dragging an endpoint away. This gives you the capability to create simple flowcharts in Excel. (See Figure 18.15.)

Figure 18.15

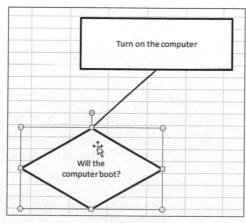

Flowchart items.

The Least You Need to Know

- Microsoft Office 2010 includes ClipArt already installed on your system. More ClipArt is available on the web, which you can quickly browse or search using the ClipArt feature.

- The Clip Organizer keeps your ClipArt neatly arranged in folders.

- Shapes can add another dimension of professionalism to your spreadsheets. You can control their shape, size, fill, and more. Use them to create basic flow-charts, signs, and so on.

SmartArt and Screenshots

In This Chapter

- Creating SmartArt graphics to display information visually
- Building an organization chart for your business
- Capturing images from the screen and placing them in your spreadsheets

Continuing with our look at the variety of illustrations and graphics objects that are available in Excel, we now look at SmartArt and screenshots in this chapter.

SmartArt

SmartArt is a collection of pre-formatted, but easily editable and customizable diagrams included with Microsoft Office 2010. Several different types of SmartArt are available, and you have many variations to choose from.

Creating SmartArt

SmartArt Graphics are tools to enable you to visually communicate information. To create SmartArt, click the Ribbon's **Insert** tab and, in the Illustration group, click the **SmartArt** button.

SmartArt Types

When you click the SmartArt button, you're asked to choose a SmartArt Graphic type. You can choose from many, including a simple List, Process, Cycle, Relationship, Matrix, and so on. These different categories represent the ways in which data is displayed in each type of SmartArt graphic (see Figure 19.1).

Figure 19.1

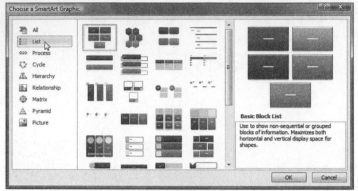

List group.

After you select a category, you can choose from many specific types of SmartArt in each group. Choose the first one in the upper-left corner: Basic Block List. Click **OK**.

Excel creates a basic, simple piece of SmartArt, which looks like a bunch of blocks. In the bulleted list window to the left of the blocks is an area to type your list items (see Figure 19.2). For this example, type in the steps for a procedure in your business (the following list is just an example):

- Discovery
- Analysis
- Consultation
- Preparation
- Execution

Notice that you have two new Ribbon tabs available under the heading of SmartArt Tools: Design and Format.

Figure 19.2

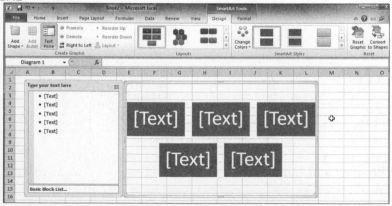

List items.

Click the Text pane to type your list. Start by typing **Discovery**, and then use the down arrow to move down to the next item. If you press Enter, you add another item to the list, creating a total of six items. Continue entering the items for your list in this way. Notice that, as you type each item, it appears on the list and in the SmartArt blocks. (See Figure 19.3.)

Figure 19.3

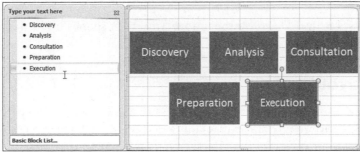

Entering list items.

After you enter all your items, press **Enter** after the last one and add it. If you decide you don't want an item, you can delete the text to delete the box.

> **TIP**
>
> The Ribbon also includes an Add Shape button on the SmartArt Tools > Design tab, in the Create Graphic group. This button enables you to add a new item to the list after or before the current item.

You can add bulleted items under your bulleted items (a second or third level) if you want to create a hierarchy. To insert sub-bullets, click the **Discovery** item and then click the **Add Bullet** button. Type the sub-bullet text here. (See Figure 19.4.)

Figure 19.4

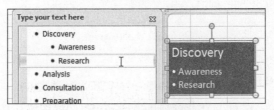

Inserting sub-bullets.

Use the Promote and Demote buttons on the Ribbon (on the SmartArt Tools > Design tab, Create Graphic group) to *promote* bulleted items a level (all the way to their own SmartArt shape) or *demote* items a level.

DEFINITION

To **promote** an item in an outline is to move it up to a higher level in the hierarchy of the outline. To **demote** an item is to move it down to a lower level, generally becoming a sub-header under a previous item.

The Right to Left button changes which way the SmartArt graphics flow (with the first item on the right or left, respectively).

The Reorder Up and Down buttons move SmartArt shapes up or down in the list order.

SmartArt Layouts

To experiment with different shape layouts, use the Layouts gallery (SmartArt Tools > Design tab > Layouts) to pick a layout. Try some of the different layouts: your data remains the same—just the presentation changes. (See Figure 19.5.)

Figure 19.5

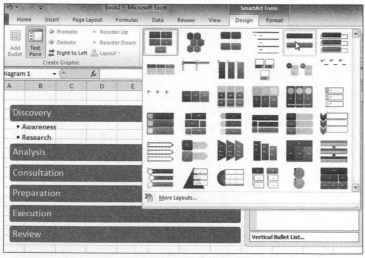

Different shape layouts.

Inserting Pictures

Some of the SmartArt layouts have places to insert pictures. To insert a picture, click the picture icon in the SmartArt graphic.

In Figure 19.6, you can see a picture of a forest for the Discovery item. You can add whatever pictures you want. Just browse your computer to select them.

Figure 19.6

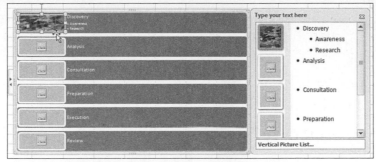

Inserted picture.

TIP

You should have some sample pictures (that come with Windows) in your "Sample Pictures" folder. If not, you can use the sample pictures in the Chapter 17 folder on your CD.

SmartArt Colors and Styles

Use the Change Colors button (SmartArt Tools > Design > SmartArt Styles > Change Colors) to change the color scheme (see Figure 19.7). You can choose from a wide variety of color schemes.

Figure 19.7

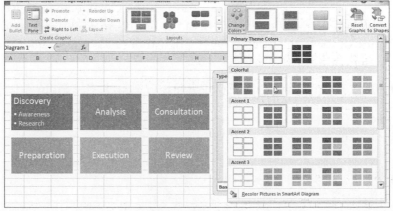

Change Colors button.

Likewise, you can choose from several different effect styles (see Figure 19.8).

Figure 19.8

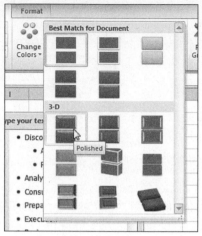

Change Effects.

The Reset Graphic button erases all the style changes you make to the SmartArt Graphic and returns it to its default state.

The Convert to Shapes button changes the object from SmartArt to a collection of shapes that you can manipulate freely.

Changing the Shape of SmartArt Objects

Moving over to the Format SmartArt Tools tab, the Change Shape button enables you to change the shape of one or more of the objects inside your SmartArt group. This is handy if, for example, you've got a bunch of rectangles in your group, and you want to change one of them to an oval.

For example, you can change the Analysis box to a circle (see Figure 19.9).

Figure 19.9

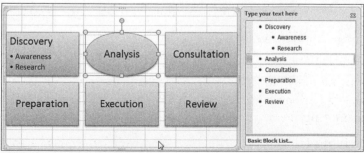

Changing the shape to a circle.

To select more than one shape to manipulate at the same time, click the first shape, hold down the **Shift** key, and then click the remaining shapes.

The Larger and Smaller buttons make the selected shape larger or smaller than the other shapes in incremental steps (see Figure 19.10). You click the **Larger** button to continue making the shape larger and the **Smaller** button to make it smaller.

Figure 19.10

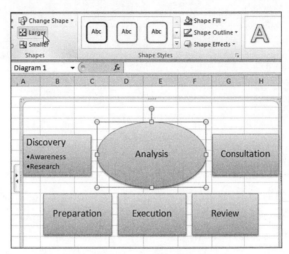

The Larger button and the Smaller button.

Changing SmartArt Shape Styles

The Shape Styles group enables you to change the styles of individual shapes. You can set a base style using the gallery and then manipulate the fill color, outline, and shape effects manually. See Chapters 17 and 18 for more details on how these features work; they're similar to how Shapes work.

The WordArt Styles group acts similar to how the Shapes WordArt Styles work (refer to Chapter 18). You can change the style, text fill, outline, and effects.

Finally, Arrange and Size buttons let you manipulate how the shapes are arranged and how big they are.

In the Organizational Chart (under the Hierarchy group), you can add new people by adding new bullet points (see Figure 19.11). Organize the people by reordering or promoting/demoting them.

To add an assistant for someone, click that shape, click the **Add Shape** button, and select **Add Assistant**. It's that easy. Enjoy, and have fun playing with SmartArt.

Figure 19.11

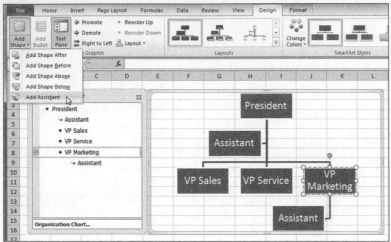

Organizational chart.

Screenshots

New in Excel 2010 is the capability to take a picture of what's on your screen. You can choose from several open windows or take a shot of a piece of the whole screen itself. Click **Insert > Screenshot**.

Notice that one or more open windows display in the drop-down box. If you click one of these, a screenshot image of the whole window appears embedded in your spreadsheet (see Figure 19.12).

If you click **Screen Clipping** (under the Screenshot drop-down button) instead of one of the windows, you can select any rectangular area on your screen that you want to clip. When your screen washes out white and your mouse becomes a crosshair, click and drag to select any region of your screen. Release the mouse, and that area is pasted into your sheet.

NOTICE

Interestingly, you cannot take a screen capture of your current Excel document. You can, however, open Word (or another Excel workbook) and get a screen capture from there.

Figure 19.12

A screenshot embedded.

With screen captures, anything that you can get on your screen you can now use as an image in your Microsoft Office documents.

TIP

You can use an old-school way to get a screen clipping, too. Click the **Print Screen** button (sometimes labeled as PrtScn). The screen capture appears on the Windows Clipboard. Go to Excel, Word, Paint, or any program that supports it and click **Paste**.

The Least You Need to Know

- You can use SmartArt to display information visually in your spreadsheet.
- You can choose from several types of SmartArt, including lists, processes, diagrams, and organizational charts.
- You can capture anything you can see on the screen using the Screen Capture feature.

In This Chapter

- Creating a simple column chart
- Graduating to more complex 3-D chart types, pie charts, bar charts, and more
- Editing chart options
- Changing chart layouts, types, styles, and more

A *chart* is a graphical illustration of one or more series of data. You can use a chart to make your data more understandable, to convey a message visually, to spot trends, or even to persuade your audience during a presentation (tilt the chart a little bit, and your slumping sales don't look so bad).

As with everything in Excel, you have a million different options for creating charts. In this chapter, we start with a simple column chart and work our way up to the more complex ones.

A lot of the options that are available with charts (such as filling the columns with color or patterns) are the same features that you learned in Chapters 17 through 19, so be sure to review those chapters as well.

Creating a Simple Column Chart

Let's begin by creating a simple column chart with one *data series*.

You can have multiple series of data on a chart, but for now, let's keep it simple and work with one data series.

Each data series is made up of a collection of *data points*.

DEFINITION

A **data series** is a single set of data that you want to chart. For example, if you're tracking sales for multiple stores, one data series would be the sales for one of your stores.

A **data point** represents one bit of data in a data series. For example, of the sales from one store, the sales from a specific quarter makes up one data point (for example, one cell of data).

Open the file "Sales Data" from the Chapter 20 folder on the accompanying CD. It's a simple sheet of sales for different stores for the four quarters of 2009. It also includes totals for each store and for each quarter. (See Figure 20.1.)

Figure 20.1

	A	B	C	D	E	F
1	Store	1Q	2Q	3Q	4Q	Totals
2	Buffalo	56	65	73	94	288
3	Key West	57	64	75	92	288
4	Miami	54	63	71	97	285
5	Los Angeles	52	69	57	43	221
6	Chicago	53	62	72	89	276
7	Totals	272	323	348	415	1358

Sales data.

To create a chart, select the data that you want to appear in the chart (including any labels) and then click the **Insert** tab of the Ribbon. Notice the Charts group with several different chart types.

For the first example, let's chart only the sales from the first quarter. Select the range A1:B6. You want the labels on the top of the column, but you don't want the totals at the bottom.

Here you'll make a simple 2-D column chart. After you've selected the range, click **Column** and then click the first **2-D Column** button. (See Figure 20.2.)

Figure 20.2

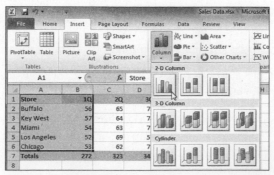

2-D column chart.

Notice that Excel creates the chart for you, using a set of default options. The chart is then placed as an embedded object on your spreadsheet. (See Figure 20.3.)

Figure 20.3

Embedded chart.

Most charts are made up of the same components:

- **Category axis:** Also known as the x-axis or horizontal axis, this represents the label for each of your items. In the example, the category axis represents the store names.

- **Value axis:** This is the y-axis, or vertical axis, representing the value for each of the data points. In your chart, it's the sales amount for each store.

- **Chart title:** The large bit of text above the chart gives the chart a descriptive title. Like many of the other objects in the chart, this is optional and can be turned off.

- **Legend:** This box on the side of the chart shows which data series are what colors. The sample chart in Figure 20.3 has only one series, so there's only one box labeled "1Q." The legend is optional.

- **Plot area:** This is the region of the chart that includes the data. It does not include the axes, titles, or legend.

- **Chart area:** This area covers the entire chart object and everything you see in it. You can select the chart area to change the chart's background color, for example.

- **Gridlines:** You can have horizontal and vertical gridlines behind your chart's data series. Gridlines make the chart more readable.

Editing Chart Objects

You can move, resize, and delete a chart just like any other Illustrations object (pictures, clipart, shapes, and so on). Click and drag to move a chart or resize it, and press the **Delete** key to get rid of it.

> **TIP**
>
> To move the chart, make sure you see the four-way arrow when you click and drag on it. (See Figure 20.4.)

Figure 20.4

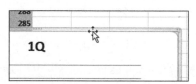

Moving a chart.

To resize the chart, make sure you have the double-arrow that appears when you hover the mouse over any corner or side of the chart.

After you select the chart, you can click any of the individual objects inside the chart to format or edit those as well. This can be a bit tricky for beginners: if the chart isn't currently selected, you have to click once to select the chart object itself and then click a second time on any object inside the chart.

For example, click cell A1 so that you do *not* have the chart selected. Then click the chart. This selects the entire chart object. Finally, if you want to edit any of the objects inside the chart, click those objects. For text objects (like the labels), you have to click them another time to go into text edit mode.

For example, let's change the title of the chart from "1Q" to "1Q Sales." Click the chart, and click the title to select it. Now click the title again to go into text edit mode (notice a blinking cursor). It seems awkward until you get used to it, but then it becomes second nature.

Fortunately, you can manipulate chart objects in other ways using the Ribbon. Click the **Chart Tools**, **Layout** tab.

Notice the Current Selection group all the way to the left side of the Ribbon. Click the drop-down box in this group to select a specific part of the chart. For example, if you want to select the chart title, select it from the drop-down menu (see Figure 20.5).

Figure 20.5

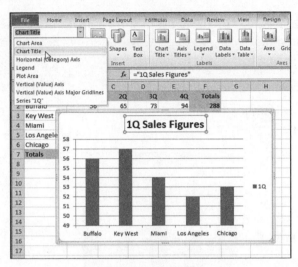

Select Chart Title.

Also notice that the selection goes the other way, too. When you click some part of the chart itself, the drop-down menu changes to tell you what object is currently selected.

When you have a piece of the chart selected, you can click the **Format Selection** button. This opens the Format dialog menu and enables you to change several options for that selected object. We come back to formatting the chart objects a little later in this chapter.

Chart with Noncontiguous Data

Now let's delete this chart and create another, slightly more complicated chart. To delete the chart, click the outside of the chart border to select the entire chart and then press **Delete**.

Let's say that you want to make a chart that shows the store names and their annual sales totals. To do this, select two ranges on the sheet that are *noncontiguous*.

> **DEFINITION**
>
> Two ranges are **noncontiguous** if they're not adjacent (next to) each other. For example, the ranges A1:A5 and D8:D10 are noncontiguous ranges.

Start by selecting A1:A6, which is a list of store names. Then release the mouse button. Press and hold down the **Ctrl** key while selecting the next range you want to chart. In this case, it's F2:F6 for the annual totals.

After you select the data, click **Insert > Column > 3-D Clustered Column** chart.

Figure 20.6 shows a simple 3-D chart.

Figure 20.6

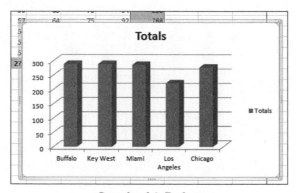

Completed 3-D chart.

The "clustered" part of the chart name simply means that if you have multiple data series, they would each be clustered together. Let's create a chart with multiple data series so you can see an example.

Chart with Multiple Data Series

Delete the current chart. Now let's make a chart showing all four quarters of the sales for all the stores. Select everything from A1 to E6. You don't want the sales totals on this chart.

Select the 3-D Column chart (see Figure 20.7), which gives you a chart with three different axes. You still have the x- (category) and y- (value) axes, but now you also have a z-axis representing each quarter.

Figure 20.7

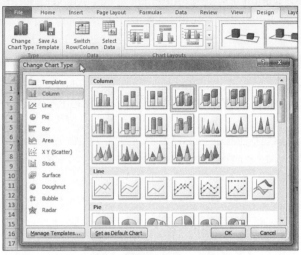

3-D Column chart.

Now that you know a quick way to build a simple chart, let's go through some options for working with charts.

Types of Charts

Starting with the Design tab of the Chart Tools section, the left-most button on the Ribbon is the Change Chart Type button (see Figure 20.8). Several chart types are available.

Figure 20.8

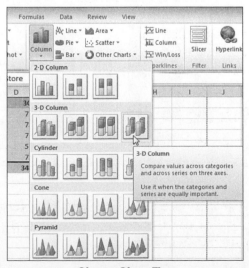

Change Chart Type.

You can easily switch among different chart types by selecting one from this menu. Let's take a look at some of the chart types.

Column Charts

The options on this menu basically enable you to replace simple columns with cylinders, cones, and pyramids. Figure 20.9 shows a 3-D pyramid chart.

Figure 20.9

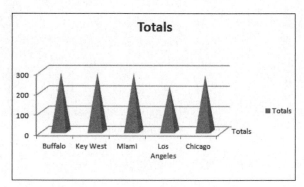

3-D pyramid column chart.

The stacked options that you see on some of the charts simply mean that the data points of a series are stacked on top of each other instead of set apart in a separate axis. This is good for viewing totals of a series. Figure 20.10 shows the stacked 3-D column chart, for example.

Figure 20.10

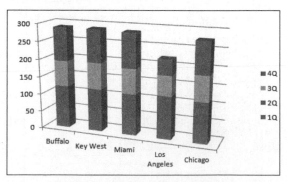

Stacked 3-D Column chart.

There's also a less used 100% stacked chart, in which each column is the same height, representing 100 percent of the series' total value. The individual values show as a percentage of the whole.

Line Charts

Line charts are straight-forward. These are lines representing each data series. You can also see options for stacked lines, lines with markers, 100 percent stacked lines, 3-D line charts, and so on (see Figure 20.11).

Figure 20.11

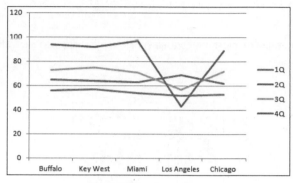

Line chart.

Pie Charts

Pie charts work with only one data series. If you change your chart type from a multiseries chart to a pie chart, for example, you'll find that it graphs only the first data series (see Figure 20.12).

Figure 20.12

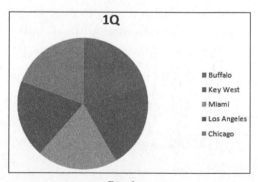

Pie chart.

With pie charts, you can carefully pull out the slices of the pie by dragging them away from the center of the pie.

If you want to split apart all of the pie slices, click once on the pie itself, hold down the mouse button, and then drag away from the center of the pie. This pulls all the pie slices apart from each other.

Notice that all of the pie slices have dots around them. This means that they're all selected. Now click and drag to move them all back toward the center, and repair the pie.

If you want to work with an individual pie slice, click one of the slices a second time. This selects just that piece of the pie, and you can drag it away from the middle by itself. (See Figure 20.13.)

TIP

If you find that you can't easily reselect all the pie slices, just click off the chart and try again.

Figure 20.13

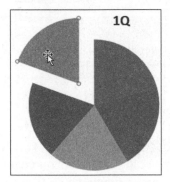

Pie chart separate one slice.

Some odd pie chart types exist, like "pie of pie" and "bar of pie." These are handy when you have several pie slices that you want to group together into one slice—usually because they represent a tiny amount of the overall pie. This "bar of pie" chart splits off the three stores that make up a very small percentage of the total sales.

The "pie of pie" chart in Figure 20.14 just makes a second pie chart to represent the same data.

Figure 20.14

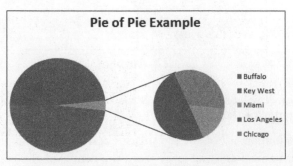

"Pie of pie" chart.

To control the number of items that are separated out into the bar or second pie, right-click the pie itself and select **Format Data Series**. In the Series Options group, notice several different ways to split the data series. For example, you could say that you want all items with a value of less than 5 to show up in the second plot.

Bar Charts

The bar chart is basically the column chart turned on its side. (See Figure 20.15.) There's not a whole lot that's different about it. It's really a matter of personal preference whether you want to use a vertical column chart or a horizontal bar chart.

Figure 20.15

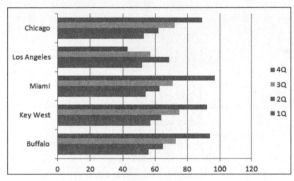

Bar chart.

Area Charts

The area chart is basically a line chart with the area below the line filled in with a solid color. The area chart enables you to show overlaps in the data. In Figure 20.16, you can see that the data for 4Q is almost always higher than that of the other quarters. You can rearrange the data series so you can see 4Q in the back and the lower quarters in the foreground.

Figure 20.16

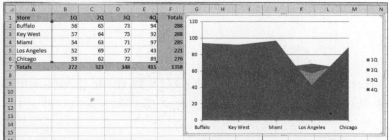

Area chart.

To do this, on the Chart Tools Design tab, in the Data group, click the **Select Data** button.

The Select Data Source dialog menu opens (see Figure 20.17). You can see the chart data range at the top of the menu. In this case, it shows '2009 Sales'!$A$1:$E$6. This means that the sheet name is "2009 Sales" and that we're dealing with the range A1:E6.

Figure 20.17

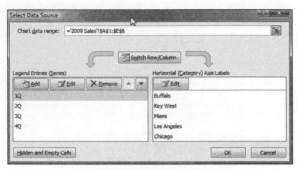

Select Data Source menu.

The data series is on the left side of this menu, and the axis labels are on the right side. You can switch them by clicking the **Switch Row/Column** button (which does the same thing as the Switch Row/Column button on the Ribbon). (See Figure 20.18.)

Figure 20.18

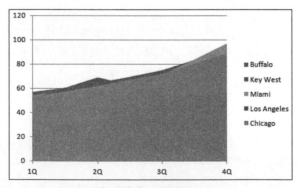

Switch Row/Column.

Now, let's rearrange the data series so that 4Q is in the back, followed by 3Q, 2Q, and finally 1Q. Click the 4Q item, and then click the up arrow a few times to move it to the top of the list. (See Figure 20.19.)

Figure 20.19

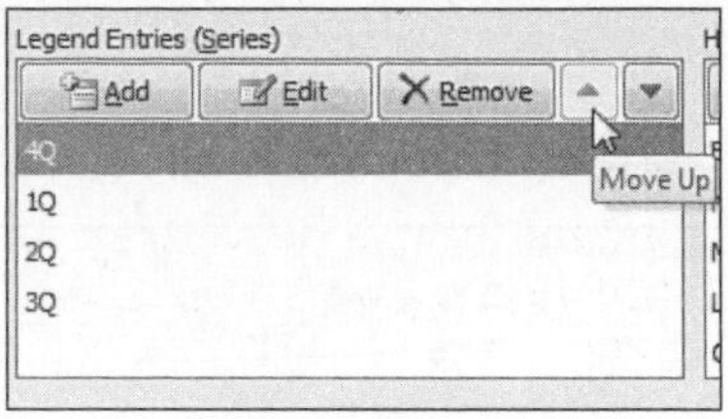

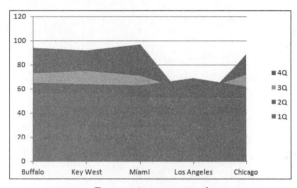

Move item up.

You can do something similar for 3Q and 2Q to rearrange them. When you're done, your chart will look like Figure 20.20.

Figure 20.20

Data series rearranged.

You can also use this dialog menu to add more series to your chart or remove something you don't want on there. Perhaps you're planning to close the Los Angeles store, so you don't need its sales figures for this chart. Click **Los Angeles** and then **Remove**.

Scatter Charts

Scatter charts show lines and markers. The lines can be smooth or straight. The markers are different for each data series. Figure 20.21 shows an example of a "smooth lines with markers" scatter chart.

Figure 20.21

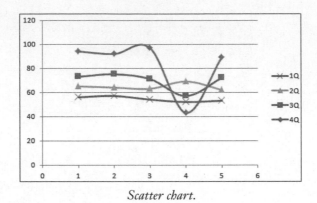

Scatter chart.

Doughnut Charts

A doughnut chart is basically a pie chart with multiple series. Each data series shows up as a concentric ring inside the doughnut. (See Figure 20.22.) These charts are good for gauging percentages of a whole.

Figure 20.22

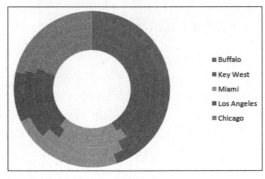

Doughnut chart.

Other Chart Types

A few other, lesser-used chart types exist: the stock, surface, bubble, and radar charts. The stock chart is used for tracking stock prices. The others are used for more advanced statistical analysis.

Chart Layouts

When you settle on a specific type of chart, it's time to work on the layout. Next to the Data group on the Chart Tools, Design tab, you'll find the Chart Layouts gallery.

Each of the items in this gallery is specific to the type of chart you pick. The different layouts enable you to specify where items on the chart go and what items are visible.

The layout in Figure 20.23 changes the chart slightly by moving the legend to the top of the chart and placing data labels on each data point so you can see their values.

Figure 20.23

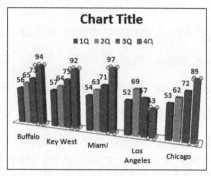

Layout 2.

The layout in Figure 20.24 adds a *data table*, which shows a mini spreadsheet with the chart so you can see all the data items. It also adds an *axis title* for the vertical axis. You can click that to change it (as well as change the chart title).

Figure 20.24

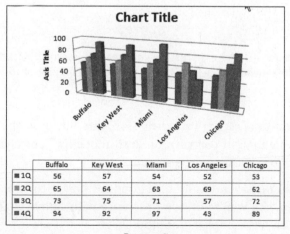

Layout 5.

Chart Styles

After you choose a type of chart and layout, you can pick a chart style. Just like normal styles and themes, chart styles allow us to set different colors and effects for the charts based on existing templates. (See Figure 20.25.)

Figure 20.25

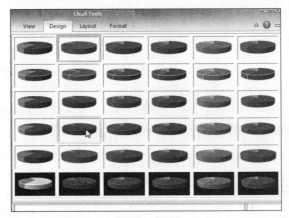

Chart styles.

Note that there's usually a black-and-white (grayscale) style for you to pick from in the options for each chart type. This is great if you have only a black-and-white printer (or don't want to waste color ink).

NOTICE

Keep in mind that these chart styles change with the workbook's theme. If you change the theme on the Page Layout tab, you'll change all of your available styles, too.

While on the subject of saving ink, there's a Draft button in the Mode group of the Chart Tools, Design tab. If you turn on draft mode for your chart, it won't print as sharply or show up as nicely on the screen.

This is used as an ink saver, but it's also good for slower computers that can't render complex graphics. You won't notice a difference with simple charts, but when you start working with big, complex graphical charts, you'll see it.

Finally, if you want more room to work with your chart, you can change it to a full-page chart. On the **Chart Tools**, **Design** tab, find the **Location** group. Click the **Move Chart** button.

You can use this menu to move the chart as an object inside of a different sheet, or you can create a full sheet out of it. Select the **New Sheet** option, and type a different name for the chart or leave it as the default name. Click **OK**.

Notice that the chart now takes up its own page. It's still linked to the data on the original sheet, but this gives you much more room to work with if you're planning to make full-page charts for a printed publication or presentation.

Custom Chart Layout

Now that you've selected a chart type, a general layout, and a style, you're ready to tweak the chart and make it look exactly like you want it. Click the **Chart Tools, Layout** tab and notice several options that let you change every specific thing about the chart that you want to.

You already looked at the Current Selection group, where you can pick a chart element.

Next comes the Insert group, where you can insert a picture, shape, or text box inside the chart. This is handy if you want to put some descriptive text somewhere in your chart. Figure 20.26 shows what a properly placed shape with some text in it can look like.

Figure 20.26

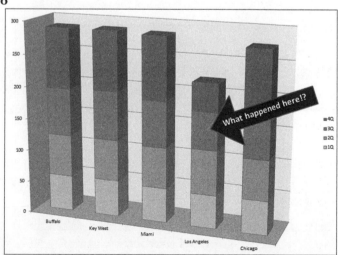

Add shapes to chart.

Whether or not your layout has a chart title, you can create one with the Chart Title button. You can make your title centered over the top of the chart, and either push the rest of the chart down or just have it float over the chart.

To edit the chart title's text, click it until you get the "I" text cursor, and feel free to use any formatting you like (color, font, and so on). (See Figure 20.27.)

Click the **More Title Options** selection for additional settings for your chart title. You can control the fill, border color, styles, shadow, glow, 3-D effect, and lots more.

Figure 20.27

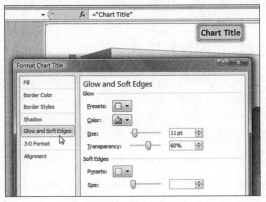

Chart Title Options.

Next is the button to create axis titles. Figure 20.28 shows a rotated vertical axis title. Again, several options are available.

Figure 20.28

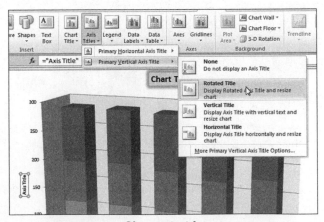

Chart axis titles.

The next button enables you to change the placement of the legend (up, down, left, right, and so on).

Data labels are numbers that show up next to the data points (see Figure 20.29). On some charts, they're helpful; on other charts, they can make your chart look really cluttered.

Figure 20.29

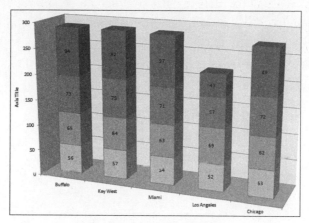

Data labels on a column chart.

Sometimes you can turn on a data label and then pull it away from the chart a bit. Just click the data label until you have only one selected, and then click and drag. You get a *leader line* that points from the chart to the data label. (See Figure 20.30.)

Figure 20.30

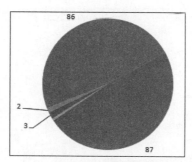

Data labels separated from a pie chart.

Notice also that the Data Labels menu is different for pie charts than it is for column charts and others.

Finally, in the Labels group, you can turn the Data Table on or off. This is a mini-spreadsheet used to show you the actual data values for each point.

Next, in the Axes group, you have the Axes button. For the horizontal axis, you can set whether you want to see the axes labels (see Figure 20.31). You can choose to have the values go from left to right (default) or right to left. Finally, you can show the axis without labels.

Figure 20.31

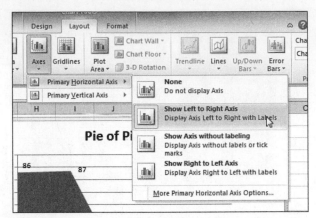

Horizontal axis. You can set vertical axis values in thousands, millions, or billions, or with a logarithmic (base 10) scale.

For additional options, click the **More Primary Vertical Axis Options** selection (see Figure 20.32).

Figure 20.32

More Primary Vertical Axis Options.

Aside from the normal formatting options, this menu gives you several ways to display the data. For example, normally the axes values range from zero to a little over your maximum value.

If most of your values are within a certain range (say, test scores that all fall between 64 and 100), you can manipulate the axis values here. Because the lowest sales figure is 43, let's set the minimum value to 40 and the maximum value to 100. (See Figure 20.33.)

Figure 20.33

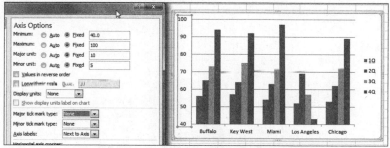

Axis Options, minimum and maximum values.

Notice in Figure 20.33 that, with a little adjusting, we've made the differences between the stores' sales look huge. Los Angeles looks like it had a bad fourth quarter.

We also changed the major and minor units to a fixed 10 and 5, respectively. These are the lines you see in the background. Right now, only the major lines are on. Let's turn on the minor lines, too.

Click **Gridlines > Primary Horizontal Gridlines > Major & Minor Gridlines** to turn on the fat, big major lines and the thin, whispy minor lines. And, of course, there are several options for these as well.

If you switch to a 3-D chart, you can play with the wall and floor settings in the Background group. You can also have some fun with the 3-D Rotation settings (see Figure 20.34).

Figure 20.34

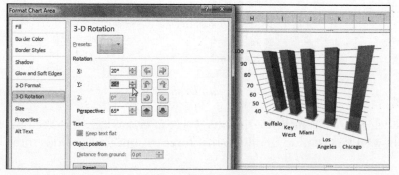

3-D Rotation settings.

For the Analysis section, you can create trendlines, droplines, high/low lines, up/down bars, and error bars.

A trendline is best with column or bar charts. You can use a trendline to spot trends and to forecast results into the future. For example, Figure 20.35 shows a simple linear trendline for the Key West store. Switch the rows and columns, click **Trendline > Linear**, and then select **Key West**.

Figure 20.35

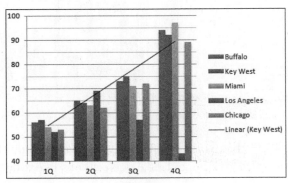

Trendline.

You can add multiple trendlines for different series. You can also forecast results. Pick the Linear Forecast trendline (see Figure 20.36). To delete a trendline, click the line itself and press the **Delete** key.

Figure 20.36

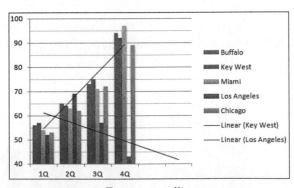

Forecast trendline.

If you click **More Trendline Options**, you can create a custom trendline. Figure 20.37 shows a logarithmic trendline that forecasts out four periods into the future.

Figure 20.37

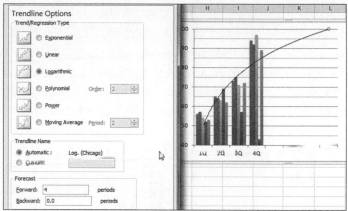

Forecast logarithmic trendline.

Change the way the trendlines are calculated to better suit the message you want to convey with the chart. If you want to show that sales will even out over time, use a logarithmic trendline. If you want to show that they're exploding, use an exponential line.

Drop lines on a line chart show where the data points meet the x-axis. (See Figure 20.38.)

Figure 20.38

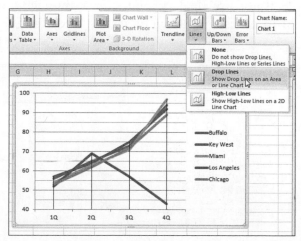

Drop lines.

Finally on the Chart Tools, Format page, you find some of the same formatting options you already looked at with other types of illustrations (pictures, shapes, and so on). Here you can change the shape styles, WordArt styles, arrangement of objects, and more.

Remember, to format an object, right-click it and select Format [object type]. For example, if you right-click any one of the columns in a chart, you get "Format Data Series." This changes the whole data series. In Figure 20.39, we made Miami solid black.

Figure 20.39

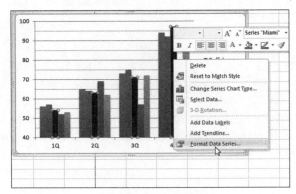

Format data series.

To highlight a specific column in the chart, click it while the series is already highlighted, which selects just a single data point. Now right-click and select **Format Data Point**. In 20.40, we used a pattern fill just on Miami's 3Q column.

Figure 20.40

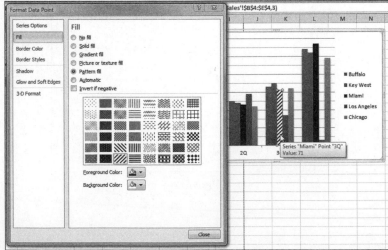

Format Data Point.

The Least You Need to Know

- You can create a very professional-looking and detailed chart in Excel with just a few clicks.

- Use the Ribbon to change your chart layout, styles, and adjustments. This alone usually gives you the chart you're looking for.

- Want even more customization? Spend some time exploring the format menu options to see the little tweaks and enhancements you can make to charts.

Formulas and Functions

You learned about a couple of the more popular functions back in Chapter 2. This part covers functions in more detail.

In Chapter 22, you learn different ways to create formulas. We cover relative and absolute references, named cells and ranges, references to values on other sheets, how to link cells together, and formula errors.

Chapter 23 shows you how to manipulate text strings. You learn how to see if two cells are the same and how to concatenate two text strings (like first name and last name). We also cover functions to determine information about a text value: LEN, LEFT, RIGHT, MID, FIND, and SEARCH. Finally, you learn how to convert between upper- and lowercase.

In Chapter 24, you work with date and time values. You see how Excel stores date values internally and how to determine the current date and time.

Chapter 25 is about logical functions. You learn about NOT, TRUE, FALSE, AND, and OR. You learn how to make your formulas smart with the IF function. You also see how to determine the contents of a cell with functions.

In Chapter 26, you look at one of my favorite functions: VLOOKUP. You can use this powerful function to look up values from another range in your workbook.

Chapter 27 focuses on math and statistics functions. You find out how to do more with the SUM function and you learn about the SUMIF function. You also learn how to round values properly, and you work with other lesser-used math functions, such as POWER, ABS, and RAND.

In Chapter 28, you learn how to calculate monthly payments for a loan using the PMT function and how to calculate the future value of an investment using FV. You also get to play the "What's My Interest Rate?" game with the RATE function, and you learn how long it will take for you to become a millionaire with the NPER function.

Other Objects

In This Chapter

- Inserting new objects into your Excel sheets
- Making fancy text with text boxes and WordArt
- Learning why math teachers love the Equation Editor
- Using Sparklines to create mini charts in your sheet

In addition to pictures, ClipArt, SmartArt, screenshots, and charts, you can insert other object types into your spreadsheets to enhance them. We look at many of them in this chapter.

Text Boxes

If you want to put a block of random text somewhere on your sheet, such as a short note to the spreadsheet user, the best tool to use is the Text Box button. You can find it on the Insert tab. This feature is handy for adding some notes or other descriptive text to your spreadsheets.

After you click the Text Box button, your mouse changes to an upside-down "t" pointer. Click and drag a box to place the text box wherever you'd like (see Figure 21.1). Then type some text.

Figure 21.1

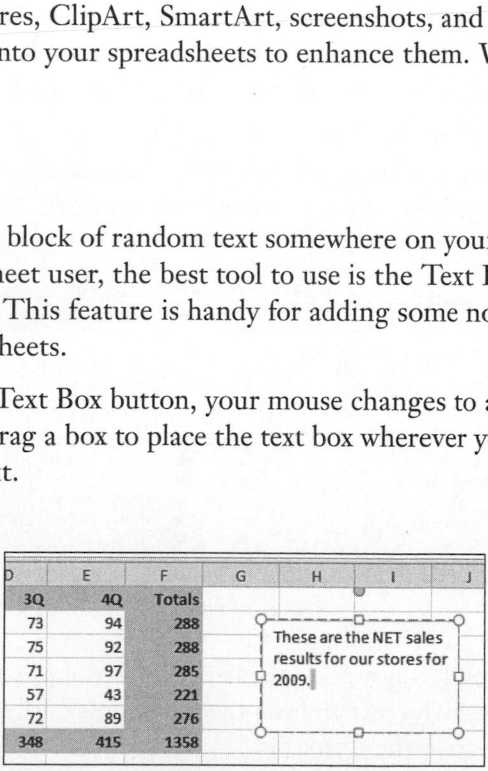

D	E	F	G	H	I	J
3Q	4Q	Totals				
73	94	288				
75	92	288	These are the NET sales results for our stores for 2009.			
71	97	285				
57	43	221				
72	89	276				
348	415	1358				

Text box with text.

Treat this object just like any normal illustration object. You can move it, delete it, resize it, rotate it, change the font formatting, modify the fill color, change the border color, and so on. In Figure 21.2, the text box has a selected style, an increased font size, and a drop shadow. Refer to Chapter 17 for more information on these techniques.

Figure 21.2

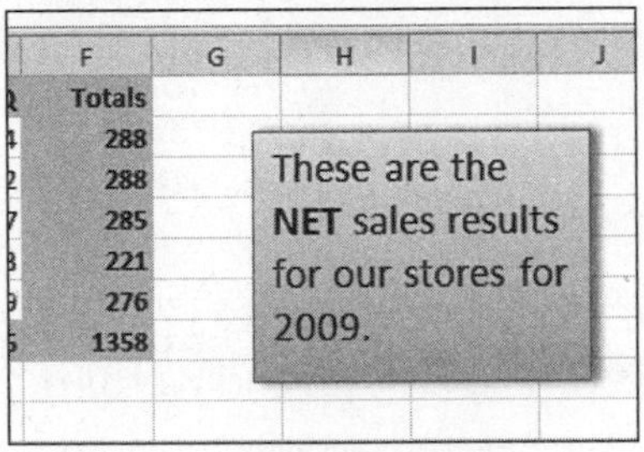

A formatted text box.

WordArt

Use the WordArt tool to create attention-getting text for your sheet. You can use it for titles, to draw attention to something, or just to have fun. Click **Insert > Text > WordArt** and then choose a style of WordArt that you like.

In Figure 21.3, a piece of WordArt has been inserted and the rest of the sheet data has been moved down by simply inserting some blank rows. The style of the WordArt has been changed and there's a soft glow effect.

Figure 21.3

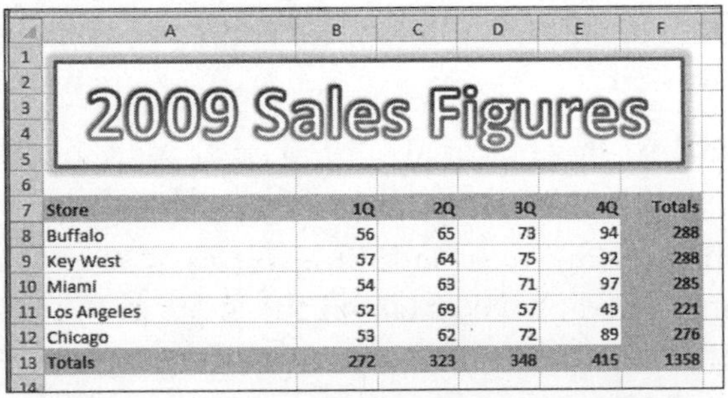

WordArt header.

It's important to note that just resizing the WordArt object frame does not resize the text. You have to select the text and use the Font tools (either the mini pop-up toolbar or the Ribbon) to change the font size.

Signature Line

The signature line has two uses. First, you can use it to simply place a nice-looking X with a line and the signer's name and title beneath it (see Figure 21.4). This way, when you print the sheet, the signer can sign it. This makes the sheet look professional.

Figure 21.4

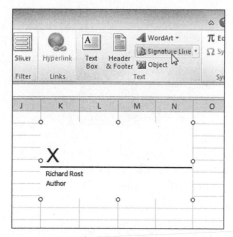

A signature line.

Another use for a signature line is to enable you to embed a *digital signature* into the spreadsheet to verify its authenticity. This way, if anyone else changes the sheet, the signature is invalidated and everyone will know that the sheet has been edited.

Setting up a digital signature is beyond the scope of this book. You have to purchase a digital signature from one of the various authorities that provide them. They're not cheap, but if you need to authenticate documents, it might be a worthwhile investment.

Equations

Math teachers will love the Equation Editor feature. Click the **Insert > Equation** button to access the Equation Tools tab on the Ribbon. You can use this tool to create many different kinds of custom math equations that you can print out.

NOTICE

Remember, these math formulas aren't functional. They're for display only. Excel will not actually calculate anything. These are just display objects.

If you want to type math formulas or symbols, you have several to choose from. Let's do a simple cube root problem. Click the **Radical** button. You'll find it on the Equation Tools > Design tab. Then select the **Radical With Degree** option.

A radical sign with two boxes displays. Type the numbers where needed by clicking the boxes (see Figure 21.5). Voilà! There's your radical.

Figure 21.5

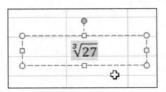

Completed radical.

After the radical, press the spacebar and then a plus sign, followed by another space. Notice that the equation is just an object inside a text box. Now let's add more to the math problem. Click **Insert > Equation** again. Let's add a fraction. Click **Fraction** and then **Stacked Fraction**.

Now you can enter numbers for the numerator and denominator. Different types of math equations are possible: brackets, limits, logarithms, matrices, integrals, and several math symbols.

> **NOTICE**
>
> Keep in mind that the formula is text inside a text box, so if you want to increase the size of the text, you can't just resize the box. Use the font buttons to increase the size.

If you click the down arrow next to the Equation button, you'll find templates for popular types of equations: area of a circle, binomials, the Pythagorean theorem, and so on (see Figure 21.6).

Figure 21.6

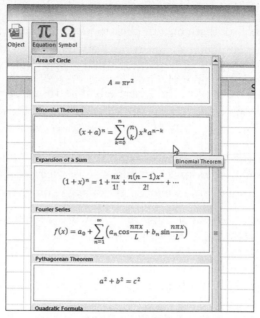

Formula templates.

Symbols

Looking for a copyright notice sign or the marker for a euro? Just click the **Insert > Text > Symbol** button (see Figure 21.7). You can scroll through several symbols that you can insert into your spreadsheet.

Figure 21.7

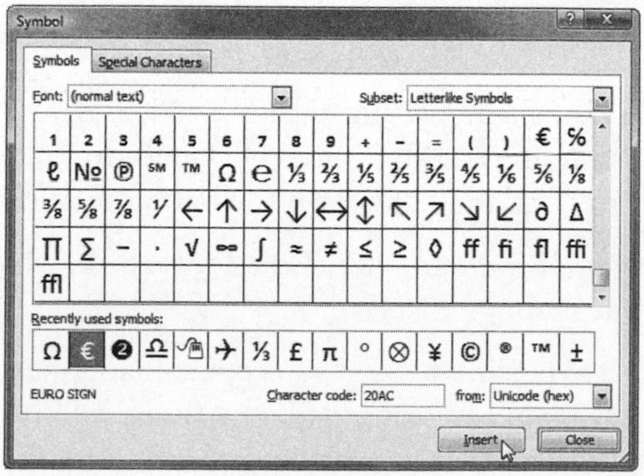

Insert symbols.

Hyperlinks

A hyperlink is a text link that you can click to jump to another location. That location can be a file on your computer or network, a place in the current document (specified with a bookmark), an e-mail address (to send an e-mail), or a web page.

Click the **Hyperlink** button on the Insert tab. The Insert Hyperlink dialog box displays. The first option on the left under "Link to" says, "Existing File or Web Page." Choose this option to select a file from your computer or a web page.

Buttons on the left side of the Insert Hyperlink dialog box enable you to choose files from the current folder or from recent files you've accessed. Also notice a Browsed Pages button that enables you to choose a web page you've recently visited.

Let's make a link to a web page. Type the following web address into the Address bar: **http://www.CIGExcel.com**. At the top of the window, type **CIG Excel Web Site** into the Text to Display box. This is what the user actually sees in the sheet (see Figure 21.8).

Figure 21.8

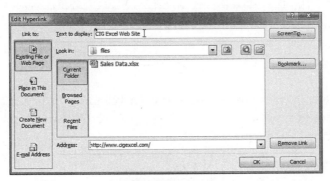

CIG Excel web link.

Notice on the sheet that the hyperlink has been added. If you hover the mouse over the link, you get instructions telling you to click once to follow the link (load it in your web browser), or click and hold down the button to select the cell.

To edit the link, right-click it and select **Edit Hyperlink**, which brings up the Insert Hyperlink dialog box again.

You can also create a hyperlink to send someone e-mail. Specify the text that's visible for the hyperlink, the recipient's e-mail address (Excel adds the "mailto:" in front of it), and an optional subject line for the e-mail.

Sparklines

Sparklines are a new feature in Excel 2010. They enable you to create embedded charts inside cells, and they provide a quick way to visualize data trends. Let's see them in action.

The Sparklines group is located on the Insert tab just to the right of the Charts group.

You can create three different types of Sparklines: line, column, and win/loss. Let's create a line Sparkline. Open the Sales Data workbook from the Chapter 21 folder on your CD. To create Sparklines:

1. First, select a range of cells that represents the data series you want to chart. Unlike regular charts, don't select the labels, too. Select B2:E6.

2. Now click the **Line** button in the Insert > Sparklines group.

3. The Create Sparklines dialog box appears. Because you had a range selected, the Data Range is filled in for you.

4. Specify the Location Range, or where the Sparklines are to be placed. Type **G2:G6** (or use the selector button).

5. Click **OK** when finished. Your Sparklines appear (see Figure 21.9).

Figure 21.9

Completed Sparklines.

Notice that each line represents the values in your range. If you look at Figure 21.9, for example, you can see that Los Angeles went up from Q1 to Q2, and then went straight down in Q3 and Q4. That's just what the line looks like.

You can choose among several styles for your lines. You can change the colors manually as well. You can also turn on indicators for the high point, low point, negative points, first point, and last point. The markers represent the individual data points.

To switch from a line to a column or win/loss Sparkline, click the appropriate buttons in the Type group (see Figure 21.10).

Figure 21.10

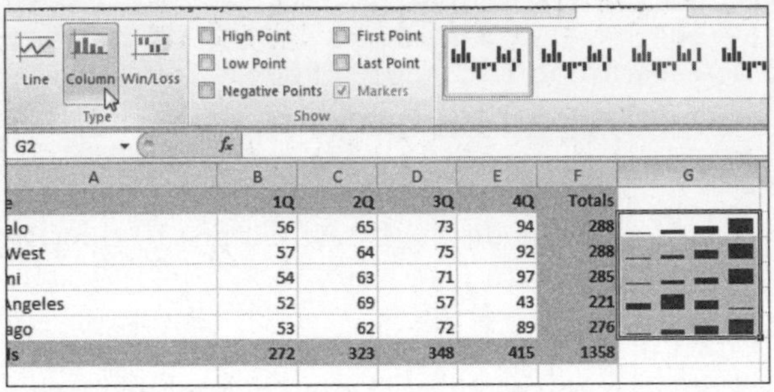

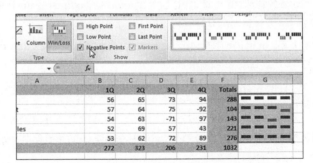

Column Sparklines.

The win/loss Sparklines show different values only if you have negative numbers. If you want to see an example, change some of your numbers to negatives and then click the Negative Points option in the Show group (see Figure 21.11).

Figure 21.11

Win/loss Sparklines.

The Least You Need to Know

- Insert a text box or WordArt to add descriptive text to your sheets.
- Use the Equation Editor to insert complex math formulas for display or printing only in your sheets.
- Insert hyperlinks into your sheets to launch web pages, send e-mail, or load other documents.
- Sparklines are a quick and easy way to add visual representations of your data to your sheets.

Working with Formulas and Functions

In This Chapter

- Different ways to create formulas
- Discovering the difference between relative and absolute references
- Using named cells and ranges to make referring to specific cells easier
- Referring to cell values on other sheets
- Understanding formula errors

We talked about basic formulas and functions in Chapters 5 and 6, but we only scratched the surface of what functions can do. You learned about the basic, most popular functions: SUM, AVERAGE, COUNT, MAX, and MIN. In this chapter, you learn more techniques for working with formulas. In the next couple chapters, you explore new functions.

Methods for Creating Formulas

Remember that you can create a function by typing the name of the function itself (either directly into a cell or the Formula bar), or by using the AutoSum button to insert popular functions like SUM and AVERAGE.

Because there are a ton of different functions, you might not always remember their names. Fortunately, Excel has bundled them together in categories on the Formulas tab of the Ribbon.

The functions are organized based on category. For example, the financial functions are organized under the Financial button. There are buttons for logical functions, text-manipulation functions, date and time functions, and so on.

The functions you used recently can be found under the Recently Used button. Anything that doesn't fit neatly into one of these major categories can be found under the More Functions button.

You can insert a function into the currently selected cell by clicking the Category button and then selecting the function name. For example, if you want to insert a SUM function, you can click on the Math and Trig button and then find the SUM function in the list. If you're not sure which function is the right one, just hold your mouse over the function name to get a pop-up tip with the function description.

Let's start with a blank spreadsheet. Type in six random numbers in both columns E and F (see Figure 22.1).

When you click the **SUM** function, the Function Arguments dialog box displays. The SUM function can be used to sum up multiple ranges of cells. You used it for only one range so far, but you can enter multiple ranges if needed.

Type a range into the Number1 box—for example, E1:E6. Notice that Excel shows the values in those cells and adds them up in the dialog box (see Figure 22.1).

Figure 22.1

	A	B	C	D	E	F	G	H
1					5	3		
2	(e1:e6)				4	4		
3					3	2		
4					6	3		
5					7	2		
6								
7			Function Arguments					
8			SUM					
9			Number1	e1:e6		I	📷	= {5;4;3;6;7;8}
10			Number2				📷	= number
11			Number3				📷	= number
12								
13								
14								
15								= 33
16			Adds all the numbers in a range of cells.					

SUM function ranges.

As soon as you press Tab or move to the Number2 box, Excel adds a Number3 box. You can have many different ranges (or even individual cells) as parameters in these Number boxes. Add a second range in the Number2 box by clicking the **Range Selector** button just to the right of the text box (see Figure 22.2).

Figure 22.2

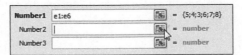

Range Selector button.

The full dialog box shrinks, enabling you to select a range of cells on the sheet. Select F1:F8 (see Figure 22.3).

Figure 22.3

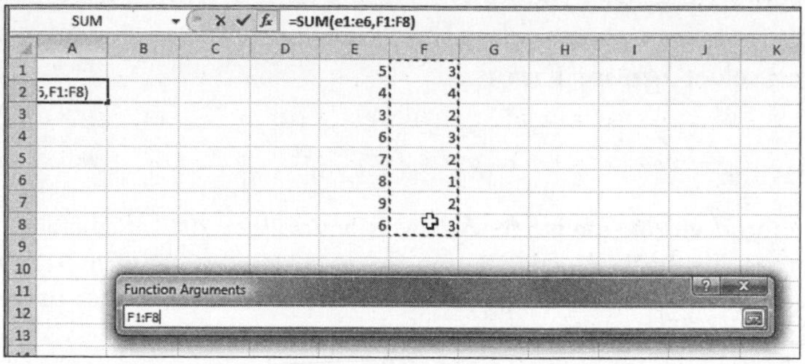

Select a range of cells.

Now click the **Selector** button again to expand the dialog box back to its original state. Click **OK**. Notice the complete formula in the Formula bar:

=SUM(E1:E6,F1:F8)

To specify multiple ranges for a function (provided that the function supports it), separate them with a comma.

You might get a warning message next to the function in the sheet. If you hold your mouse over the warning message pop-up, it says, "The formula in this cell refers to a range that has additional numbers adjacent to it." (See Figure 22.4.)

Figure 22.4

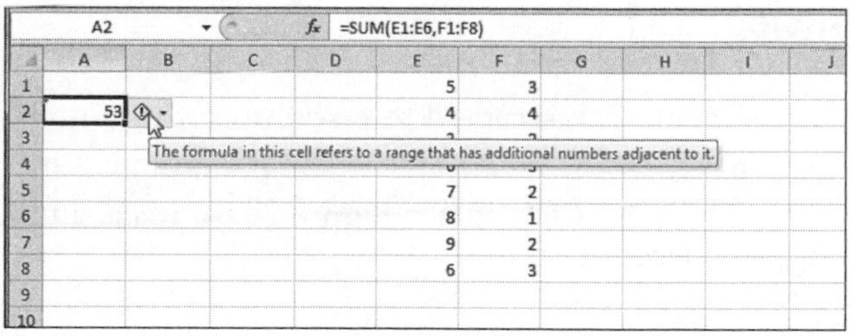

Warning message.

This is Excel's way of warning you that there are additional values in the cells adjacent to the ones you selected, and you might want to consider adding them to your range. If you do, you can adjust the range accordingly.

Adjust the range by clicking the Formula bar and then typing a new range, or double-click the cell to edit it. Notice the colored boxes around your ranges. These help you identify the data that's going into your functions. Click and drag the corners of these colored boxes to adjust the ranges. When you're happy with the result, press **Enter**.

If you don't want to update the range—you're sure that the range you entered is correct—and you want to get rid of Excel's warning message, click the down arrow next to it and select **Ignore Error**.

> **NOTICE**
>
> For those who are used to the older versions of Excel (2003 and before), you can still use the "fx" function button next to the formula bar to insert a function. Microsoft also added a bigger version of this button to the Ribbon as well. Both load the same Insert Function dialog.

In this dialog box, you can browse by categories, but you can also use the search box to look for a function. For example, if you type the word "loan" you get several financial functions for calculating loan amounts, like PMT, RATE, and so on. Don't worry about what these specific functions do right now. Our focus at this point is just to get you comfortable with functions in general. We'll study these functions in depth over the next couple of chapters.

Relative vs. Absolute References

One concept that is important to understand is relative versus absolute references in your Excel formulas. You learned how to refer to individual cells and ranges, such as A3:D9. A couple times in the previous chapters, you saw ranges that look like this:

$A$5:$B$10

Up to this point, you've been instructed to just ignore those dollar signs in the range. Now let's learn about what they mean. But first, an example. Open the Order Log file from the CD in the Chapter 22 folder (see Figure 22.5). It's a simple list of customers and their order totals.

Figure 22.5

	A	B
1	Customer	Order Total
2	Joe Smith	$ 50.24
3	Bill Jones	$ 102.45
4	Sue Watson	$ 69.54
5	Alan Williams	$ 23.11
6		

Order log.

Now add the amount of sales tax to collect for each customer. Let's say that all the sales are made in the store, so you always collect the same percentage from everyone.

Again, let's assume that the tax rate is 8 percent. So in cell C2, use the following formula to calculate the sales tax for Joe Smith:

=B2*0.08

You can then AutoFill that formula down the rest of the column to calculate the sales tax for all of the other customers. At this point, you can also calculate a grand total for each sale by adding the other two cells together:

=B2+C2

Now the sheet looks like Figure 22.6.

Figure 22.6

	A	B	C	D
			fx =B2*0.08	
1	Customer	Order Total	Sales Tax	Grand Total
2	Joe Smith	$ 50.24	$ 4.02	$ 54.26
3	Bill Jones	$ 102.45	$ 8.20	$ 110.65
4	Sue Watson	$ 69.54	$ 5.56	$ 75.10
5	Alan Williams	$ 23.11	$ 1.85	$ 24.96
6				

Order log with sales tax.

Now, it would be nice to have the sales tax amount somewhere visible where you could see it on your sheet. It's also good to place a variable like this (numbers that can change) in its own cell so you can easily change it.

With that in mind, put the words "Sales Tax Rate" in cell A9 and then add the value "8%" to cell B9. The actual location doesn't matter—just place it somewhere out of the way of the rest of your data (see Figure 22.7).

Figure 22.7

	A	B	C	D
1	Customer	Order Total	Sales Tax	Grand Total
2	Joe Smith	$ 50.24	$ 4.02	$ 54.26
3	Bill Jones	$ 102.45	$ 8.20	$ 110.65
4	Sue Watson	$ 69.54	$ 5.56	$ 75.10
5	Alan Williams	$ 23.11	$ 1.85	$ 24.96
6				
7				
8				
9	Sales Tax Rate:	8%		

Sales tax cell.

Now that the sales tax rate is in cell B9, you can refer to B9 in your calculations instead of manually typing "0.08" in all of the formulas. Delete everything from C2 to C5 and update the formula in C2 to this:

=B2*B9

The values should be exactly the same as they were before. Now AutoFill that down the column to give everyone else the right sales tax figures (see Figure 22.8).

Figure 22.8

	C3		f_x	=B3*B10	
	A	B	C	D	
1	Customer	Order Total	Sales Tax	Grand Total	
2	Joe Smith	$ 50.24	$ 4.02	$ 54.26	
3	Bill Jones	$ 102.45	$ -	$ 102.45	
4	Sue Watson	$ 69.54	$ -	$ 69.54	
5	Alan Williams	$ 23.11	$ -	$ 23.11	
6					
7					
8					
9	Sales Tax Rate:	8%			
10					

AutoFill sales tax.

Oh, wait a minute. Something's not right. What happened? Your cells are empty now. Let's take a closer look at the formula. C2 looks good. C3, however, has this:

=B3*B10

AutoFill correctly moved you down to the next row in the order log, but you wanted it to keep the sales tax rate cell the same. AutoFill tried to do its job, however, and ended up giving you something you didn't want.

When using AutoFill, all of your cell and range references are *relative* references. This means they're relative to the row and column they're in. If you AutoFill a formula down a column, all of the row references are relative to the current row. The same goes for AutoFilling across a row—the columns all move relative to the original cell.

In the case of your sales tax rate, however, you want that specific cell to always stay the same. To do this, use an *absolute* reference. This tells AutoFill to never move that cell. To do that, use dollar signs next to the row and column values:

=$B$9

DEFINITION

A **relative reference** is a cell reference that will automatically adjust when copied to adjacent rows or columns. If you copy (or AutoFill) a formula containing a relative reference down a column, the **row** part of the formula will change accordingly, and vice versa.

An **absolute reference** is a cell reference that will **not** automatically adjust when copied to adjacent rows or columns. It always refers to the **exact** cell specified.

This says that the column should always *absolutely* be column B, and the row should always *absolutely* be row 9. Don't ever move it if you AutoFill a formula that refers to this cell.

TIP

In some instances, you might want only the row or the column to be relative and the other to be absolute. You can write B$7 or $B7. Most of the time, you'll make both absolute.

So replacing C2 with "=$B$9" and then AutoFilling that down the column fixes everything. If you examine the other cells, notice that the reference to B9 never changes. Be sure to leave B2 relative, though, because you want that to change as you AutoFill down the rest of the cells (see Figure 22.9).

Figure 22.9

	C4		*fₓ*	=B4*$B$9	
	A	**B**	**C**	**D**	**E**
1	Customer	Order Total	Sales Tax	Grand Total	
2	Joe Smith	$ 50.24	$ 4.02	$ 54.26	
3	Bill Jones	$ 102.45	$ 8.20	$ 110.65	
4	Sue Watson	$ 69.54	$ 5.56	$ 75.10	
5	Alan Williams	$ 23.11	$ 1.85	$ 24.96	
6					
7					
8					
9	Sales Tax Rate:	8%			
10					

AutoFill corrected.

Named Cells and Ranges

There's an easier way to refer to a single location on your spreadsheets, which involves creating a *named cell* or *range*.

DEFINITION

A **named cell** is a specific cell that has been assigned a name by you. This way instead of having to always refer to the cell containing your sales tax amount as $B$9 in your calculations, you can assign it a name like **SalesTaxRate**. Likewise, a **named range** is a range that has similarly been assigned a name.

Sometimes you'll have a cell, like the sales tax rate, that you want to be able to refer to in your calculations. If you have a big sheet and several different values like this, you probably don't want to have to stop and figure out that the sales tax rate is in cell B9. Wouldn't it just be easier if you could refer to it in your formulas with a memorable name, such as "SalesTaxRate"? Well, you can.

Let's assign a name to cell B9.

1. First click the cell you want to define a name for. Click cell B9.

2. Then, on the Formulas tab, in the Defined Names group, click the **Define Name** button.

3. Excel sees that you have a label right next to that cell that says "Sales Tax Rate," so it provides a name for the defined cell. It uses "Sales_Tax_Rate" originally, which is perfectly acceptable. You can shorten it by deleting the underscores to just "SalesTaxRate."

WARNING

You cannot use spaces in your defined names. Stick to just letters, numbers, and the underscore character.

4. Next, choose the scope of the name (the limit of where this name is valid). The default is the entire workbook, but you can limit it to just one sheet.

5. You can also leave a comment and change what this name refers to here. Right now, it refers to Sheet1, cell $B$9. It's an absolute reference, of course.

6. Finally, click **OK**.

Notice at this point that the *name box* to the left of the Formula bar says "SalesTaxRate" instead of B9 whenever you click this cell. (See Figure 22.10.)

That's now the name of the cell. You can still refer to it as B9, but you can now also refer to it as SalesTaxRate in your calculations. Let's try it.

Figure 22.10

SalesTaxRate	▾	f_x	8%	

◢	A	B	C	D
1	Customer	Order Total	Sales Tax	Grand Total
2	Joe Smith	$ 50.24	$ 4.02	$ 54.26
3	Bill Jones	$ 102.45	$ 8.20	$ 110.65
4	Sue Watson	$ 69.54	$ 5.56	$ 75.10
5	Alan Williams	$ 23.11	$ 1.85	$ 24.96
6				
7				
8				
9	Sales Tax Rate:	⊕ 8%		
10				
11				

Name box.

Update the formula in C2 again to:

=B2*SalesTaxRate

Now AutoFill that formula down the column. Because SalesTaxRate is a named cell, there's nothing for AutoFill to change. It always references the same cell.

> **NOTICE**
>
> As soon as you start typing "=B2*Sal," a helper pops up with "SalesTaxRate" in it. Double-click that pop-up to fill in the named cell automatically.

The best part about using a named cell is that you don't have to remember cell addresses. If you have several values that you want to be able to refer to throughout your sheet (InterestRate, MinimumGrade, TeamBattingAverage, and so on), you can just start creating named cells.

Also, if your cell happens to move, the name automatically updates. If you cut and paste, or click and drag that cell somewhere else, the name is updated for you.

Defined Names Manager

In the Defined Names group, you can click the Name Manager (see Figure 22.11) to create, edit, or delete your defined names. Generally, you use this only if you want to change or delete an existing defined name.

Figure 22.11

Name Manager.

You can also create named ranges. Instead of referring to individual cells, a name can refer to a range. You can define a name to refer to all of the order totals, for example (see Figure 22.12).

Then, later in the sheet, if you want to refer to the SUM of all your orders, all you have to say is this:

=SUM(OrderTotals)

It's a simple example, but it illustrates the point of how to use a named range.

Figure 22.12

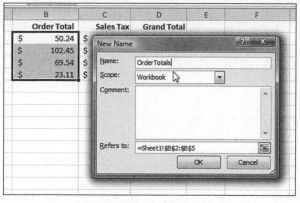

Named range.

Now that you have two named ranges, here's a neat trick: you can use the name box as a drop-down box to quickly jump between the ranges. Open the box and select SalesTaxRate, and you move there (see Figure 22.13).

Figure 22.13

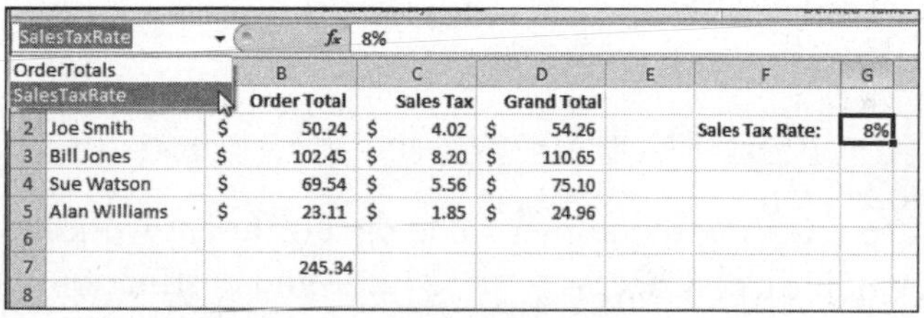

Name box to select cells.

Values on Other Sheets

Finally, it's important to understand how to refer to values that are on other sheets in your workbook, or in entirely different workbook files altogether.

You might, for example, have all of your sales figures for each month on separate sheets in a workbook. They might be called JanuarySales, FebruarySales, MarchSales, and so on. You can then create a summary sheet where you show the totals for each month on one sheet. To do this, you'll need to know how to look up a value on a different sheet.

Essentially, you can refer to a value on another sheet with the following syntax:

=SheetName!CellName

For example, to refer to the value in cell B2 on Sheet3, you would say:

=Sheet3!B2

If the sheet name includes spaces, you must enclose the name in single quotes, like this:

='December Sales'!B2

If you want to refer to a value in a different workbook file than the one that's currently open, it gets a little more tricky. You put the workbook file name inside square brackets, like this:

=[WorkbookName]SheetName!CellName

For example:

=[Workbook2]Sheet1!B2

Paste Link

For a shortcut to referring to another value on a different workbook, open both workbooks so that you have easy access to the source and destination sheets (the sheets you're copying values from and to). Go to the source file and copy the data you want to reference to your Clipboard.

Now go to the destination sheet and click **Paste**. In the pop-up toolbar, select **Paste Link**.

This creates a link to your original workbook file, sheet, and cell name. This value is now linked to the original, so if the original value changes, the link is automatically updated.

This is how you can create summary sheets. For example, you might have all of January's sales data on Sheet1, February on Sheet2, and so on. On Sheet13, you could make a summary for each month's sales to view at a glance. Plus, if the values are linked, if you edit/update any of the sales, the linked copies are automatically refreshed.

For example, rename Sheet1 to January (refer to Chapter 3). Rename Sheet2 to February. Rename Sheet3 to Summary. Move the SalesTaxRate cell and its label to your Summary sheet by cutting and pasting it. Notice that the calculations on the January sheet still work, because the named cell has Workbook scope (it's visible from the whole workbook).

Next, create a Total row for the January sheet so that you can refer to these values on the summary sheet. This is just a simple SUM function. Make sure that you sum B2:B5 and don't refer to the OrderTotals named range that you created earlier (see Figure 22.14).

Figure 22.14

	A	B	C	D
	B7		f_x =SUM(B2:B5)	
1	Customer	Order Total	Sales Tax	Grand Total
2	Joe Smith	$ 50.24	$ 4.02	$ 54.26
3	Bill Jones	$ 102.45	$ 8.20	$ 110.65
4	Sue Watson	$ 69.54	$ 5.56	$ 75.10
5	Alan Williams	$ 23.11	$ 1.85	$ 24.96
6				
7	Total:	$ 245.34	$ 19.63	$ 264.97
8				

Total row.

Now copy and paste the data from January to February (just to keep the same structure) and change the numbers a bit to simulate different sales figures (see Figure 22.15).

Figure 22.15

	A	B	C	D	E
	G6		f_x		
1	Customer	Order Total	Sales Tax	Grand Total	
2	Joe Smith	$ 90.20	$ 7.22	$ 97.42	
3	Bill Jones	$ 45.20	$ 3.62	$ 48.82	
4	Sue Watson	$ 102.20	$ 8.18	$ 110.38	
5	Alan Williams	$ 11.33	$ 0.91	$ 12.24	
6					
7	Total:	$ 248.93	$ 19.91	$ 268.84	
8					
9					
10					
11					

January   **February**   Summary

Ready

February sales.

Finally, go to the Summary sheet to enter data. Copy the header row (A1:D1) from either one of the monthly sheets and paste it into the Summary sheet; then change column A to a list of months. (See Figure 22.16.)

Figure 22.16

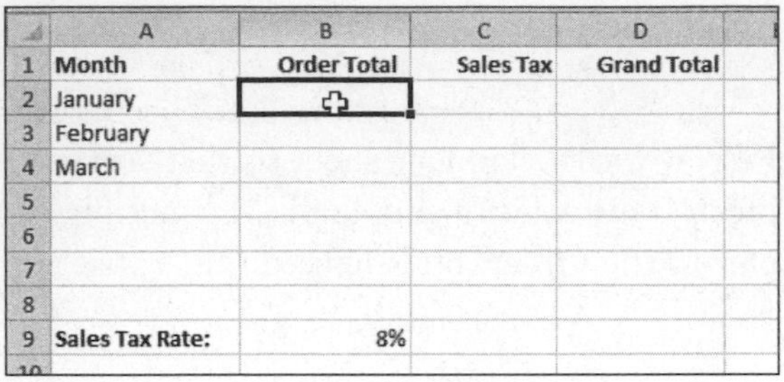

Summary sheet.

Next, get the January sales totals into this sheet, which includes a link to them so that if the totals change, this page is updated. Go back to the January sheet and copy B7:D7 to your Clipboard. Switch back to the Summary sheet and paste a link into the appropriate cells.

Notice that before you click the Link button on the pop-up menu, you see a #REF! error in the cells. This means that you're trying to refer to a cell that doesn't exist. It goes away after you select the Link option from the Paste menu. (See Figure 22.17.)

Figure 22.17

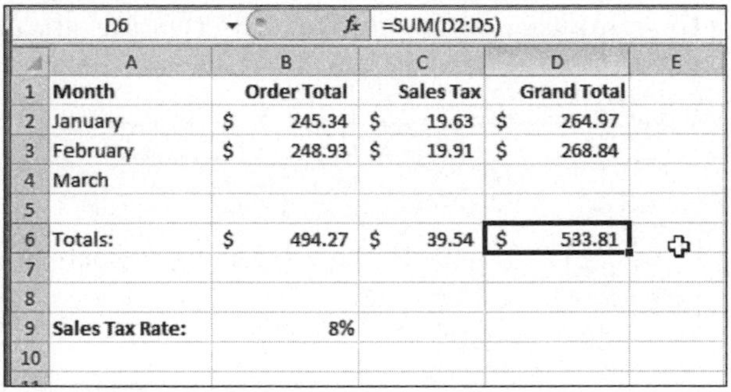

Summary sheet completed.

To finish, add a Totals row. Your summary sheet is complete. Notice that if you change the values on the January or February sheet, the summary sheet is automatically updated.

Understanding Formula Errors

In the previous section, you experienced a #REF! error because you were referring to a cell that didn't exist when you copied and pasted a formula. Table 22.1 lists some common errors you might encounter.

Table 22.1 Common Error Codes

#####	This isn't an error, really. Pound signs in a cell mean that the cell is too narrow to display the data. Just make the column wider.
#REF!	You're referring to a cell that doesn't exist. This usually happens when you copy data from one sheet to another.
#NAME?	You used an invalid name. Usually this is caused by misspelling a function name, such as "AVRAGE," or a named cell, like "SalesTaxRat."
#VALUE!	You used the wrong type of value for a function. This can happen if you used text instead of a number, like saying =SUM("Bob"). It's the wrong type of value.
#NUM!	Your calculation results in a number that's too large or too small for Excel to handle, such as =1000000^1000000 (that's one million to the one-millionth power).
#N/A!	A value that Excel is looking for isn't available. This generally occurs with lookup functions such as VLOOKUP.
#DIV/0	You tried to divide by zero, which fifth-grade math teachers everywhere will constantly remind you that you can't do.

You might encounter one other type of error message, called a *circular reference*. This happens when a cell attempts to refer to itself. For example, you get a circular reference if you put the following in cell A1:

=A1+5

Excel can't tell you what A1+5 is because A1 refers to the cell itself. It creates an endless loop of logic.

The Least You Need to Know

- You can create a formula by manually typing it in, by using the Insert Function button next to the Formula bar, or by using the Function gallery on the Ribbon.
- You can use absolute references to force your formulas to always refer to a specific cell.
- Create a defined name or range for an easy way to refer to unique cells or ranges in your formulas.
- To refer to a value on another sheet, use the SheetName!CellName reference, or paste a link.

Text Functions

In This Chapter

- Comparing two text strings
- Concatenating two text strings by putting first name and last name together in one cell
- Getting the left or right characters from a cell
- Breaking apart a full name into first and last names
- Finding one text string inside another
- Substituting and replacing text inside a cell

In the next couple chapters, we go over many of the most popular functions in Excel. This book is by no means a comprehensive guide covering all the functions that Excel has to offer. Excel has thousands of functions, and whole books are dedicated to covering functions.

This book attempts to cover all the functions that you'll use on a regular basis or that you'll need to perform the most common function-related tasks in Excel.

This chapter covers functions to manipulate and work with text, or strings. Computer programmers refer to text as strings because they're groups of characters strung together.

Comparing Text Strings

There may come a time when you want to compare two text strings to see if they're the same or different. To determine whether two text strings are the same, you can compare them by simply saying:

    =A1=B1

If the strings are the same, you get a TRUE value. If not, you get FALSE (see Figure 23.1).

Figure 23.1

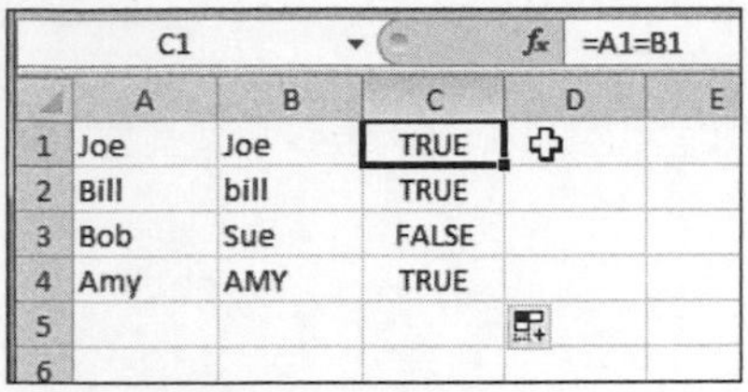

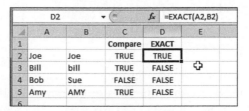

Comparing strings.

As you can see in Figure 23.1, this method of comparison doesn't care about case sensitivity. "Bill" and "bill" are considered the same.

If you need case sensitivity, use the EXACT function:

=EXACT(A2,B2)

Figure 23.2

Exact strings.

Notice in Figure 23.2 that only Joe from row 2 shows up exact. All the others are slightly different.

Concatenation

Excel makes it easy to put two entities, like first and last name, together in one cell. It's not quite so easy to separate them.

You can *concatenate* two strings by adding them together with an ampersand between them:

=A1&B1

DEFINITION

The act of putting two text strings together is called **concatenation**.

In the case of a "first name, last name" situation, however, this gives you JoeSmith, without any spaces between the names. To add a space, or any literal characters, enclose them inside double quotes, like this:

=A1&" "&B1

Figure 23.3

	A	B	C	D	E
			C2	fx	=A2&" "&B2
1	First	Last	Together		
2	Joe	Smith	Joe Smith		
3	Amy	Jones	Amy Jones		
4	Bill	Williams	Bill Williams		
5	James	Kirk	James Kirk		
6					

First and last name.

As you can see in Figure 23.3, this gives you the effect you're looking for. To add a middle initial (or middle name), add more to your formula (see Figure 23.4):

=A1&" "&B1&" "&C1

Figure 23.4

	A	B	C	D	E
				D2	fx	=A2&" "&B2&" "&C2
1	First	Middle	Last	Together	
2	Joe	E.	Smith	Joe E. Smith	
3	Amy	Ann	Jones	Amy Ann Jones	
4	Bill	P.	Williams	Bill P. Williams	
5	James	T.	Kirk	James T. Kirk	
6					

First, middle, and last.

You can also use a CONCATENATE function, which provides the same level of functionality. Instead of using ampersands, separate the strings with commas (see Figure 23.5).

=CONCATENATE(A2," ",B2," ",C2)

Figure 23.5

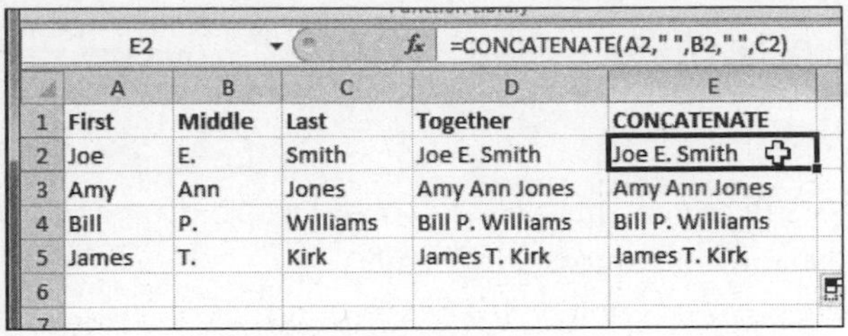

	A	B	C	D	E
	First	Middle	Last	Together	CONCATENATE
1	First	Middle	Last	Together	CONCATENATE
2	Joe	E.	Smith	Joe E. Smith	Joe E. Smith
3	Amy	Ann	Jones	Amy Ann Jones	Amy Ann Jones
4	Bill	P.	Williams	Bill P. Williams	Bill P. Williams
5	James	T.	Kirk	James T. Kirk	James T. Kirk

CONCATENATE function.

Finding Information About a String

A couple useful functions help you find information about a text string. Use the LEN function to determine how long a string is (including spaces and any other characters) (see Figure 23.6).

> =LEN(A1)

Figure 23.6

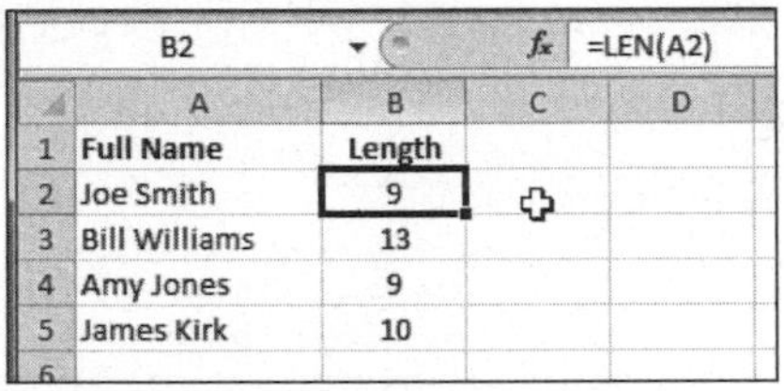

	A	B	C	D
1	Full Name	Length		
2	Joe Smith	9		
3	Bill Williams	13		
4	Amy Jones	9		
5	James Kirk	10		

LEN function.

You can use the LEFT and RIGHT functions to get the left or right X characters in a string (see Figure 23.7). For example, to find the left 3 characters of a string, say:

> =LEFT(A1,3)

Similarly, this is how you would find the right 3 characters (see Figure 23.7):

> =RIGHT(A1,3)

Figure 23.7

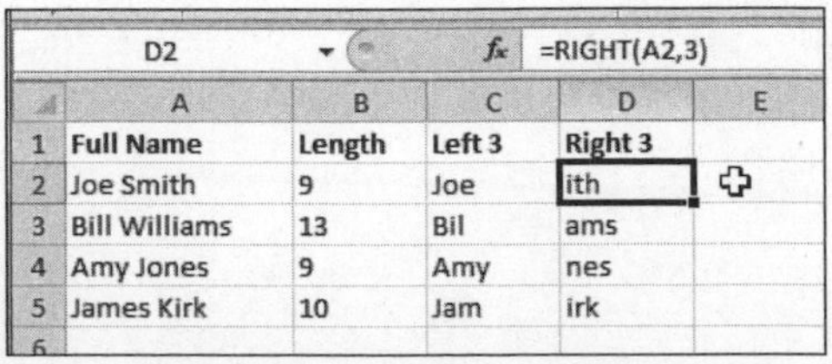

	A	B	C	D	E
1	Full Name	Length	Left 3	Right 3	
2	Joe Smith	9	Joe	ith	
3	Bill Williams	13	Bil	ams	
4	Amy Jones	9	Amy	nes	
5	James Kirk	10	Jam	irk	

LEFT and RIGHT functions.

There's also a function to return X characters from position Y inside a string. This is good for picking characters out of the middle of a string. For example, let's say you want to get characters 2, 3, 4, and 5 out of the middle of a string. Start at position 2 and return 4 characters. Use the MID function for this (see Figure 23.8):

=MID(A1,2,4)

Let's say you have a list of products, and the serial numbers are all in the format XX-YYYY-ZZZ. You need to figure out what the YYYY numbers are for all your products (perhaps it's the manufacturer code). You can say:

=MID(A1,4,4)

Assuming that your product is in A1, you want to start at the fourth character and return 4 characters from the code.

Figure 23.8

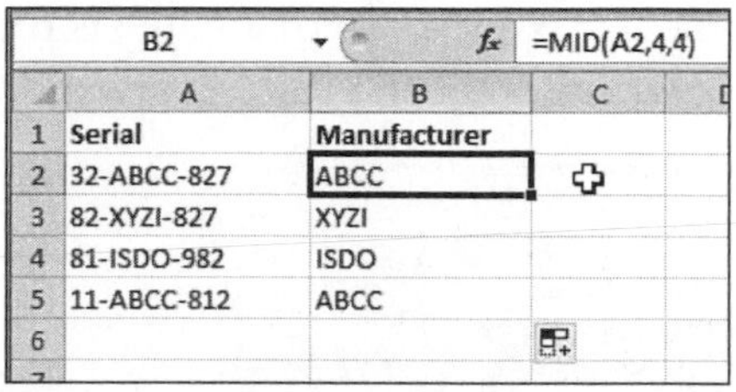
B2 =MID(A2,4,4)

	A	B	C
1	Serial	Manufacturer	
2	32-ABCC-827	ABCC	
3	82-XYZI-827	XYZI	
4	81-ISDO-982	ISDO	
5	11-ABCC-812	ABCC	
6			

MID function.

Finding Text

Of course, the previous examples work only if all of your data conforms to the same specifications (in the same format). What if you need to be able to find the location of one character or string inside another text string? In that case, you can use the FIND function.

Let's go back to your list of full names (see Figure 23.9). In this spreadsheet, the first and last names are together in one cell. You need to split them apart so you can create a mailing later and be able to say "Dear Bob" in it.

First, locate where the SPACE character is inside the cell. To do that, use the FIND function:

=FIND(" ",A2)

The FIND function takes two bits of information. First, what are you trying to find (a single space, in the example)? Second, what cell are you looking in?

Figure 23.9

	E2		f_x	=FIND(" ",A2)	
	A	B	C	D	E
1	Full Name	Length	Left 3	Right 3	Space Char
2	Joe Smith	9	Joe	ith	4
3	Bill Williams	13	Bil	ams	5
4	Amy Jones	9	Amy	nes	4
5	James Kirk	10	Jam	irk	6
6					

FIND function.

As you can see in Figure 23.9, the FIND function returns the location of that character inside the string. If the string doesn't exist, it returns a #VALUE error.

Now that you know the location of the space, you can split the cell into two pieces to get the first name and the last name. The first name is the LEFT X-1 characters. So if the space is in position 4, you want the left 3 characters (see Figure 23.10).

> =LEFT(A2,E2-1)

Figure 23.10

	F2		f_x	=LEFT(A2,E2-1)		
	A	B	C	D	E	F
1	Full Name	Length	Left 3	Right 3	Space Char	First Name
2	Joe Smith	9	Joe	ith	4	Joe
3	Bill Williams	13	Bil	ams	5	Bill
4	Amy Jones	9	Amy	nes	4	Amy
5	James Kirk	10	Jam	irk	6	James
6						

Determine first name.

The last name is more complex. You know the length of the string and where the space character is. The last name is the RIGHT length-space characters in the string (see Figure 23.11).

> =RIGHT(A2,B2-E2)

Figure 23.11

	NOT		X ✓ f_x	=RIGHT(A2,B2-E2)			
	A	B	C	D	E	F	G
1	Full Name	Length	Left 3	Right 3	Space Char	First Name	Last Name
2	Joe Smith	9	Joe	ith	4	Joe	(A2,B2-E2)
3	Bill Williams	13	Bil	ams	5	Bill	Williams
4	Amy Jones	9	Amy	nes	4	Amy	Jones
5	James Kirk	10	Jam	irk	6	James	Kirk

Determine last name.

Most of the time, it's easier to break apart your formulas into multiple columns. You can always hide them later if you don't want to see them. However, you can also put all of that together into one long formula.

=RIGHT(A2,LEN(A2)-FIND(" ",A2))

You get the same result, but it's more difficult to figure out.

The SEARCH Function

A SEARCH function is available that's similar to FIND. The differences are that the SEARCH function allows the use of wildcard characters and is not case sensitive. FIND is case sensitive and does not allow wildcard searches.

In a wildcard search, any number of characters can result in a positive hit for your search results. For example, let's say you're looking for any name that includes the word "Jon." You might want Jon, Jonathan, Jonathon, Jones, John, and so on. You can use a wildcard search (see the Search tab in the sample sheet).

=SEARCH("j*n",A1)

The asterisk (*) indicates that you want to insert any number of characters here and that you don't care what they are. So you're going to find names like John and Jon, but words like Anjelia will also trigger the search. "J" followed by any number of characters, followed by an "N" will satisfy this search, as shown in Figure 23.12.

Figure 23.12

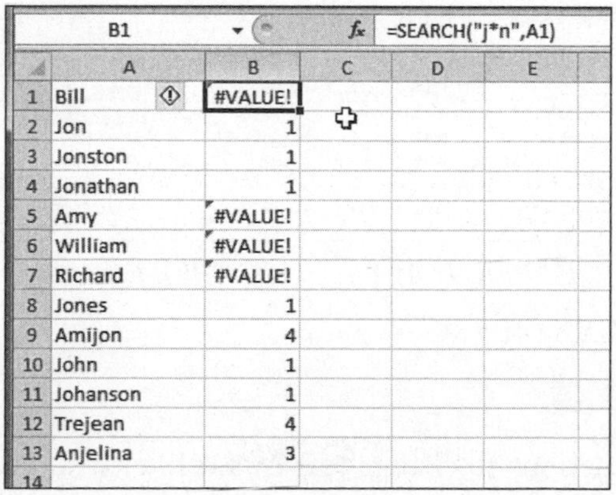

Wildcard search.

To limit the search to a specific number of characters, use the "?" wildcard. This indicates "one and only one character." So if you want Jon and Jan to trigger the results, but not John, you can say:

=SEARCH("j?n",A1)

Likewise, if you want John but not Jon, say:

=SEARCH("j??n",A1)

This means you need exactly two characters between the J and N.

Changing Cases

Three functions are useful for changing the case of text from upper to lower to proper case. Proper case makes the first letter of each word in a string uppercase; the rest of the characters are made lowercase. This is handy with names. If you were given a list of customer names and some of them are in all capitalized letters and others are all lowercase, you can use these functions to make all of the letters uniform (see Figure 23.13).

=LOWER(A1)

=UPPER(A1)

=PROPER(A1)

Figure 23.13

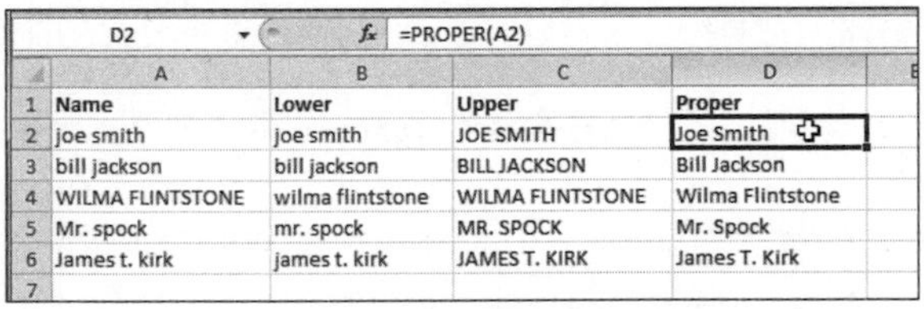

	A	B	C	D
	Name	**Lower**	**Upper**	**Proper**
1	joe smith	joe smith	JOE SMITH	Joe Smith
2	bill jackson	bill jackson	BILL JACKSON	Bill Jackson
3	WILMA FLINTSTONE	wilma flintstone	WILMA FLINTSTONE	Wilma Flintstone
4	Mr. spock	mr. spock	MR. SPOCK	Mr. Spock
5	James t. kirk	james t. kirk	JAMES T. KIRK	James T. Kirk

UPPER, LOWER, and PROPER functions.

Changing Text

You can use two functions to change text in a cell with some other text. The first is the SUBSTITUTE function. This is handy if you know the TEXT that you want to replace, but you aren't sure where it is in the cell (it can be at any position).

For example, to change "Star Wars" to "Star Trek," like in Figure 23.14, say:

=SUBSTITUTE(A2,"Wars","Trek")

Figure 23.14

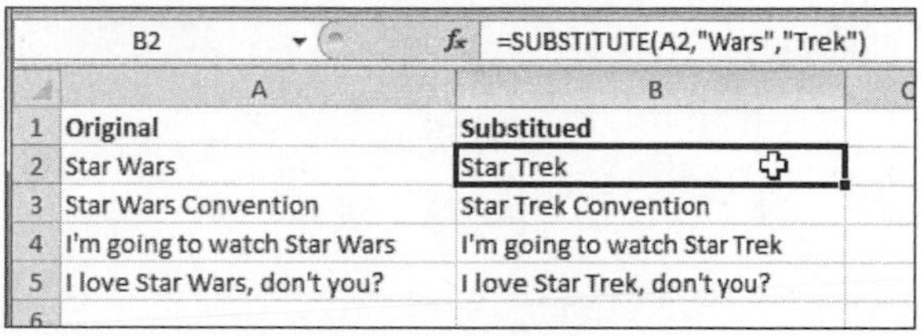

	A	B	C
	B2 ▾	fx	=SUBSTITUTE(A2,"Wars","Trek")
1	Original	Substitued	
2	Star Wars	Star Trek	
3	Star Wars Convention	Star Trek Convention	
4	I'm going to watch Star Wars	I'm going to watch Star Trek	
5	I love Star Wars, don't you?	I love Star Trek, don't you?	
6			

SUBSTITUTE function.

This substitutes all instances of "Wars" with "Trek."

The other function is REPLACE, which is helpful if you know the position of the text, but you don't care what characters are already there. For example, let's go back to the example on the Products tab. Let's say you want to replace all of the manufacturer codes with a different code (see Figure 23.15). You could say:

=REPLACE(A2,4,4,"LMNO")

Figure 23.15

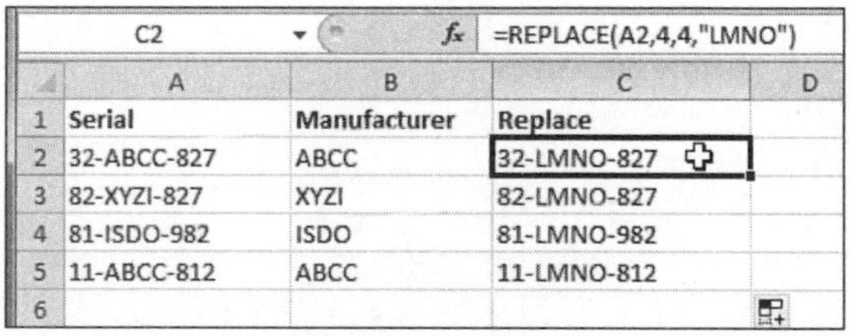

	A	B	C	D
	C2 ▾	fx	=REPLACE(A2,4,4,"LMNO")	
1	Serial	Manufacturer	Replace	
2	32-ABCC-827	ABCC	32-LMNO-827	
3	82-XYZI-827	XYZI	82-LMNO-827	
4	81-ISDO-982	ISDO	81-LMNO-982	
5	11-ABCC-812	ABCC	11-LMNO-812	
6				

REPLACE function.

This says to take cell A2, go 4 characters in, and replace the next 4 characters with "LMNO."

Use the TRIM function to remove unnecessary space characters from the beginning or end of a string. So if the first names have spaces after them, you can use TRIM to clean them. (See Figure 23.16.)

=TRIM(A2)&" "&TRIM(B2)&" "&TRIM(C2)

Figure 23.16

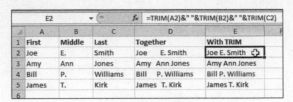

TRIM function.

The Least You Need to Know

- Use the EXACT function to determine whether two text strings are exactly the same.
- Concatenation enables you to easily put two text strings together into one.
- Use the LEFT, RIGHT, and MID functions to pull information out of a text string.
- FIND and SEARCH can tell you whether a specific text string occurs in a cell.
- UPPER, LOWER, and PROPER can convert the case of your text.
- SUBSTITUTE and REPLACE can change the contents of your text strings.

Date and Time Functions

24

In This Chapter

- Learning valid date/time formats
- Understanding how Excel stores dates internally
- Identifying the different parts of a date/time value
- Assembling dates from their component parts
- Adding and subtracting date/time values
- Determining the difference between two dates or times

There are a lot of different functions to deal with dates and times. You can take date/time values apart to find their components (for example, what year does this date fall in?) or go the other way. In this chapter, you learn how to work with dates and times in Excel.

Valid Excel Date/Time Formats

You have a choice of many valid formats when entering dates and times in Excel. The following are some ways you can represent August 30, 2010. Note that these are set up for American dates in the format MM/DD/YY (as opposed to the European standard of DD/MM/YY):

- 8/30/2010
- 8-30-2010
- 8/30/10
- 30 AUG 2010
- AUG 30, 2010

- August 30, 2010
- 8/30
- 2010/08/30
- 30-Aug-10

If you omit the year, Excel assumes the current year (based on your computer's clock). If you type a two-digit year from 00 to 29, Excel assumes 2000 to 2029. If you type a two-digit year from 30 to 99, Excel assumes 1930 to 1999.

> **TIP**
>
> This two-digit year is a Windows-level property that you can change in your Control Panel under the Regional Settings.

Of course, many valid formats also exist for time values. The following are some of the ways in which you can represent 9:30 P.M.:

- 9:30 PM
- 09:30 PM
- 9:30:00 PM
- 21:30

If you type "9:30," you get 9:30 A.M. You can also mix and match dates and times in any of the valid formats, separated by a space. For example:

- 8/30/2010 9:30 PM
- August 30, 2010 9:30:00 PM
- 30-Aug-10 21:30

Understanding Excel and Dates

Excel might display dates in a format that you're familiar with, such as 5/31/2010, but internally, dates and times are stored as numbers. Specifically, dates are stored as the number of days since January 1, 1900. For example, 1/1/2000 is stored internally as the number 36526.

This enables Excel to treat dates and times as any other number. You can add and subtract dates and times easily if you know that a day is given a value of 1. Times are fractions of a day. In fact, you can refer to the value as a date/time value because they're really the same thing.

Consider a couple of examples. Open a blank new spreadsheet. Type the date 5/30/2010 into cell A1. Now, in cell B1, type:

    =A1+1

You get the date 5/31/2010. Excel took the first date and added one whole day to it. Now, in cell C1, type:

    =B1+0.5

You still see just the date 5/31/2010, because Excel uses a specific kind of date format for this cell called "Short Date." This displays dates in the familiar MM/DD/YYYY format. You can see a list of common cell formats in the drop-down box in the Home tab, Number group.

Let's convert it to show the date and time so we can see exactly what's in that cell.

Right-click C1 and select **Format Cells**.

Select one of the date formats that shows both a date and a time, such as the format shown in Figure 24.1.

Figure 24.1

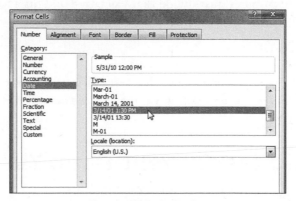

Format Cells dialog box.

Now when you return to the sheet, you might have to make the column a little wider ("######" means that the column is too narrow to fit the data). Widen the column, and then you should see the value:

> 5/31/10 12:00 PM

This is because you took the date from B1 and added half of a day to it. Half of a day brings you to noon of the same day. Any date without a time portion assumes midnight of that day. So if you add half a day, that equals 12 hours, or noon.

Let's add an hour to this time. In cell D1, type:

> =C1+(1/24)

Now D1 says "40329.54167." What does this mean? Remember that Excel stores dates and times *internally* as the number of days since 1/1/1900.

You need to convert this number to a date/time format. You can either right-click the cell and go to Format Cells again, or you can use the Format Painter (refer to

Chapter 14). Click cell C1, click the **Format Painter**, and then click D1. This copies the format from C1.

Notice that D1 is formatted as a date/time. So while you're working with dates and times, if you get a really strange and big number, don't panic. Excel is just showing you an internal date value. Just change the format to display it however you want.

Now, why did we use (1/24) in the date calculation? Why should we bother to do the math when Excel can easily do it? The fraction 1/24 is equal to one hour (it's one twenty-fourth of a day). If you want to add two hours, make it 2/24 (or 1/12, if you want to get picky, but this way you can easily see that it represents 2 hours).

If you want to add minutes, just divide that value by 60. This adds 8 minutes to the time in D1:

=D1+(1/24/60*8)

Again, you can simplify the math, but this makes it easy for you to see that you are working with minutes and that you want to add 8 of them. Let Excel do the math—that's what it's getting paid to do.

Determining the Current Date/Time

Want to know what time it is? Use the NOW function.

=NOW()

This function doesn't take any values in; it just spits out the current date/time.

Just plug that function into any cell of your sheet, and you'll instantly know the current time. It's often useful to know the current date or time so that you can calculate how old something is. You can also format that cell to include seconds. You have to use a custom date/time format to see both the date and the time to seconds.

Right-click the cell and select **Format Cells**. On the Number tab, select **Custom** under the category. On the right side, in the text box immediately above the list of available formats, type:

mm/dd/yyyy hh:mm:ss

This gives you a custom date/time format that shows the month and day (two digits) and a four-digit year, followed by a two-digit hour, minute, and second (see Figure 24.2).

Figure 24.2

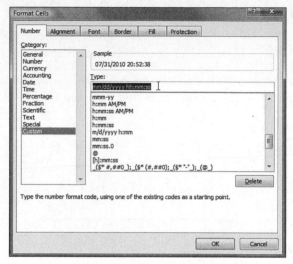

Custom date/time format cells.

When you have your custom date on the sheet showing seconds, you can press the F9 function key to automatically recalculate the functions on your sheet. This includes updating the date/time functions.

If you want the current date without the time portion, you can use the TODAY function, which gives you today at midnight.

=TODAY()

If you want to calculate the current time, but you don't want the day portion, say this:

=NOW()-TODAY()

This takes the full date/time and subtracts the date at midnight, leaving the time only. Excel likely gives this to you as a number, which you can then apply a time format to.

TIP

Keep in mind that it's almost always beneficial to keep the date portion even if you don't want it. You can always display the time with the appropriate format and not show the date.

Identifying Parts of a Date/Time Value

Want to find out the day of the month? How about the month of the year? You can use the YEAR, MONTH, and DAY functions to pull apart any date.

For example, put the date 8/30/2010 in cell A1. Now, using the YEAR, MONTH, and DAY functions, you can deconstruct that date (see Figure 24.3):

> =YEAR(A1)
>
> =MONTH(A1)
>
> =DAY(A1)

Figure 24.3

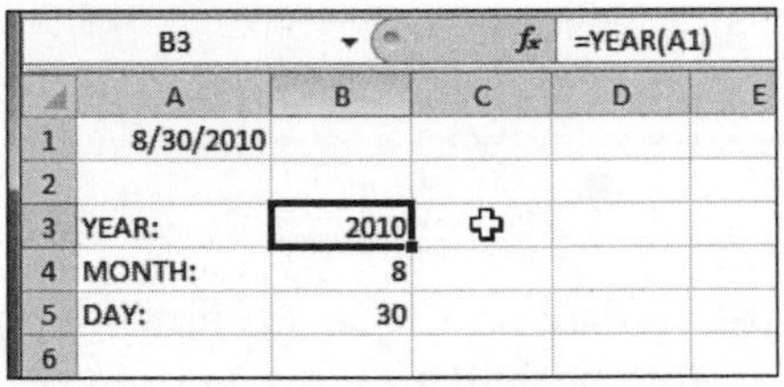

YEAR, MONTH, and DAY functions.

A similar set of functions is available for times. You can use HOUR, MINUTE, and SECOND accordingly. Change the value in A1 to include a time portion, and see how those functions work.

A WEEKDAY function can tell you what day of the week a date falls on.

> =WEEKDAY(A1)

WEEKDAY returns a number from 1 to 7, where 1 is Sunday, 2 is Monday, and so on. There's an optional second parameter where you can change this.

Putting Dates Together

In the previous section, we took a date apart. What if you need to put a date back together again? Let's say that we know the month, day, and year, and now we just need to make a valid date out of it. Perhaps a customer has given you a list of family members with their birth month, day, and year in separate columns, and you need to put them together into a valid Excel date/time value.

This is where the DATE and TIME functions come into play. The DATE function is used to build a Date value, and the TIME function is used for putting together Time values:

=DATE(year, month, day)

=TIME(hour, minute, second)

Taking a look at the DateTimeParts sheet again (sample workbook on the CD), you've already deconstructed the date/time value in A1. Let's put it back together now. In cell B12, create a new date from it:

=DATE(B3,B4,B5)

This gives you the same date as in A1, but it illustrates how to build a date from the component pieces (see Figure 24.4).

Figure 24.4

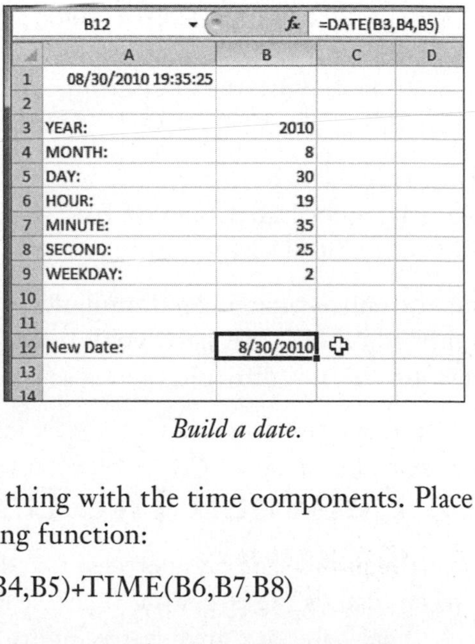
B12 | =DATE(B3,B4,B5)

	A	B	C	D
1	08/30/2010 19:35:25			
2				
3	YEAR:	2010		
4	MONTH:	8		
5	DAY:	30		
6	HOUR:	19		
7	MINUTE:	35		
8	SECOND:	25		
9	WEEKDAY:	2		
10				
11				
12	New Date:	8/30/2010		
13				
14				

Build a date.

You can do the same thing with the time components. Place them in a new cell or build on to the existing function:

=DATE(B3,B4,B5)+TIME(B6,B7,B8)

Of course, you get the correct value (see Figure 24.5).

Figure 24.5

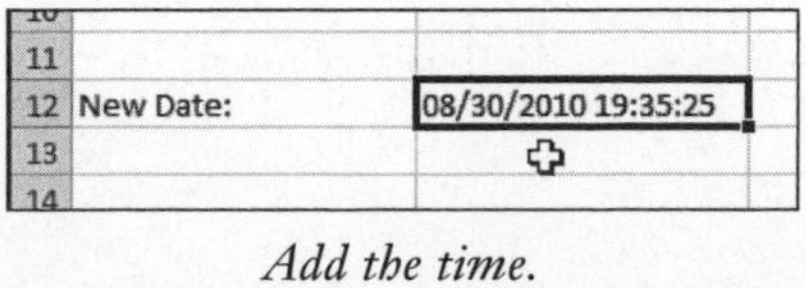

11		
12	New Date:	08/30/2010 19:35:25
13		
14		

Add the time.

Adding Dates with the DATE Function

The beauty of knowing how to perform these kinds of date/time calculations is that you can easily manipulate the date with these functions. For example, let's say that you have someone's hire date, and you want to know when that person's one-year anniversary is. You can easily say:

=A1+365

If it's a leap year, you want to be able to add a whole year to the date. So in this case, say:

=DATE(YEAR(A1)+1,MONTH(A1),DAY(A1))

Note that days "spill over" into months, and months spill over into years. So if you decide to add 90 days to a date using the following method, Excel properly adds 90 days to the date as a whole, which is from 8/30/2010 up to 11/28/2010:

=DATE(YEAR(A1),MONTH(A1),DAY(A1)+90)

Of course, everything you can do with the DATE function, you can do with the TIME function and time values. To SUBTRACT 15 minutes from a time, use the following method:

=DATE(YEAR(B1),MONTH(B1),DAY(B1))+TIME(HOUR(B1), MINUTE(B1)-15,SECOND(B1))

Notice that if you want the entire time minus 15 minutes, you have to create the DATE part first and then add the TIME part. With the TIME function, however, you subtract the 15 minutes. It's not difficult, as long as you remember to put all the pieces in the right place.

The Difference Between Two Dates

If you want to figure out the number of days between two dates, just use simple math. Remember, the most recent date is the larger one, because dates are stored as numbers internally in Excel. Older dates are smaller (see Figure 24.6).

=B2-A2

Figure 24.6

	A	B	C
	C2	f_x	=B2-A2
1	Start Date	End Date	Number of Days
2	1/1/2010	1/15/2010	14
3	1/1/2010	3/1/2010	59
4	1/1/2010	6/1/2010	151

Number of days difference.

This is handy, for example, if you want to calculate how many days late an invoice is, or how many days you have to go until someone's birthday.

Figuring out someone's age, as a function of years, is a simple task (see Figure 24.7), assuming that the full birthday is in cell B2, you can use the following formula:

=YEAR(NOW())-YEAR(B2)

When you first type this formula, Excel might give you a date/time format. Just convert it to a number format, and you'll get the right value.

Figure 24.7

	A	B	C	D	E
	C2		f_x	=YEAR(NOW())-YEAR(B2)	
1	Name	Birthdate	Current Age		
2	Lynn	10/31/1990	20		
3	Maude	2/7/1971	39		
4	Ronald	2/18/1992	18		
5	Ralph	10/23/1972	38		
6					

Current age.

A nice hidden function in Excel called DATEDIF enables you to find the number of days, months, or years between two dates. Why is it hidden? Microsoft put it in Excel years ago, to be compatible with older spreadsheet programs like Lotus 123, and just left it in there. You can still use it—it just doesn't show up on any of the menus, function wizards, or help tips.

=DATEDIF(Date1, Date2, Interval)

The Interval can be either "m" for month, "y" for year, or "d" for days. Days is useless because you can just subtract the two values for days. Months is really the only thing you can use this function for.

=DATEDIF(B2,TODAY(),"m")

This figures out how many months each person has been alive. Note that you can't just multiply the value in C2 by 12 because that represents how many years. What if the person has been alive for 6 months on top of that? The DATEDIF function is more exact in this case (see Figure 24.8).

Figure 24.8

	D2		▼	f_x	=DATEDIF(B2,TODAY(),"m")	

▲	A	B	C	D	E
1	Name	Birthdate	Current Age	Months Alive	
2	Lynn	10/31/1990	20	237	✛
3	Maude	2/7/1971	39	473	
4	Ronald	2/18/1992	18	221	
5	Ralph	10/23/1972	38	453	

DATEDIF function.

You can also set up a timesheet in Excel. If you want to have a start time and an end time, and calculate the number of hours someone worked, just subtract the two times and multiply the result by 24. Remember, you have to format the result as a number, not a date/time (see Figure 24.9):

=(B2-A2)*24

Figure 24.9

	C2		▼	f_x	=(B2-A2)*24

▲	A	B	C	D
1	Time In	Time Out	Hours Worked	
2	9:00 AM	2:00 PM	✛ 5.0	
3	9:30 AM	6:00 PM	8.5	
4	11:00 AM	4:00 PM	5.0	
5				
6				

Timesheet.

This works just fine as long as everyone starts work in the morning and finishes in the afternoon. It doesn't work so well if you have someone who works second shift. If that person starts work at 6 P.M. and finishes at 2 A.M., you can't just subtract the times.

In this case, you have two choices: either store the complete date and time that the person started and finished work, (which is recommended) or use the IF function to determine if their shift crosses midnight. You learn how to do this later when we get to logic functions in Chapter 25.

Fixing Date/Time Errors

If you have data files where the dates or times are not in a valid Excel date/time format, you have to take a ton of time to convert them over so you can perform calculations on them.

If the dates are in the format YYYYMMDD use the LEFT, RIGHT, and MID functions to separate out the year, month, and day pieces from this bad date (see Figure 24.10):

YEAR:	=LEFT(A2,4)
MONTH:	=MID(A2,5,2)
DAY:	=RIGHT(A2,2)

Figure 24.10

	C2		f_x	=MID(A2,5,2)
	A	B	C	D
1	Bad Date	Year	Month	Day
2	20101030	2010	10	30
3	20100814	2010	08	14
4	20091201	2009	12	01
5	19991031	1999	10	31
6				

Fixing a bad date.

Now that you have the individual components separated, you can recombine them into a proper date with the DATE function:

    =DATE(B2,C2,D2)

Now you have a valid Excel date that you can use in calculations.

TIP

If you want to keep these dates and work with their values, and even possibly discard the original bad dates after you've fixed them, just copy these to the Clipboard and then paste them somewhere else. When the paste tool pops up, select Paste Values and Number Formatting, which pastes just the values in the source cells (not the functions) and keeps the date format.

The Least You Need to Know

- Excel stores dates internally as a number representing the days since 1/1/1900.
- Use the NOW and TODAY functions to get the current time and date.
- Use the YEAR, MONTH, DAY, HOUR, MINUTE, and SECOND functions to deconstruct the parts of a date/time value.
- Use the DATE and TIME functions to put a date/time value back together again.
- An undocumented function called DATEDIF makes it easy to find the difference between two dates in years, months, and days.

Logical Functions

In This Chapter

- Learning the basic Boolean logic functions NOT, AND, and OR
- Teaching Excel how to make decisions with the IF function
- Assigning letter grades to students (A, B, C, D, F)
- Fixing the time clock to include shifts that go past midnight
- Calculating overtime pay for employees
- Dealing with divide-by-zero errors

Excel is powerful enough without logical functions, but after you learn how to make your spreadsheets make decisions with the IF function, a whole new world of possibilities opens up. In this chapter, you learn how to make your spreadsheets smart with logic functions.

Simple Logic Functions

Logic functions deal with TRUE and FALSE values, also called Boolean values. Once you know whether a condition is TRUE or FALSE, you can then use that information to have Excel make decisions. For example, "if a specific customer is from New York, then charge him sales tax."

When working with nontext values in Excel, anything that returns the value of 0 is considered FALSE. Anything else is considered TRUE. So the number 17 is considered TRUE. The value –1 is considered TRUE. The date 1/1/2010 is considered TRUE. Zero is FALSE.

In addition to this, and to make two unambiguous values use Boolean logic, you can refer to two specific values, TRUE and FALSE, in your formulas and functions. TRUE is not the same as the text string "TRUE." It is a special value in Excel.

The three core logic functions are AND, OR, and NOT. AND returns TRUE if all of the values sent to it are true; otherwise, it returns FALSE. OR returns TRUE if any of the values sent to it are false.

NOT simply returns the opposite of what you send it. If A1 has any TRUE value in it, then the following returns a FALSE:

=NOT(A1)

Figure 25.1 shows a simple logic table involving two variables, X and Y.

=AND(A2,B2)

=OR(A2,B2)

Figure 25.1

	D5			f_x	=OR(A5,B5)	
	A	B	C	D	E	F
1	X	Y	AND	OR		
2	1	1	TRUE	TRUE		
3	1	0	FALSE	TRUE		
4	0	1	FALSE	TRUE		
5	0	0	FALSE	FALSE		
6						

Logic table.

Instead of 1 and 0 values, you can use TRUE and FALSE. Remember, any nonzero numeric value is considered TRUE. Here you can see that when X and Y are both TRUE, the AND condition is TRUE. When either X or Y is TRUE, the OR function returns TRUE.

You can use multiple values with AND and OR. You're not limited to just two choices. Here's a hypothetical example of the AND function with four values:

=AND(A2,B2,C2,D2)

You can also include equations inside your AND and OR functions. For example, let's say you have a list of your customers who are past due. You also know which customers are local. You want to plan a visit to your local customers to kindly remind them to pay their bill.

You can use the AND function to see which customers are both local and past due (see Figure 25.2). This AND function will return TRUE only if B2 is TRUE (the customer is local) AND if C2 (the due date) is earlier than today's date.

=AND(B2,C2<TODAY())

Figure 25.2

	A	B	C	D	E
				D2 ▾ *fx* =AND(B2,C2<TODAY())	
1	Customer	Local	Due Date	Local and Past Due	
2	Joe	TRUE	1/1/2010	TRUE	
3	Sue	FALSE	2/1/2010	FALSE	
4	Bill	TRUE	10/1/2010	FALSE	
5	Jim	FALSE	11/5/2010	FALSE	
6					

Past-due customers.

Consider another example. You have a list of orders that need to be shipped. You can't ship the orders until the boxes are packed, so you have a PACKED column that the workers mark as TRUE when they're ready. In addition, you're responsible for mailing only the UPS packages; someone else in the office handles the local deliveries and the USPS and FedEx packages. You need to figure out which orders are ready to be packed and are going via UPS.

The formula in Figure 25.3 will return TRUE if the value in B2 is TRUE (the order is packed) AND the value in C2 is equal to "UPS."

=AND(B2,C2="UPS")

Figure 25.3

	A	B	C	D	E
				D2 ▾ *fx* =AND(B2,C2="UPS")	
1	OrderID	Packed	Method	Ready?	
2	14343	TRUE	UPS	TRUE	
3	14344	TRUE	FedEx	FALSE	
4	14345	TRUE	UPS	TRUE	
5	14346	FALSE	Delivery	FALSE	
6	14347	FALSE	USPS	FALSE	

UPS shipments ready.

Look over one more example. You have a list of your sales. You want to determine which credit card sales should be deposited in your bank account for this batch of transactions. Credit card sales could be AmEx, Visa, or MasterCard, and the order has to be paid.

=AND(D2,OR(C2="Visa",C2="MasterCard",C2="AmEx"))

Notice how we *nested* an OR function inside the AND function. The innermost function is evaluated first, and then that value is fed to the outer function. In the case of C2, the OR function evaluates to FALSE because this is a cash sale, so the whole thing evaluates to FALSE (see Figure 25.4).

DEFINITION

A **nested** function is a function that's included inside another one. The inner-most function is evaluated first. For example:

AND(X,OR(Y,Z))

The OR function would be evaluated first, and then that result would be used to evaluate the AND function.

Figure 25.4

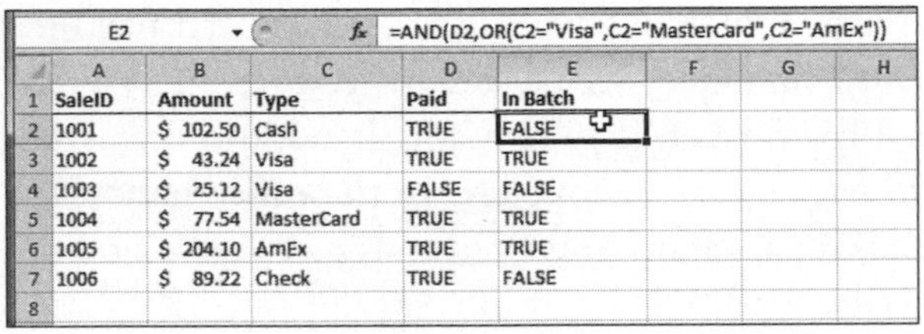

	A	B	C	D	E	F	G	H
	E2			f_x	=AND(D2,OR(C2="Visa",C2="MasterCard",C2="AmEx"))			
1	SaleID	Amount	Type	Paid	In Batch			
2	1001	$ 102.50	Cash	TRUE	FALSE			
3	1002	$ 43.24	Visa	TRUE	TRUE			
4	1003	$ 25.12	Visa	FALSE	FALSE			
5	1004	$ 77.54	MasterCard	TRUE	TRUE			
6	1005	$ 204.10	AmEx	TRUE	TRUE			
7	1006	$ 89.22	Check	TRUE	FALSE			
8								

Nested functions.

Making Decisions with the IF Function

Now that you know which sales will be in your credit card batch for the evening, you can add them so you know what your batch amount is going to be.

Use the IF function to have Excel make a decision on which value to provide. The basic syntax is:

=IF(expression, value if true, value if false)

For example, assume that cell A1 has the number 5 in it. Put the following function into cell B1:

=IF(A1=5, "Elephant", "Baboon")

Now cell B1 should say "Elephant" because A1=5 evaluates to TRUE. If A1 were any value other than 5, B1 would say "Baboon."

For computer programmers, the IF function is essentially shorthand for this:

IF A1 = 5 THEN

   B1 = "Elephant"

ELSE

   B1 = "Baboon"

END IF

Knowing this, you can look at your sales log and say, "IF the transaction is in the credit card batch, THEN I want to add this value in my batch total—ELSE, I don't." You can do this with a simple IF function, as follows:

=IF(E2,B2,0)

Figure 25.5

	A	B	C	D	E	F	G
					fx	=IF(E2,B2,0)	
1	SaleID	Amount	Type	Paid	In Batch	Add to Batch	
2	1001	$ 102.50	Cash	TRUE	FALSE	$ -	
3	1002	$ 43.24	Visa	TRUE	TRUE	$ 43.24	
4	1003	$ 25.12	Visa	FALSE	FALSE	$ -	
5	1004	$ 77.54	MasterCard	TRUE	TRUE	$ 77.54	
6	1005	$ 204.10	AmEx	TRUE	TRUE	$ 204.10	
7	1006	$ 89.22	Check	TRUE	FALSE	$ -	
8							
9						$ 324.88	
10							

IF function.

This simply says, "IF E2 is TRUE, set this cell equal to B2; otherwise, set it equal to 0." For this specific example, E2 is FALSE, so F2 is set to 0.

For the next row, however, E3 is TRUE, so the amount from B3 gets placed in F3. AutoFill this function down the whole column, and then add the following simple function on the bottom. You now know exactly how much money from credit card sales will be in the nightly batch this evening.

=SUM(F2:F8)

Student Grades

Let's take a look at another example.

NOTICE

IF is a very important function and I use it all the time, so I want to make sure you fully understand it.

In Figure 25.6, we have a sheet that's a list of student names and their final grades for a class.

Figure 25.6

Student grades.

You want to assign each student either a PASS or a FAIL, based on his or her grade. Students need to achieve a 65 or higher to pass; otherwise, they fail (see Figure 25.7).

=IF(B2>=65,"Pass","Fail")

Figure 25.7

Pass or fail.

Notice that the students with grades below 65 have "Fail" marks. The rest passed. Notice also that "Pass" and "Fail" are inside quotes because we put the text "Pass" or "Fail" into the cell—not a value or named reference called Pass or Fail.

Imagine that you want to grade on a curve and you want to set the passing grade equal to the class average. If a student scored higher than the class average, that student passes.

Start by calculating the class average:

=AVERAGE(B2:B6)

Now use this value in your IF function, but remember to make it an absolute reference; otherwise, when you AutoFill it down, the formula references will change.

=IF(B2>=$B$8,"Pass","Fail")

Better yet, set up cell B8 as a named cell and call it ClassAverage. Then you can refer to that in your functions.

=IF(B2>=ClassAverage,"Pass","Fail")

Now the professor decides that he was a little harsh. "Okay," he says, "let's make it that your grade has to be at least 90 percent of the class average for you to pass. That should make it a little easier."

To do this, create two more cells. Create a value to represent the difficulty factor—in this case, 90 percent—and then create a second cell as a named cell called PassingGrade, which multiplies the difficulty with the class average (see Figure 25.8).

> PassingGrade = ClassAverage * Difficulty

Figure 25.8

	A	B	C	D	E	F
	PassingGrade	▼	fx	=ClassAverage*Difficulty		
1	Student	Final Grade	Pass/Fail			
2	Bob	95	Pass			
3	Sue	80	Pass			
4	Sally	72	Pass			
5	Mark	64	Fail			
6	Ralph	52	Fail			
7						
8	Average:	72.6				
9	Difficulty:	90%				
10	Passing Grade:	65.34				
11						

Difficulty.

This makes the passing grade a little lower and helped one more student pass.

Using IF to Assign a Letter Grade

You can use the IF function to assign a letter grade to each student. To do this, you have to nest multiple IF statements. Let's say that you want to give each student an A, B, C, D, or F grade. Ninety gives you an A, 80 a B, and so on, down to the passing grade for D. Below that, the student gets an F.

> =IF(B2>=90,"A",IF(B2>=80,"B",IF(B2>=70,"C",IF(B2>=PassingGrade,"D","F"))))

First, check to determine whether the grade is greater than or equal to 90. The first test is greater, so an A is assigned and you're done.

For the next student (Sue), check to determine whether her grade is greater than 90. It's not, so the next IF is evaluated. Is her grade more than 80? Yes, so she gets a B.

This happens all the way to the last IF function, which checks to determine whether the grade is above the PassingGrade named cell (which is 65.7 at this point). Unfortunately, Ralph got a 52, so he gets an F (see Figure 25.9).

> **NOTICE**
>
> Another way to assign letter grades is to use the VLOOKUP function, which you learn about in the next chapter. IF works okay if you have only a small number of parameters, but if you have more than five or six, your functions start to get messy.

Figure 25.9

	A	B	C	D	E	F	G	H	I	J
	D2		f_x =IF(B2>=90,"A",IF(B2>=80,"B",IF(B2>=70,"C",IF(B2>=PassingGrade,"D","F"))))							
1	Student	Final Grade	Pass/Fail	Letter Grade						
2	Bob	95	Pass	A						
3	Sue	80	Pass	B						
4	Sally	72	Pass	C						
5	Mark	66	Pass	D						
6	Ralph	52	Fail	F						
7										
8	Average:	73								
9	Difficulty:	90%								
10	Passing Grade:	65.7								
11										

Yes, I cheated and changed Mark's grade to 66.

Fixing the Time Clock with IF

Now that you know how to use the IF function, you can revisit the time clock from Chapter 24. Recall that it works great as long as the time in is less than the time out. If you have a shift that straddles midnight and your time out is less than the time in, you have a problem.

You can fix this with the IF function. Here's what it looks like:

$$=IF(A2<B2,(B2-A2)*24,((1-A2)+B2)*24)$$

First, check to determine whether A2 (time in) is less than B2 (time out). If that's the case, use the simple subtraction formula to figure out the number of hours (time out minus time in, times 24 to get hours).

Now, if the time in is greater than the time out, you have a shift that crossed midnight. In this case, you need to figure out how many hours the employee worked before midnight and then add that to how many hours he worked after midnight.

The number of hours he worked after midnight is easy: that's just the value of time out. If he worked until 6 A.M., that's 6 hours.

The number of hours he worked before midnight is a little trickier. Recall that one full day is assigned a value of 1 in Excel. So to figure out the hours before midnight, subtract the time in from 1.

Then add these two values and multiply by 24 to get the total hours:

(1-A2)+B2)*24

Put this all together in the IF function. The time sheet is now fixed and takes into account shifts that go past midnight. (See Figure 25.10.)

Figure 25.10

	C2			f_x	=IF(A2<B2,(B2-A2)*24,((1-A2)+B2)*24)		
	A	B	C		D	E	F
1	Time In	Time Out	Hours Worked				
2	9:00 AM	2:00 PM	5				
3	9:30 AM	6:00 PM	8.5				
4	11:00 AM	4:00 PM	5				
5	11:00 PM	2:00 AM	3				
6	10:00 PM	6:00 AM	8				
7							
8							

Fixed time clock.

Calculating Overtime Pay

Another great example of the IF function is calculating overtime pay. Let's say you have a list of employees, the number of hours they worked for the week, and their hourly rate.

First, figure out how many regular hours and how many overtime hours each employee worked. Overtime hours are any hours over 40 for the week, and the employee is paid time-and-a-half.

Regular hours are:

=IF(B2<40,B2,40)

This says, "If the employee has worked less than 40 hours, then the regular hours worked is the same as the total number hours he or she worked; otherwise, it's 40." (See Figure 25.11.)

Figure 25.11

	D2			f_x	=IF(B2<40,B2,40)	
	A	B	C	D		E
1	Employee	Hours	Pay Rate	Regular Hours		
2	Sue	25	9.25	25		
3	Mark	30	9.50	30		
4	Joe	40	10.00	40		
5	Sam	42	10.00	40		
6	Dave	52	20.00	40		
7						

Regular hours worked.

Overtime hours are:

=IF(B2>40,B2-40,0)

This says, "If the employee has worked more than 40 hours, then the overtime hours worked is the difference between the total hours and 40; otherwise, it's zero."

As you can see from Figure 25.12, Sue has worked 25 regular hours and 0 overtime hours; Dave has worked a total of 52 hours, of which 40 are regular and 12 are overtime.

Figure 25.12

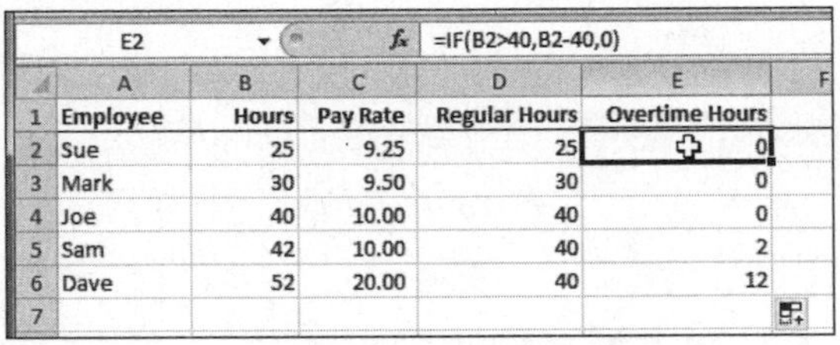

Overtime hours worked.

To calculate each employee's paycheck, multiply his or her regular hours by the pay rate and then add to that 1.5 times the overtime pay times the overtime hours. To make it easier to spot and fix errors, break it down into two columns (see Figure 25.13).

Regular Pay: =C2*D2

Overtime Pay: =C2*E2*1.5

Total Paycheck: =F2+G2

Figure 25.13

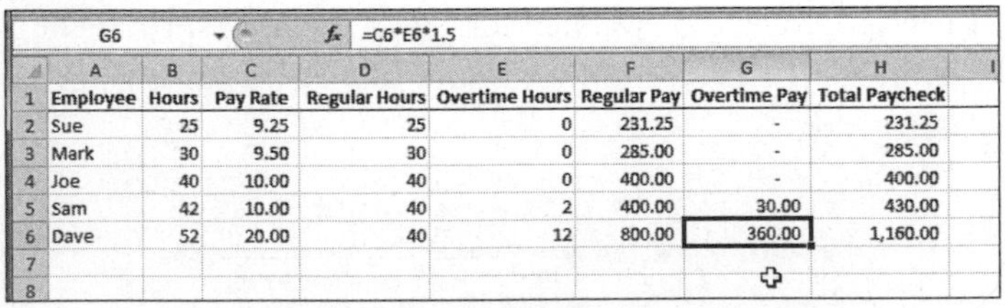

Total paycheck.

IS Functions

No discussion of logic functions is complete without talking about the wide range of IS functions that are available in Excel. IS… functions are functions that try to determine if a value IS something specific, like a blank cell or an error message.

Here's the rundown:

ISBLANK—Returns TRUE if the cell is blank/empty

ISERR—Returns TRUE for any error other than #N/A

ISERROR—Returns TRUE for any error

ISNA—Returns TRUE if the cell contains an #N/A error

ISEVEN—Returns TRUE if the cell has an even value (2, 4, 6, 8, and so on) or is zero

ISODD—Returns TRUE if the cell has an odd value (1, 3, 5, 7, and so on)

ISLOGICAL—Returns TRUE if the value given is either TRUE or FALSE

ISNONTEXT—Returns TRUE if the cell contains any nontext value (number, date, and so on)

ISNUMBER—Returns TRUE if the cell contains a numeric value (including dates)

ISTEXT—Returns TRUE if the cell contains a text string value

Here is a quick example. Remember back in Chapter 23, we put together first name, middle initial, and last name using string concatenation? Well, what if the person has no middle initial listed? You end up with two spaces in the name. You can fix that with an ISBLANK inside an IF function (see Figure 25.14).

=A2&" "&IF(ISBLANK(B2)," ",B2&" ")&C2

Figure 25.14

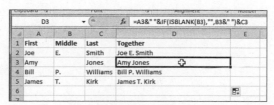

Double space problem.

This basically says, "The full name is going to be the first name (A2) followed by a space. If the middle name (B2) is blank, put nothing here (empty quotes); otherwise, put the middle name followed by a space here. Finally, add the last name (C2)."

IFERROR Function

The IFERROR function is basically a mix of ISERROR and an IF function. It's a quick value replacement for something if an error occurs.

For example, this is great if you have a situation where a "divide by zero" error could ruin your whole day. As you know, you cannot divide something by zero, as doing so will result in an error. Just wrap that inside an IFERROR function and set the value to zero manually.

=IFERROR(A1/A2,0)

This evaluates the cell to be A1/A2 unless an error occurs, in which case you get the zero.

The Least You Need to Know

- Use the basic logic functions AND and OR to check for simple conditions.
- The IF function enables Excel to provide a value based on one or more criteria that you specify.
- Many different functions, like ISTEXT, help you determine the type of value in a cell.

Lookup Functions

In This Chapter

- Finding values in a lookup table using VLOOKUP
- Looking up weekday names, student letter grades, and employee data
- HLOOKUP, MATCH, and INDEX

A *lookup function* is a function that enables you to look up a value from a list, another sheet, or even a whole different workbook file. You can use lookup functions to look up product information, employee pay rates, customer phone numbers, or anything else you can think of. For example, if you have a filing cabinet with all of your customer records in neat, organized files, you can easily "look up" a particular customer's phone number from his file. This is, in a nutshell, what Excel's various lookup functions do.

VLOOKUP

My personal favorite lookup function is VLOOKUP, because it's the most versatile and easiest to use. The *V* in *VLOOKUP* stands for "vertical." This just means that you're looking up a value from a list where the records go up and down in columns.

VLOOKUP has a close cousin, named HLOOKUP, which is designed to look up values from horizontal rows. The two work almost identically. For now, this chapter focuses on VLOOKUP.

Name of Weekday

Let's take a look at a simple example. In Chapter 24, you learned about the WEEKDAY function, which returns the day of the week that a particular date falls on. The number 1 equals Sunday, and 7 equals Saturday. If you want to convert that number to a full weekday name, you can use VLOOKUP for this task, as shown in the following steps:

1. In a blank sheet, enter a list of order numbers in column A.

2. Type in some order dates in column B (the actual values don't matter).

3. Use the WEEKDAY function in column C to determine what day of the week each date falls on, as shown in Figure 26.1.

Figure 26.1

	A	B	C	D	E
	C2		f_x =WEEKDAY(B2)		
1	Order ID	Order Date	Weekday		
2	1001	1/1/2010	6		
3	1002	3/1/2010	2		
4	1003	6/1/2010	3		
5	1004	6/15/2010	3		
6	1005	6/30/2010	4		
7	1006	8/1/2010	1		
8	1007	8/15/2010	1		
9					

Orders and weekdays.

Easy enough so far. Now you need to set up a lookup table. This is a range of cells that you use to provide the data that's being looked up. Consider it a reference table.

In cell F1, create a lookup table of numbers and their corresponding days of the week. Why F1? No real reason—it's far enough away to not bother the rest of the data. Here are the steps for creating the lookup table:

1. Starting in cell F2, type in the numbers 1 to 7 in column F.

2. Starting in cell G2, type in the days of the week, starting with Sunday.

3. Put the column headers "Weekday" and "Name" at the top of the lookup table.

4. Add color and format as you desire.

TIP

Remember, you can type in "Sunday" and then AutoFill down the column, and Excel will complete the series of days for you.

Here's where the VLOOKUP function comes into play. You want to take the Weekday value from each order and find the corresponding weekday name from the lookup table. For example, the first order in Figure 26.2 was placed on 1/1/2010. The

WEEKDAY function returns a value of 6 for this date. Looking up 6 in the lookup table tells me that this is a Friday.

You want to look up the value in C2 (the result of the WEEKDAY function) in the lookup table. After you find it, you want to return the word from the table's second column (the full name). Here's what you're going to put in cell D2:

=VLOOKUP(C2,$F$2:$G$8,2)

Figure 26.2

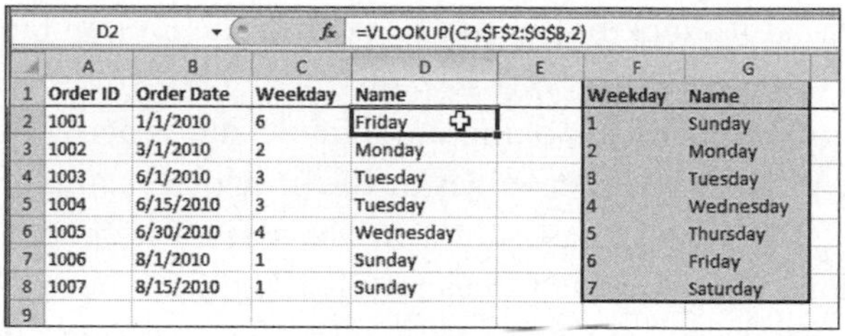

D2 =VLOOKUP(C2,$F$2:$G$8,2)

	A	B	C	D	E	F	G
1	Order ID	Order Date	Weekday	Name		Weekday	Name
2	1001	1/1/2010	6	Friday		1	Sunday
3	1002	3/1/2010	2	Monday		2	Monday
4	1003	6/1/2010	3	Tuesday		3	Tuesday
5	1004	6/15/2010	3	Tuesday		4	Wednesday
6	1005	6/30/2010	4	Wednesday		5	Thursday
7	1006	8/1/2010	1	Sunday		6	Friday
8	1007	8/15/2010	1	Sunday		7	Saturday
9							

VLOOKUP function.

This function says, "Look up the value from C2 in the table located at F2:G8, and bring back the second column." Of course, we need the absolute reference in our function so that when we AutoFill the function down the column, it doesn't get messed up (or set up a named range for the table).

Excel looks at C2 and finds the number 6. It goes to the lookup table and finds 6. What's in the second column of that table next to 6? The word "Friday." The VLOOKUP function returns the "Friday" and places it in D2.

Get it?

Let's look at another example.

Student Grades

In Chapter 25, you learned how to give students a letter grade using a set of nested IF functions. This works okay if you have only 5 letter grades, but if you've got 300 to look up, you're better off with VLOOKUP. Let's look at the same example of the students and set it up with VLOOKUP, for some practice.

Figure 26.3 shows the familiar student grades list from Chapter 25. Remove the pass/fail column and add the lookup table (in cells E1:F6) so that your sheet looks like the one shown.

Figure 26.3

⊿	A	B	C	D	E	F
1	Student	Final Grade	Letter		Grade	Letter
2	Bob	95			0	F
3	Sue	80			65	D
4	Sally	72			70	C
5	Mark	66			80	B
6	Ralph	52			90	A

Student grades.

VLOOKUP can perform two kinds of searches. It can perform an *exact* match, in which the value that it's looking for has to exist in the lookup table (as in the previous example). It can also perform a *range* lookup, in which it finds the closest value that doesn't exceed the number it's looking up. The default is actually a range lookup, but because we have only seven exact values in the previous example, it worked just fine. However, in this case with grades, you won't have *every* item that you're looking up in the table. You don't want to have values for all 100 grades here. That would be silly to have to make an entire table from 0 to 100 with the corresponding letter grade.

It would be much better to specify ranges of grades for Excel to lookup. If the student has a 69, you want Excel to know that's higher than 60, but not quite 70. That's what a ranged VLOOKUP is for. Just set up your table with the numbers that represent the limits for each range. In the case of our grade table, we start with 0, then everything up to but not including 65 gets an F. Everything from 65 up to but not including 70 gets a D, and so on.

This is very important: in the case of a range lookup, your list has to be sorted in ascending order. If not, the VLOOKUP won't work. This means that your smallest values have to be at the top of the list. Do this when you set the list up or use Excel's sort feature.

Named Range for VLOOKUP

Set up the lookup table as a *named range*, to make it easier for your calculations. This way, you don't have to worry about absolute references and all that stuff. Use your mouse to highlight E2:F6.

Here's a shortcut: instead of using the Define Name button that you learned about in Chapter 22, click in the name box next to the function bar. Type the word **LookupTable** and press **Enter** (see Figure 26.4). That's the quick and dirty way to make a named range or cell reference.

Figure 26.4

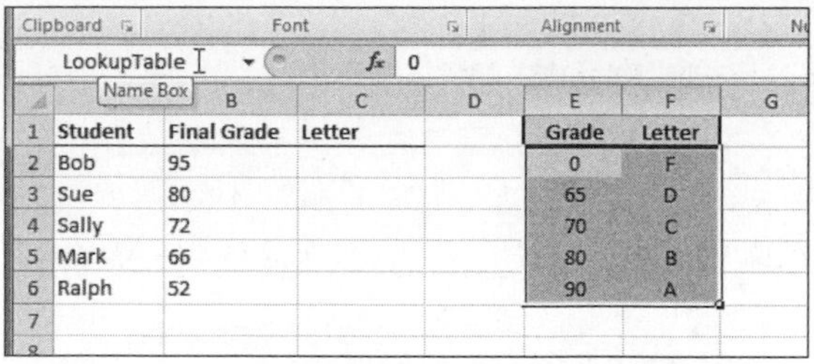

Quick named range shortcut.

Now you're ready for the VLOOKUP function. Here's how it looks:

=VLOOKUP(B2,LookupTable,2)

This says, "Look up the value in cell B2 in the LookupTable range. Return the second column." Now all the students have letter grades (see Figure 26.5). Bob has an A for his 95, Sue has a B for her 80, and so on. This is much more efficient than using nested IF statements.

Figure 26.5

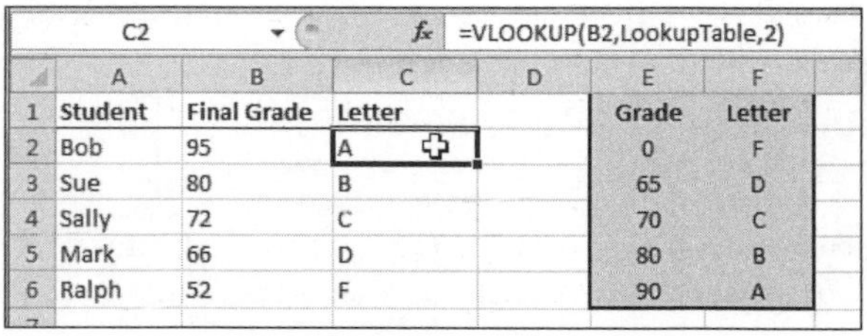

VLOOKUP letter grades.

Employee Data

For this next VLOOKUP example, let's set up a simple employee table. As you can see in Figure 26.6, this table has an Employee ID, First Name, and Pay Rate. This sheet tab is named EmployeeList and is in the sample workbook files on the CD under Chapter 26 (Sample26.xlsx).

Open the sample file, or set up the employee list as a named range from A2 to C7 on this sheet. Call it "Employees."

Figure 26.6

	A	B	C	D	E
1	Employee ID	First Name	Pay Rate		
2	101	Jo	$ 10.00		
3	102	Sue	$ 11.00		
4	103	Bill	$ 12.50		
5	104	Ralph	$ 14.00		
6	105	Mark	$ 8.75		
7	106	Ann	$ 9.00		

Name of Week Day | Gradebook | EmployeeList

Ready

EmployeeList sheet.

Now create another new, blank sheet. This is the work log where employees can put in their hours worked each day. All they have to do is type in the date, their employee ID, their start time, and their end time. Excel does the rest of the work, calculating their hours worked with a little calculation (see Figure 26.7).

Figure 26.7

E8 | fx =(D8-C8)*24

	A	B	C	D	E
1	Date	Employee ID	Start Time	End Time	Hours
2	8/2/2010	101	9:00 AM	1:00 PM	4.0
3	8/2/2010	102	9:00 AM	3:00 PM	6.0
4	8/2/2010	103	10:00 AM	6:30 PM	8.5
5	8/3/2010	101	10:00 AM	2:00 PM	4.0
6	8/3/2010	104	1:00 PM	6:00 PM	5.0
7	8/4/2010	105	2:00 PM	7:00 PM	5.0
8	8/4/2010	101	9:00 AM	1:00 PM	4.0
9					
10					

WorkLog sheet.

Add the formula to calculate each employee's hours worked (we covered this in Chapter 24). You can also set all the columns from E to K to a light blue background. This is just to visually tell the user not to type anything here. For the next column, you want to look up the employee's first name and put it in column F. You can do this with VLOOKUP. Here's what it looks like (see Figure 26.8):

=VLOOKUP(B2,Employees,2,FALSE)

This says, "Look up the value from B2 (the employee ID) in the Employees table (on the other sheet) and return column 2 (the employee name). Also make sure you perform an exact match (the FALSE parameter)."

Figure 26.8

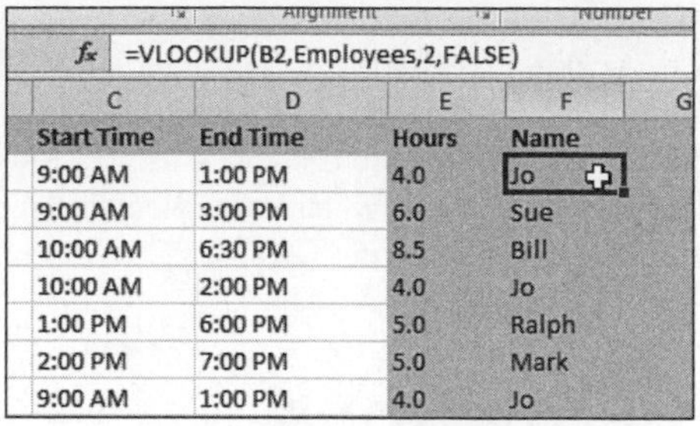

C	D	E	F	G
Start Time	**End Time**	**Hours**	**Name**	
9:00 AM	1:00 PM	4.0	Jo	
9:00 AM	3:00 PM	6.0	Sue	
10:00 AM	6:30 PM	8.5	Bill	
10:00 AM	2:00 PM	4.0	Jo	
1:00 PM	6:00 PM	5.0	Ralph	
2:00 PM	7:00 PM	5.0	Mark	
9:00 AM	1:00 PM	4.0	Jo	

fx =VLOOKUP(B2,Employees,2,FALSE)

Employee VLOOKUP.

Remember, "Employees" is a named range that, by default, has Workbook scope, meaning that you can refer to it anywhere in this workbook. Otherwise, you'd have to call it:

EmployeeList!$A$2:$C$7

This is why named cells and ranges make life easier.

Next, you might want to look up the employee's pay rate. Bring back the NEXT column (see Figure 26.9).

=VLOOKUP(B2,Employees,3,FALSE)

Figure 26.9

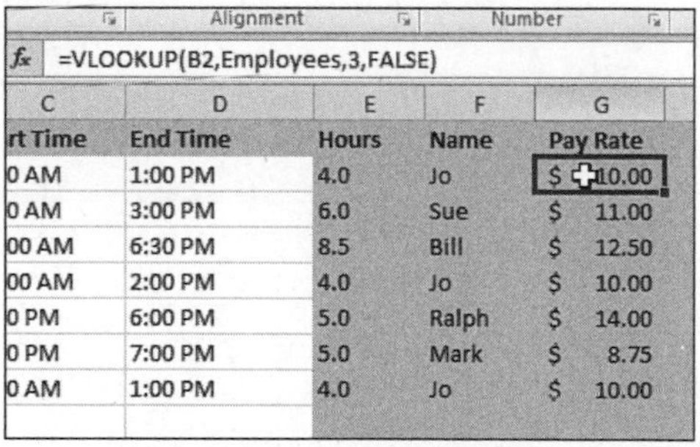

fx =VLOOKUP(B2,Employees,3,FALSE)

C	D	E	F	G
rt Time	**End Time**	**Hours**	**Name**	**Pay Rate**
0 AM	1:00 PM	4.0	Jo	$ 10.00
0 AM	3:00 PM	6.0	Sue	$ 11.00
00 AM	6:30 PM	8.5	Bill	$ 12.50
00 AM	2:00 PM	4.0	Jo	$ 10.00
0 PM	6:00 PM	5.0	Ralph	$ 14.00
0 PM	7:00 PM	5.0	Mark	$ 8.75
0 AM	1:00 PM	4.0	Jo	$ 10.00

Employee pay rate.

See how easy it is to bring back exactly the column that you want? Just specify the column number in the VLOOKUP function. Now you're all set to do whatever other calculations you need to do (total pay for the day, overtime, and so on).

> **NOTICE**
>
> If the value you're looking up doesn't exist in the lookup table, and you're using an EXACT match lookup, you'll get an #N/A error. This is good. It tells you that you need to add that value to the table. If you're using a RANGE lookup, you'll get the next-closest value above it, which can yield weird results. Always make sure you specify the right lookup type.

Other Lookup Functions

In addition to VLOOKUP, there are a couple of other lookup functions that you can use. There are HLOOKUP, LOOKUP, MATCH, and INDEX. You will probably use VLOOKUP most of the time, but it's handy to also learn these additional functions, too.

HLOOKUP

As mentioned earlier, the HLOOKUP function works almost the same as VLOOKUP, except that it's on the side, horizontally. This is useful if the data you're looking up happens to be stored in columns instead of rows, like in Figure 26.10.

=HLOOKUP(C2,$F$4:$L$5,2)

Figure 26.10

	A	B	C	D	E	F	G	H	I	J	K	L	M
1	Order ID	Order Date	Weekday	Name									
2	1001	1/1/2010	6	FRI									
3	1002	3/1/2010	2	MON									
4	1003	6/1/2010	3	TUE		1	2	3	4	5	6	7	
5	1004	6/15/2010	3	TUE		SUN	MON	TUE	WED	THU	FRI	SAT	
6	1005	6/30/2010	4	WED									
7	1006	8/1/2010	1	SUN									
8	1007	8/15/2010	1	SUN									

D2   =HLOOKUP(C2,$F$4:$L$5,2)

HLOOKUP example.

LOOKUP

Another related function is plain old LOOKUP. LOOKUP is related to VLOOKUP and HLOOKUP. With LOOKUP, You specify a lookup vector and a result vector—that is, you give it two ranges, the range to search in and the range to return the value from, as in the following (see Figure 26.11):

=LOOKUP(C2,$F$4:$L$4,$F$5:$L$5)

Figure 26.11

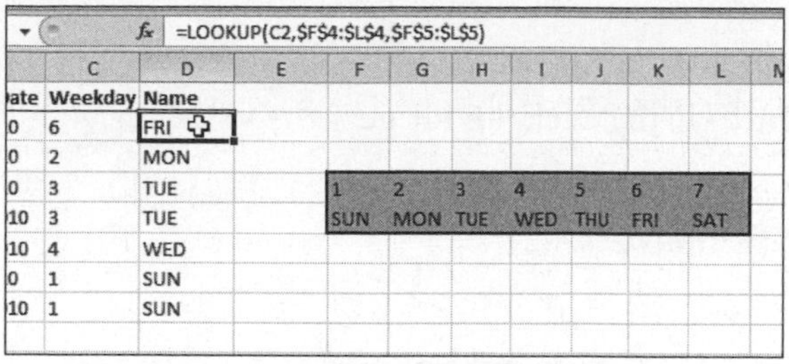

=LOOKUP(C2,$F$4:$L$4,$F$5:$L$5)

ate	Weekday	Name								
0	6	FRI								
0	2	MON								
0	3	TUE		1	2	3	4	5	6	7
10	3	TUE		SUN	MON	TUE	WED	THU	FRI	SAT
10	4	WED								
0	1	SUN								
10	1	SUN								

LOOKUP example.

In Figure 26.11, the lookup says, "Look up C2 in the range F4:L4." LOOKUP finds that value in the sixth location. Now look up whatever is in the sixth location in the result range (F5:L5), which happens to be "Friday."

As you can see, the lookup functions pretty much work the same. Just master one of these, and you'll be fine. VLOOKUP is the most popular.

MATCH

The MATCH function is handy if you want to find the location of an item in a range. For example, in our employee list, type in this (see Figure 26.12):

=MATCH("Bill",B2:B7)

Figure 26.12

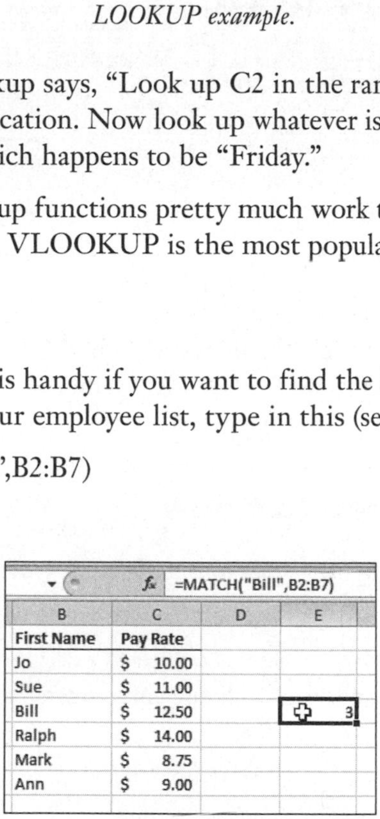

=MATCH("Bill",B2:B7)

First Name	Pay Rate		
Jo	$ 10.00		
Sue	$ 11.00		
Bill	$ 12.50		3
Ralph	$ 14.00		
Mark	$ 8.75		
Ann	$ 9.00		

MATCH example.

The MATCH function returns the number 3 because "Bill" is in the third cell of that range. There's also an optional additional parameter to return an exact match or find values that are greater than or less than the looked-up value.

You can use MATCH to see whether a value exists in a range. Make sure you specify the third optional parameter to perform an exact search—otherwise, it won't do so.

INDEX

In some ways, the INDEX function is the opposite of MATCH. You tell INDEX what cell you want to bring back, and it gets the value for you. For example (see Figure 26.13):

=INDEX(Employees,4,2)

Figure 26.13

E4 | f_x =INDEX(Employees,4,2)

	A	B	C	D	E
1	Employee ID	First Name	Pay Rate		
2	101	Jo	$ 10.00		
3	102	Sue	$ 11.00		
4	103	Bill	$ 12.50		Ralph
5	104	Ralph	$ 14.00		
6	105	Mark	$ 8.75		
7	106	Ann	$ 9.00		
8					

INDEX example.

This looks in the named range "Employees" (which is set up as A2:C7) and brings back the value in row 4, column 3, which is "Ralph."

The Least You Need to Know

- If you need to look up values in a table, stick with VLOOKUP, if you can.
- You can use the MATCH function to determine whether a value exists in a particular range.
- Use the INDEX function to pull any value from a range of cells, knowing just its row and column.

Math and Statistical Functions

In This Chapter

- Creating a running balance
- Using SUM or COUNT values only if they match a certain criteria
- Using ROUND numbers
- Generating RANDOM numbers
- Using trigonometry to calculate the height of a building

You learned about five basic functions in Chapter 6: SUM, AVERAGE, MAX, MIN, and COUNT. You're likely to use these functions 80 percent of the time you use functions. The remaining 20 percent of the time, you'll probably use IF and VLOOKUP.

A lot of other mathematical and statistical functions are similar to SUM, COUNT, and the like. In this chapter, we go over some of the more popular ones.

More with SUM

You might not know that you can use SUM with multiple ranges. You don't have to identify just one range, such as follows:

=SUM(A1:A100)

You can include several additional ranges, such as:

=SUM(A1:A100,B1:B100,F1:F100)

These ranges do not need to be contiguous (next to each other on the spreadsheet). In fact, many of the functions, such as AVERAGE and COUNT, also work with multiple ranges.

Running Balance

If you work with ledger balances, you might have a need to create a *running sum* or a running balance. You can do this with SUM and an absolute reference.

> **DEFINITION**
>
> A **running sum** is a total that is continuously updated for each record or row, much like a bank statement or balance sheet.

Take a look at Figure 27.1, which shows a simple ledger sheet with a date, a transaction amount, and a running balance. You can either open the sample sheet on the CD (Sample27.xlsx) or recreate the sheet yourself. In the first row, the balance is just the transaction amount.

Figure 27.1

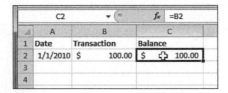

Running balance.

When you enter the second transaction, enter the following SUM formula for the running balance using an absolute reference (see Chapter 22) for the top cell of the range, cell C3 (see Figure 27.2):

=SUM($B$2:B3)

Figure 27.2

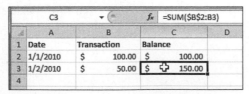

Running balance, absolute reference.

Now, when you AutoFill this formula down for the rest of the rows in this ledger, the absolute reference to $B$2 always stays the same, but the end of the range (B3) keeps moving down, adjusting for the current row. (See Figure 27.3.)

Figure 27.3

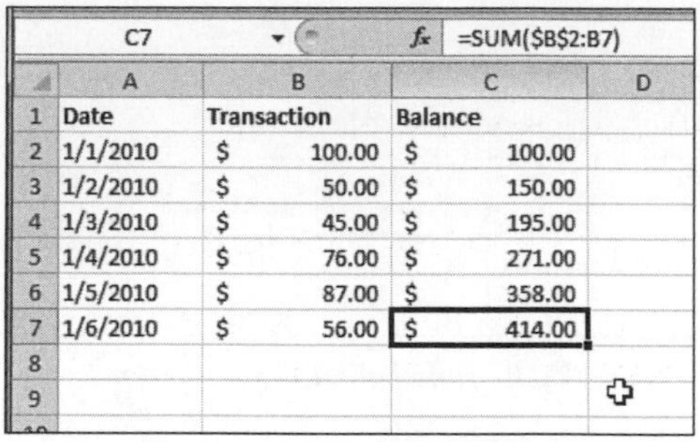

Running balance, completed.

This is how you set up a running balance in Excel.

SUMIF

SUMIF is a nifty function related to SUM. This function enables you to add up values in a range *if* they match specific criteria. Look at the sheet in Figure 27.4.

Let's say that you are calculating employee commissions. You pay commissions only on sales that are over $100. Anything less is ignored. You need to total all the individual sales that are more than $100. You can use the SUMIF function:

=SUMIF(B2:B8,">100")

Figure 27.4

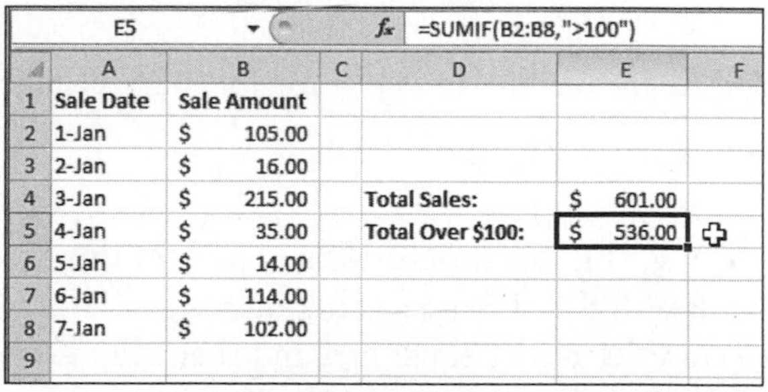

SUMIF function.

This says, "SUM up all the values in B2:B8 that are greater than 100." You can see that the total works out. You can use a number by itself if you want to find an exact match, or you can use greater than and less than inequalities.

You can even use a cell reference (see Figure 27.5):

=SUMIF(B2:B8,">"&E5)

Figure 27.5

	E6	▾ (		*f*	=SUMIF(B2:B8,">"&E5)		
	A	B	C	D		E	F
1	Sale Date	Sale Amount					
2	1-Jan	$ 105.00					
3	2-Jan	$ 16.00					
4	3-Jan	$ 215.00		Total Sales:		$ 601.00	
5	4-Jan	$ 35.00		Minimum Commission Amount:		$ 100.00	
6	5-Jan	$ 14.00		Total Over Minimum:		$ 536.00	
7	6-Jan	$ 114.00					
8	7-Jan	$ 102.00					
9							

SUMIF function with cell reference.

This enables you to specify the criteria in a different cell, and it uses a string concatenation to build the ">100" reference right inside the function. Tricky, but cool.

Figure 27.6 gives a slightly more useful variation of this example. You can actually use a second range to specify the criteria. For example, let's add employee names to this sheet to represent the sales reps.

Figure 27.6

	A	B	C
1	Sale Date	Sale Amount	Sales Rep
2	1-Jan	$ 105.00	Joe
3	1-Jan	$ 16.00	Sue
4	2-Jan	$ 215.00	Joe
5	2-Jan	$ 35.00	Bill
6	2-Jan	$ 14.00	Sue
7	3-Jan	$ 114.00	Joe
8	3-Jan	$ 102.00	Mark
9			

SUMIF with sales reps.

Now, if you want to figure out the sales just for Joe, here's the formula:

=SUMIF(C2:C8,"Joe",B2:B8)

As shown in Figure 27.7, this equation uses the optional third parameter that SUMIF supports to get the data to SUM from a different range. The function basically says, "Find all the values in C2:C8 that equal Joe, and then add up the related values next to them in B2:B8." This enables you to pick out Joe's sales from the adjacent column. The columns must match exactly, but they don't necessarily need to be adjacent.

Figure 27.7

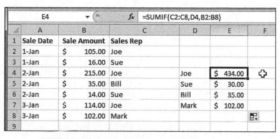

SUMIF function with optional SUM range.

Want to make this sheet a little more useful? Set up a cell for each of your sales reps:

=SUMIF(C2:C8,D4,B2:B8)

Of course, remember that you should make your ranges *absolute* references when you AutoFill them. The dollar signs are left off here, to make the formulas easier to read (see Figure 27.8).

Figure 27.8

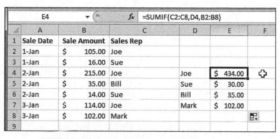

SUMIF function with variable sales rep.

This now makes the sales rep criteria variable. The function looks in cell D4 to get the name of the sales rep and then uses that value for the lookup.

NOTICE

There are similar and related functions, called COUNTIF and AVERAGEIF, that work just like SUMIF, except that they calculate a count and an average, respectively.

SUMIFS

A new function was added in Excel 2007, called SUMIFS (and related AVERAGEIFS and COUNTIFS). The SUMIFS function works similarly to SUMIF, except that it enables you to specify multiple criteria.

For example, using the previous sales rep chart, let's say that you want to figure out how much commissionable sales each sales rep has. This would be sales for each employee, but remember the total sale amount has to be over $100 (see Figure 27.9).

=SUMIFS(B2:B8,C2:C8,D4,B2:B8,">100")

Figure 27.9

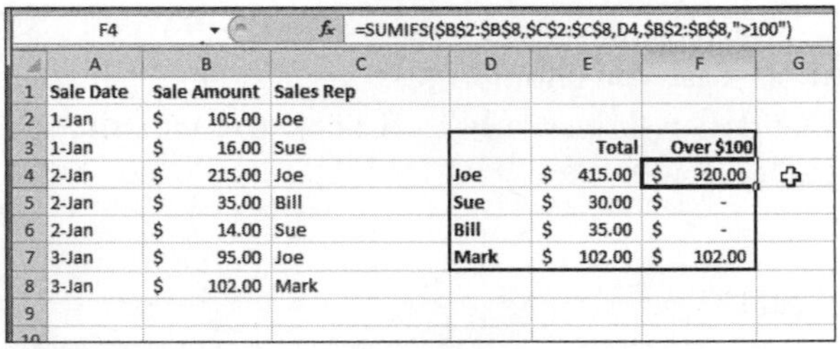

F4 =SUMIFS($B$2:$B$8,$C$2:$C$8,D4,$B$2:$B$8,">100")

	A	B	C	D	E	F	G
1	Sale Date	Sale Amount	Sales Rep				
2	1-Jan	$ 105.00	Joe				
3	1-Jan	$ 16.00	Sue		Total	Over $100	
4	2-Jan	$ 215.00	Joe	Joe	$ 415.00	$ 320.00	
5	2-Jan	$ 35.00	Bill	Sue	$ 30.00	$ -	
6	2-Jan	$ 14.00	Sue	Bill	$ 35.00	$ -	
7	3-Jan	$ 95.00	Joe	Mark	$ 102.00	$ 102.00	
8	3-Jan	$ 102.00	Mark				
9							

SUMIFS.

Looks complicated, eh? It sets up the variables differently than SUMIF. SUMIFS wants the range that you're adding up first. Then it wants pairs of criteria ranges and criteria values—you can specify many of them, if you want.

Here's what this formula says: "Add up values in B2:B8. The first criteria range is C2:C8 (the sales rep names). The first criteria value is found in D4 (which is Joe). The second criteria range is B2:B8 (the sale amounts). The second criteria value is sales over $100."

Now Excel finds all the sales for Joe that are over $100 and adds up those values. This is pretty cool stuff! Before Microsoft added this function to Excel, you had to do a lot of work with a lot of extra columns to get these results.

More Counting Functions

While we're talking about counting functions, you'll likely use a couple of functions often. The first is COUNTA. It's similar to COUNT, which counts just numeric data, whereas COUNTA counts all nonblank cells. Of course, there's also a COUNTBLANK function that counts the blank cells.

In Figure 27.10, you can see 10 values of random types: 5 numeric values (remember, dates are considered numeric values), 9 total nonblank cells, and 1 blank cell.

Figure 27.10

	A	B	C	D
1	5			
2	10			
3	Joe			
4	Alpha		COUNT:	5
5	1/5/2010		COUNTA:	9
6			COUNTBLANK:	1
7	6			
8	5.6			
9	Mark			
10	Sue			

Counting functions.

Remember, you can use logical functions such as ISBLANK and ISTEXT to find out what a specific cell is. We covered these functions in Chapter 25.

Rounding Functions

You might find that you need to round off values in Excel. For example, if you're calculating student grades and you only want whole numbers (without decimals) you can round the results. Be aware that what you see in a cell isn't always exactly the value that is stored in the cell. If you have reduced the number of visible decimal places (with the Increase/Decrease Decimal button), you might see a visually rounded number, but that's not the number that's stored in the cell.

Look at Figure 27.11, for example. The values from column A into column B are copied and pasted, and then the Decrease Decimal button was clicked for each value in column B. The numbers in rows 1 and 3 look different, but they're the same value. In fact, if you click B1 and look in the formula bar, you'll see the exact value stored in the cell. Be careful of this.

Figure 27.11

B1 | *fx* 100.005

	A	B	C	D	E
1	100.005	100.01			
2	10.5	10.50			
3	100.009	100.01			
4	10.9	10.90			
5	14.1	14.10			
6	14.2	14.20			
7	14.9	14.90			
8	14.5	14.50			
9					

What you see might not be what you get.

If you need to round off a number so that you can use VALUE in your cells, you have to use one of the rounding functions. The ROUND function is the most basic of the functions. It performs the kind of rounding that you were taught in grade school. You specify the number and how many digits you want to round off to. Anything from 1 to 4 gets rounded down; 5 to 9 gets rounded up. Negative numbers are the opposite. This will round the value in A1 to zero decimal places, as shown in column C of Figure 27.12.

=ROUND(A1,0)

This rounds off a number to zero decimal places (nearest integer), according to the rules.

Figure 27.12

	A	B	C	D
1	100.005	100.01	100	100
2	10.5	10.50	11	10.5
3	100.009	100.01	100	100
4	10.9	10.90	11	10.9
5	14.1	14.10	14	14.1
6	14.2	14.20	14	14.2
7	14.9	14.90	15	14.9
8	14.5	14.50	15	14.5
9	-10.1	-10.10	-10	-10.1
10	-10.9	-10.90	-11	-10.9
11				
12	Original Numbers	Decrease Decimal	Round to 0 digits	Round to 1 digit
13				

ROUND function.

If you want to specify whether all fractional components get rounded up or down, you can use the ROUNDUP or ROUNDDOWN functions, as follows:

=ROUNDUP(A1,0)

ROUNDUP rounds *any* fractional component up to the next largest integer value (or down, if negative). In Figure 27.13, you can see the ROUNDUP function in use in column E, and ROUNDDOWN in column F.

Figure 27.13

	A	B	C	D	E	F	G
	E3	▾		fx	=ROUNDUP(A3,0)		
1	100.005	100.01	100	100	101	100	
2	10.5	10.50	11	10.5	11	10	
3	100.009	100.01	100	100	101	100	
4	10.9	10.90	11	10.9	11	10	
5	14.1	14.10	14	14.1	15	14	
6	14.2	14.20	14	14.2	15	14	
7	14.9	14.90	15	14.9	15	14	
8	14.5	14.50	15	14.5	15	14	
9	-10.1	-10.10	-10	-10.1	-11	-10	
10	-10.9	-10.90	-11	-10.9	-11	-10	
11							
12	Original Numbers	Decrease Decimal	Round to 0 digits	Round to 1 digit	Round Up	Round Down	
13							

ROUNDUP and ROUNDDOWN functions.

If you want to round to a multiple of something, you can use the MROUND function. Let's say you want to round to the nearest multiple of 5. You would use the following (see Figure 27.14, column G):

=MROUND(A1,5)

Figure 27.14

	A	B	C	D	E	F	G
	G1	▾		fx	=MROUND(A1,5)		
1	100.005	100.01	100	100	101	100	100
2	10.5	10.50	11	10.5	11	10	10
3	100.009	100.01	100	100	101	100	100
4	10.9	10.90	11	10.9	11	10	10
5	14.1	14.10	14	14.1	15	14	15
6	14.2	14.20	14	14.2	15	14	15
7	14.9	14.90	15	14.9	15	14	15
8	14.5	14.50	15	14.5	15	14	15
9	-10.1	-10.10	-10	-10.1	-11	-10	#NUM!
10	-10.9	-10.90	-11	-10.9	-11	-10	#NUM!
11							
12	Original Numbers	Decrease Decimal	Round to 0 digits	Round to 1 digit	Round Up	Round Down	Mround 5
13							

MROUND function.

Notice that the MROUND function apparently doesn't like negative numbers. Similar to MROUND are the CEILING and FLOOR functions that round numbers up and down to the nearest multiples. If you want to round down to the nearest multiple of 3, just use the following:

=FLOOR(A1,3)

You can use the INT function to round any number down to the nearest integer:

=INT(A1)

You can use the TRUNC function to chop off (truncate) any number of digits from a number. For example, the following keeps one digit after the decimal point and truncates the rest, performing no rounding (see Figure 27.15, column I):

=TRUNC(A1,1)

Figure 27.15

	I10	▾	f_x	=TRUNC(A10,1)					
	A	B	C	D	E	F	G	H	I
1	100.005	100.01	100	100	101	100	100	100	100
2	10.5	10.50	11	10.5	11	10	10	10	10.5
3	100.009	100.01	100	100	101	100	100	100	100
4	10.9	10.90	11	10.9	11	10	10	10	10.9
5	14.1	14.10	14	14.1	15	14	15	14	14.1
6	14.2	14.20	14	14.2	15	14	15	14	14.2
7	14.9	14.90	15	14.9	15	14	15	14	14.9
8	14.5	14.50	15	14.5	15	14	15	14	14.5
9	-10.1	-10.10	-10	-10.1	-11	-10	#NUM!	-11	-10.1
10	-10.9	-10.90	-11	-10.9	-11	-10	#NUM!	-11	-10.9
11									
12	Original Numbers	Decrease Decimal	Round to 0 digits	Round to 1 digit	Round Up	Round Down	Mround 5	Int	Trunc 1
13									

INT and TRUNC functions.

Miscellaneous Math and Statistics Functions

There are some lesser-known math and statistics functions that you may never use. However, for those of you who work heavily with math in Excel, you should review this section.

MEDIAN and MODE

If you're familiar with statistics, you might have heard of the MEDIAN and MODE functions. MEDIAN finds the middle value in a set. MODE finds the most common value in a set. Both are used often when tracking sales in the housing market or reporting on incomes, for example. As you can see from Figure 27.16, the MEDIAN function returns the value in the middle.

Figure 27.16

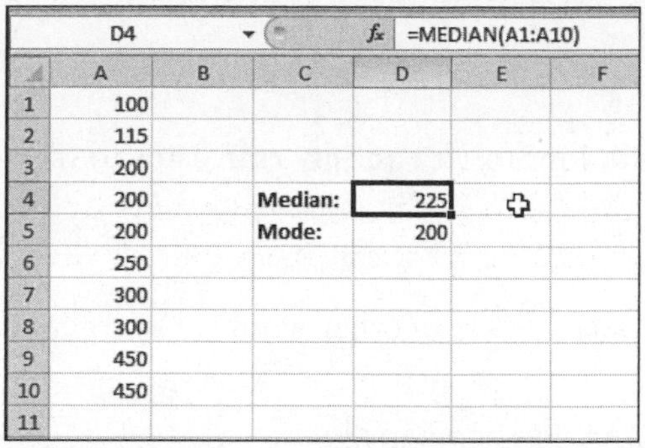

MEDIAN and MODE functions.

If there is an odd number of values, it returns a single value. Because there are an even number of values, it averages the two in the middle.

The MODE function returns the most common value in the set. In this case, it's 200, because there are 3 of them, which is more frequent a value than any other value listed.

PRODUCT and Scientific Notation

The PRODUCT function is just like the SUM function, except that it multiplies all the values in a range. Let's throw it on this sheet because it gives me a chance to talk about *scientific notation*.

You'll see in Figure 27.17 that all the numbers in column A were multiplied together with the PRODUCT function:

Figure 27.17

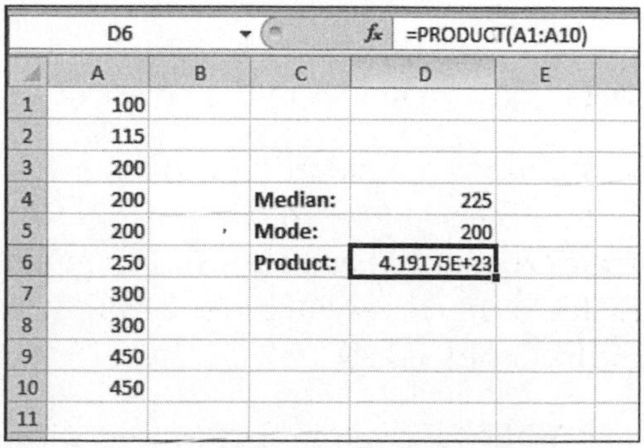

PRODUCT function.

The PRODUCT function returned something weird:

4.19175E+23

What does that number mean? It basically translates to this:

4.19175×10^{23}

Yes, that's 10 to the 23rd power. In other words, it's larger than the number 4 with 23 zeros after it:

419,175,000,000,000,000,000,000

That's called scientific notation, and it's generally used for very large or very small numbers.

POWER and SQRT

Speaking of large and small numbers, you can use the POWER function to raise a number to a power, and the SQRT function to find the square root of a number. These two examples show 10 to the 2nd power, and the square root of 100.

=POWER(10,2)

=SQRT(100)

You don't really need the POWER and SQRT functions, because you can raise a number to a power using the carat (^) symbol. This is 10 to the 2nd power:

=10^2

This results in 100. If you raise a number to the power of $\frac{1}{2}$, you get its square root:

=100^0.5

That gives you the square root of 100, which is 10.

Integer Division

You can use the QUOTIENT function to perform *integer division*. For example:

=QUOTIENT(10,3)

> **DEFINITION**
>
> **Integer division** is a simple division problem, but the result is also an integer (a number without a decimal component).

This results in a value of 3. If you divide 10 by 3, the result is 3 with 1 left over (3 × 3 = 9). This is useful for determining, for example, how many whole slices of pizza everyone would get if you have 3 people and 10 slices. Each person receives 3 slices, with 1 slice left over. If you want to get the remainder from that integer division, use the MOD function (short for modulus).

=MOD(10,3)

That results in 1. There is your left-over slice of pizza.

ABS and SIGN

You can use the ABS function to calculate the absolute value of a number. This is basically a number's distance from zero on a number line. Essentially, it multiplies all negative numbers by –1.

For example, the absolute value of 1 is 1. The ABS of 0 is 0. The ABS of -5 is 5 because it's 5 steps away from 0 on the number line.

=ABS(1)	1
=ABS(0)	0
=ABS(-5)	5

You use the SIGN function to figure out whether a number is positive, negative, or zero. SIGN returns a 1, –1, or 0 value, respectively.

=SIGN(10)	1
=SIGN(0)	0
=SIGN(-200)	–1

Yes, you might be able to tell whether a number is positive or negative by looking at it, but if you need to determine this for another formula (an IF statement, perhaps), you can use the SIGN function.

Random Numbers

Need to generate random numbers in Excel? You can use the RAND and RANDBETWEEN functions. Random numbers are handy for assigning random IDs to customers or products, generating passwords, randomly sorting data, and so on.

The RAND function generates a random number between 0 and 1. This can result in numbers such as 0.1827372.

If you want to create more normal-looking random numbers, use the RANDBETWEEN function. You can specify a lower and upper limit, and get integer numbers between them. For example, if you want to roll dice, you can say:

=RANDBETWEEN(1,6)

You'll get all numbers from 1 to 6 when the random number is generated (1, 2, 3, 4, 5, 6). This would be handy, for example, if you're generating a simple dice game in Excel (see Figure 27.18, column B).

Figure 27.18

Random functions.

The dice can be rerolled each time the sheet is recalculated. You can force a manual recalculation by pressing F9 on your keyboard.

Trigonometry Functions

Finally, Excel supports all the different trigonometric functions, such as SIN, COS, TAN, ASIN, ACOS, and so on. There's even a function you can use to get the exact value of PI, accurate to 15 digits, as shown in the following:

=PI()

Don't forget the () after the PI, or it won't work. PI() is a function. It takes no values in, but it returns the value of Pi (3.1415 …). It works very much the same as TODAY() and NOW() by returning a value.

> **WARNING**
>
> This section assumes you know basic high school trigonometry, and want to apply what you know to your Excel spreadsheets.
>
> If you don't remember your high school trig, and want to learn it, I would recommend picking up a math book that covers the subject in more detail, such as *The Complete Idiot's Guide to Precalculus* by Alpha Books.

When working with trig in Excel, keep in mind that Excel uses radians, not degrees, to perform its calculations. If the angle you're working with is in degrees, you need to convert it to radians first. You can use the RADIANS function for this. You can also use DEGREES to convert radians back to degrees.

As a quick example, let's say you are trying to figure out the height of a building. You know that the building is exactly 100 meters from your current location. You get out your handy surveyor's theodolite and measure the angle from your position to the top of the building as 30 degrees, which is 0.523599 radians (see Figure 27.19).

Figure 27.19

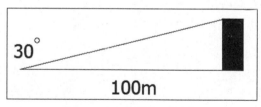

Measuring building height.

Since we know trigonometry, we know that the tangent function represents the ratio of the opposite side to the adjacent side of a right triangle. So the formula is:

=B3*TAN(B5)

This gives you a building height of almost 58 meters, as shown in Figure 27.20.

Figure 27.20

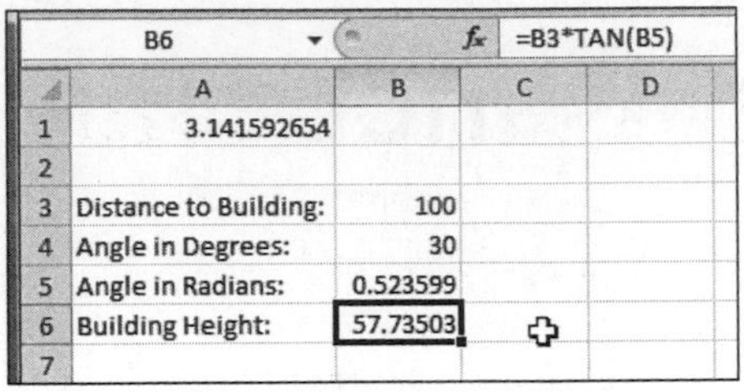

Building height.

The Least You Need to Know

- The SUMIF, COUNTIF, and AVERAGEIF functions (and their IFS cousins) can perform calculations on ranges of cells based on criteria you specify.

- Many different types of ROUNDING functions exist, and all behave slightly different. Pick the one that works for your needs.

- Whether you need to work with statistics, random numbers, trigonometry, or advanced math, Excel has the functions for you.

Financial Functions

In This Chapter

- Learning the basic, popular financial functions: PMT, PV, FV, RATE, and NPER
- Calculating a monthly mortgage payment
- Determining how much your investments will yield
- Figuring out how long until you're a millionaire

In this chapter, we explore Excel's five basic financial functions. You can use them for many different financial calculations, including figuring out a monthly loan payment, determining the future value of an investment, and lots more.

Understanding Excel's Financial Terms

Excel has five basic financial functions: PV, FV, PMT, RATE, and NPER. To use them, you need to understand what they represent.

Keep in mind that these functions work equally well for money coming in and money going out. Whether you're depositing money in the bank and collecting interest or you're paying on a mortgage, the concepts are the same. This chapter generally uses the example of you paying on a loan.

Here are the most popular financial functions. There are many more, but these are the ones you'll use on a regular basis:

- **PV (present value):** This is also known as the principal amount, the initial value of the loan. If you take out a $30,000 mortgage, the initial PV is $30,000.

- **FV (future value):** This is the amount due on your loan at some future point in time. It's usually based on an interest rate over a number of payment periods. Using this function, for example, you can calculate how much is due on your 30-year mortgage after only 10 years of payments.

- **PMT (payment):** This is the amount you're paying every period (for example, each month) on your loan. You can use this function to break down how much your monthly payment is going to be based on your term, amount of loan, and interest rate.

- **RATE (interest rate):** This is how much money the bank is making off you. It's usually represented as an annual interest rate.

- **NPER (number of periods):** This is the term of the loan. For example, the typical 30-year mortgage is made up of (30 × 12) 360 months of payments.

Understanding Interest Rates

If you loan money to a friend, chances are, you're not going to collect interest on it. If you loan a friend $100, and he pays you back $100, then you've collected 0 percent interest.

Banks, however, are in business to make money. So if you borrow $1,000 from a bank, they're generally going to collect some interest from you. Let's say they decide to give you a 5 percent APR (annual percentage rate). That means they're going to charge you 5 percent interest over the course of a year. If you pay back that $1,000 in a year, then you have to pay the bank an extra $50. That's an example of *simple* interest.

When you deposit money in a savings account, however, the bank usually gives you *compound* interest. That means they will give you a 3 percent annual interest rate, but they compound it monthly (or sometimes more often). They usually figure out what your average daily balance is and add that money to your account every month. This makes you more likely to keep your money in the bank.

Simple interest is easy to calculate. Compound interest gets a little tricky. That's why Excel has all these nifty financial functions—they do the hard work for you.

Mortgage Calculator (PMT)

Let's use Excel to calculate the monthly mortgage payment for a typical home loan. You will find the mortgage calculator on your CD (Samples28.xlsx). It looks like Figure 28.1.

Figure 28.1

	B9	▼	*fx*	=PMT(B7/12,B6,B3)

	A	B	C
1	Amount of Loan:	$ 100,000.00	
2	Down Payment:	$ 10,000.00	
3	Amount to Finance:	$ 90,000.00	
4			
5	Number of Years:	30	
6	Number of Months:	360	
7	Interest Rate:	7%	
8			
9	Monthly Payment:	($598.77)	
10			

Mortgage calculator.

Figure 28.1 shows a simple mortgage calculator. Let's start with a typical home that's worth $100,000 (cell B1). Assume that you're putting down a down payment of $10,000 (cell B2). This means you are financing $90,000. That's just simple subtraction. In cell B3, put:

= B1 – B2

Enter the number of years for the loan into cell B5. This is a 30-year mortgage, so type in 30. The PMT function, however, wants this number expressed in months, so in cell B6, we'll convert years to months by multiplying by 12:

= B5 × 12

The bank is giving you a 7 percent interest rate, so put that in cell B7. Now you have all the required information to calculate the monthly payment amount. The final PMT function for cell B9 looks like this:

= PMT (B7 / 12, B6, B3)

The PMT function first wants the interest rate, but it wants it divided up into the number of periods per year (in this case, it is 12 monthly payments). If you make weekly payments, you'd divide it up by 52. If you pay bi-monthly, you'd make it 6.

The second parameter is the total number of periods. In this case, it's 360 months. Finally, the third parameter is the amount of the loan. The amount we're financing is in B3.

This gives us a value of –$598.77 as the monthly payment. The PMT returns a *negative* number because it assumes that this is money *out* that you're paying. If you don't like it, multiply the result by –1 and you'll get a positive value.

Investment Calculator (FV)

Consider another example. Let's say that you have $5,000, and you want to park it in an investment (such as a simple savings account) that pays 8 percent (unrealistic, I know), and you're going to leave it in there for five years. You want to know how much it's going to be worth after those five years. Use the FV function to calculate a future value, as shown in Figure 28.2:

= FV (B2, B3, 0, B1)

Figure 28.2

	A	B	C	D
1	Initial Deposit:	-5000		
2	APR:	8%		
3	Years:	5		
4				
5	Future Value:	$7,346.64		
6				

fx =FV(B2,B3,0,B1)

Investment calculator.

Now, here the initial deposit is negative because you're giving that money away to the bank. Remember, it's relative to you as the depositor. If you don't remember this, that's okay. The final result just shows up as negative.

The interest rate is 8 percent, and the number of years is 5. There's no regular payment being made beyond the initial deposit, so leave the PMT parameter of this function as 0. Yes, you could set up a more complicated example where you're putting in an additional $100 a month into this investment, but we'll leave that for the next book.

You can see that, after five years, the $5,000 will turn into just over $7,346 if the investment pays 8 percent interest. Very nice.

What's the Interest Rate? (RATE)

Not sure what your interest rate is? You can use the RATE function to reverse-engineer it. Let's say that you invested $10,000 in a friend's business three years ago. You need some money, so you ask him to buy you out. He offers you $20,000. You want to know what kind of an interest rate that is (see Figure 28.3):

= RATE (B3, 0, –B1, B2)

Figure 28.3

	A	B	C	D	E
	B5		f_x =RATE(B3,0,-B1,B2)		
1	Initial Deposit:	10000			
2	Present Value:	20000			
3	Years:	3			
4					
5	Interest Rate:	26%			
6					
7					

Interest rate calculator.

The first thing RATE needs is the number of periods. In this case, that's three years. There are no regular monthly payments (PMT), so that's 0. My initial deposit (PV) was $10,000, which is in cell B1, but I'm giving it a *negative* value because that's what I initially paid him (money out, remember). Finally, the future value (FV) is $20,000.

It turns out that my investment in my friend's business netted me a nice return of 26 percent.

The Millionaire Calculator (NPER)

Here's something everyone wants to know: how long until you become a millionaire? Let's say you want to deposit $1,000 a month into a bank account yielding 4 percent interest a year. How many months will it be until you're worth $1 million? For this calculation, you can use the NPER function to calculate the number of periods on an investment, as shown in Figure 28.4.

= NPER (B4 / 12, –B2, B1, B3)

Figure 28.4

	A	B	C	D
	B6		f_x =NPER(B4/12,-B2,B1,B3)	
1	Initial Deposit:	$ -		
2	Monthly Deposits:	$ 1,000.00		
3	Goal Amount:	$ 1,000,000.00		
4	Interest Rate:	4%		
5				
6	Number of Months:	441		
7	Years:	36.7		
8				

Millionaire calculator.

NPER first needs to know what our interest rate is. We're getting 4 percent annually, but we're dealing with *monthly* payments, so remember that we have to divide that amount by 12. It's the interest rate per payment period.

Next, we're making $1,000 monthly payments into this account. It's money out, so that's –B2. Next, B1 represents the initial investment (PV), which is nothing. Finally, what's our goal amount? We want to be millionaires, so put 1,000,000 in cell B3.

Excel then does its magic and tells you that you have to wait 441 months, or 36.7 years before this account is worth a million bucks. It'll be a while, but retirement should be fun.

What Was the Initial Deposit? (PV)

Finally, you can use the PV function to figure out what the initial deposit in an account was if you know the current balance, the interest rate, and how long the account has been open.

Let's say that your account currently has $2,000 in it. You've had it for exactly five years and have been accumulating 3 percent interest this whole time. What was the initial deposit? Use the PV function as shown in Figure 28.5:

> = PV (B2, B3, 0, B1)

Figure 28.5

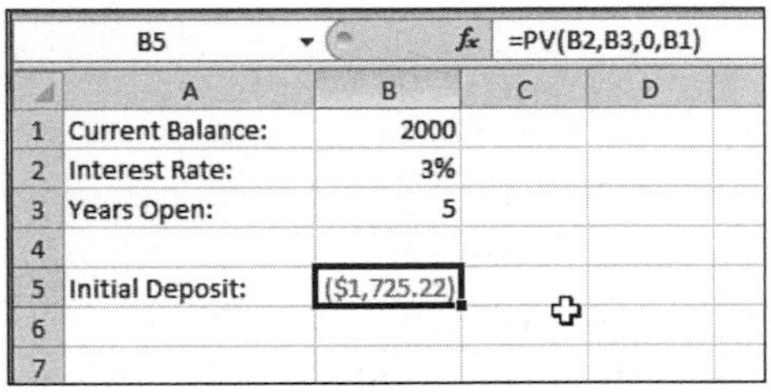

PV function.

It looks like you initially deposited $1,725.22 to start that account. Now, as you can see, these are all very simple examples. You can use a ton of additional financial functions in Excel, and you can do lots more with these five basic functions. Hopefully this gives you a small taste of what's possible with Excel.

The Least You Need to Know

- Use the PMT function to figure out a monthly payment on a loan.
- Use the FV function to calculate the future value of an investment.
- Use the PV function to figure out what the initial investment was.
- Use the NPER function to determine how long it will take to reach a financial goal.
- Use the RATE function to calculate an interest rate.

Data Analysis

You've got all the data you need. In Part 6, you learn some tricks to make more sense out of that data. It's often hard to spot trends when you have thousands of rows of information. Load that data into a PivotTable, however, and it's easy to see those trends.

In Chapter 29, you learn how to filter your data. Don't want to see all the customers from New York who have $15,000 or less in sales for the year? No problem. Just create a filter to hide them all.

In Chapter 30, you see how to create data tables. Tables help you keep your spreadsheet information in order and maintain some consistency in your columns. Plus, you can apply a formula to an entire column in your table and not have to worry about AutoFill.

Chapter 31 is all about creating a PivotTable, an extremely powerful tool for breaking down hundreds or even thousands of rows of data into useful, more recognizable information. Let's say you've got individual sale items for 10 stores in 3 states covering 10 years. A PivotTable can quickly digest that information to show you which store had the best year.

Filtering Data

In This Chapter

- Filtering a large spreadsheet to show only specific data
- Using comparison filters
- Showing your top three customers based on income
- Using number, text, and date filters

If you have a large sheet of data and want to limit the amount of information, you can use filters to "drill down" and find only data you want to see. For example, if you want to see only customers from New York with less than $100,000 in annual income, that's the perfect job for a filter.

AutoFilter

Take a look at the sheet in Figure 29.1. You can find this workbook (Sample29.xlsx) on your CD. You can see that it's a simple sheet with customer name, city, state, and income. Let's filter the list to see only customers from New York.

To turn on filtering, first select the range you want to filter, including the column headers. Select A1:E8. You can usually just click somewhere inside the range, but it's best to select the whole thing.

Figure 29.1

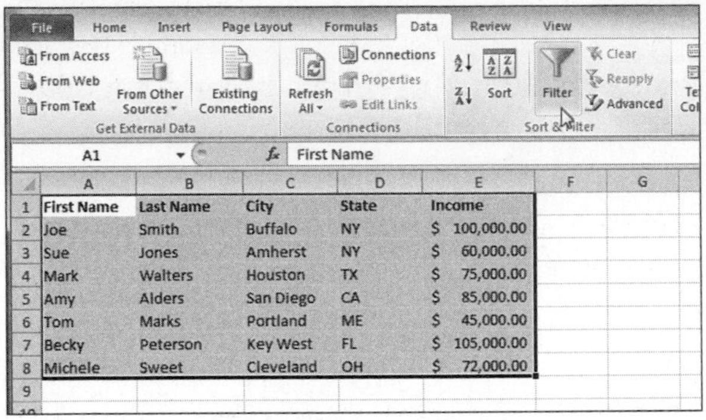

Sample sheet.

Then click **Data > Sort & Filter > Filter**. Drop-down boxes appear in all the column header cells.

Use the drop-down boxes to AutoFilter the results in the range based on your selections. First, limit the list of data to show only customers from New York. Click the drop-down box for the State column. (See Figure 29.2.)

Figure 29.2

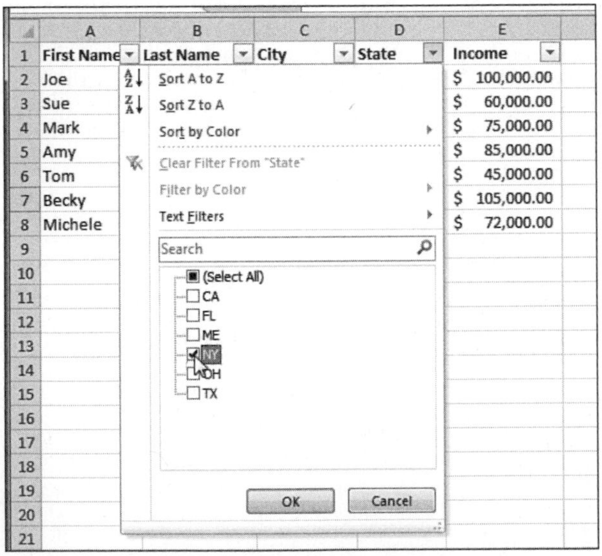

AutoFilter drop-down.

You see several options on this menu, but look toward the bottom. Notice that a list of unique options appears in this column of data. At first, they're all visible (checked on). To limit the results to just customers from New York, turn off the Select All option, which hides everything. Then click the check box next to New York to turn on the New York customers.

Notice that the rows containing customers who are not from New York are now hidden. The other headers changed to blue. This indicates that your results are filtered. Also notice that the AutoFilter drop-down box now has a funnel in the button, indicating that this column has been filtered. (See Figure 29.3.)

Figure 29.3

	A	B	C	D	E	F
1	First Name	Last Name	City	State	Income	
2	Joe	Smith	Buffalo	NY	$ 100,000.00	
3	Sue	Jones	Amherst	NY	$ 60,000.00	
9						
10						

AutoFilter rows hidden.

To add another state to the results, open the drop-down box for the State column and check the box representing that state.

Comparison Filter

Now, let's say you want to show only customers from the states who have at least $100,000 in sales. Open the AutoFilter drop-down for Income (the little drop-down box to the right of the word "Income"—see Figure 29.4).

Figure 29.4

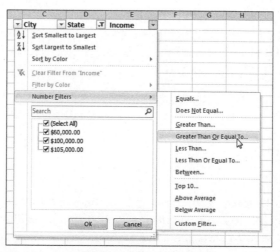

Adding Income to results.

This time, however, don't look for a specific value to add. You want a range of values, so click **Number Filters > Greater Than or Equal To.**

Use the Custom AutoFilter dialog box to get exact with your criteria for this column (see Figure 29.5). Make sure it says "is greater than or equal to," and then type "100000" in the criteria box (or you can choose from one of the existing values).

Figure 29.5

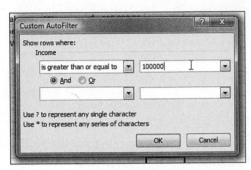

Custom AutoFilter.

> **TIP**
>
> You can also add a second criteria for the same column. For example, you might want to see customers with income of more than $50,000 but less than $100,000. We're not going to cover that in detail now, but using the steps in this section, you should be able to figure it out. Play with it, and have fun.

Now you can see your results (see Figure 29.6). You see only customers from New York or Florida who have at least $100,000 in income. Aren't filters nice?

Figure 29.6

	A	B	C	D	E
1	First Name	Last Name	City	State	Income
2	Joe	Smith	Buffalo	NY	$ 100,000.00
7	Becky	Peterson	Key West	FL	$ 105,000.00
9					

Custom AutoFilter results.

You can turn off the filter at any time by clicking the **Filter** button on the Ribbon. Note that all of your filter information is gone at this point, however. You can also click the **Clear** button to clear the filter without turning it off completely. Use the **Reapply** button to reapply the filter/sort, in case data is added or changed.

Top or Bottom Filters

Now let's say you want to see just the top three customers who have the highest incomes. Yes, you can just sort the list in descending order, but let's use a Top filter.

Turn off any existing filters. Click the **AutoFilter** drop-down for the Income column. Click **Number Filters > Top 10**.

Because you want only the top 4 items (not the 10), change the middle box to 3. Also note that you can use this to see the bottom X results, as well as the top or bottom X percent instead of items.

Notice that the filtered results are the three customers with the highest incomes (see Figure 29.7).

Figure 29.7

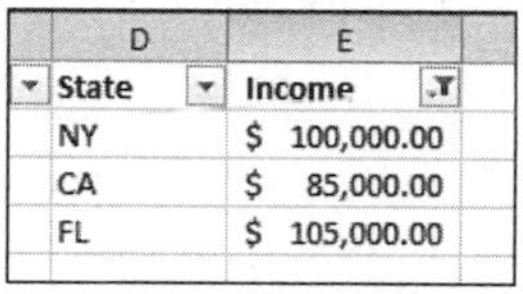

	D	E	
▼	State ▼	Income .▼	
	NY	$ 100,000.00	
	CA	$ 85,000.00	
	FL	$ 105,000.00	

Top three filter results.

Filter Options

There are different types of filter options depending on what kind of data you're working with. Numbers, text, and date values all have separate types of filter options.

Number Filters

The number filters enable you to specify the following:

- Equals
- Does Not Equal
- Greater Than
- Greater Than or Equal To
- Less Than
- Less Than or Equal To
- Between (between two values)
- Top 10 (in the top 10 values)
- Above Average (above the average of all values)
- Below Average (below the average of all values)

Text Filters

Text filters add the following options:

- Begins With
- Ends With
- Contains
- Does Not Contain

So with a text filter, you could say, "show me all of the customers whose names start with the letter A," or "show me all of the product serial numbers that contain XYZ."

Date Filters

Date filters include additional options:

- Before (a specific date)
- After (a specific date)
- Between (two dates)
- Tomorrow, Today, Yesterday
- Next Week, This Week, Last Week
- Next Month, This Month, Last Month
- Next Quarter, This Quarter, Last Quarter
- Next Year, This Year, Last Year
- Year to Date (this year, up to the current date)
- All Dates in the Period

The last option enables you to specify a period that is either a quarter or a specific month.

Filter by Color

Excel also offers a Filter by Color option. Let's say you have assigned states a certain font color (red states and blue states, for example). You can use the Filter by Color option to show or hide only specific states (see Figure 29.8).

Just click on the **AutoFilter** button for the column, then select **Filter by Color**, and pick a color to filter by.

Figure 29.8

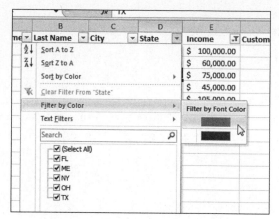

Filter by Color option.

The Least You Need to Know

- A simple AutoFilter can quickly let you "drill down" to see only the data you want.
- Use a comparison filter for additional options.
- Excel has numerous text, date, and number filters.

Tables

Chapter 30

In This Chapter

- Learn about tables, what they are, and why they're useful
- Using tables to control the style and structure of your sheets
- Utilizing table formulas to maintain consistency in your calculations

Sometimes when you put data into an Excel sheet, you don't care about the structure of the data itself. You just want to be able to enter what you want, where you want it.

However, many times you do care about the structure, and you want a nice, neat list of data where column C is always the customer's state, and column D is always the customer's ZIP code. If this is the case, there are benefits to setting up your list of data as a table.

For example, if you're going to create a mailing list, and perhaps using this data to print mailing labels in Microsoft Word, you need to make sure that the same data falls in each column (first name, last name, and so on). A table makes this easier than a free-formed spreadsheet.

Getting Started with Tables

A *table* is a structured set of data in Excel. Generally, each column represents one type of data (such as a last name, a state, or a phone number). Each row represents one record of data (one person, one employee, and so on).

Let's take another look at the spreadsheet we used in the last chapter on filtering (see Figure 30.1). It's set up perfectly to be used as a table. You will also find another copy of this workbook in the Chapter 30 folder on your CD.

Figure 30.1

	A	B	C	D	E	F
1	**First Name**	**Last Name**	**City**	**State**	**Income**	**Customer Since**
2	Joe	Smith	Buffalo	NY	$ 100,000.00	1/1/2010
3	Sue	Jones	Amherst	NY	$ 60,000.00	1/1/2000
4	Mark	Walters	Houston	TX	$ 75,000.00	3/1/1999
5	Amy	Alders	San Diego	CA	$ 85,000.00	4/5/1998
6	Tom	Marks	Portland	ME	$ 45,000.00	6/2/1989
7	Becky	Peterson	Key West	FL	$ 105,000.00	1/1/2000
8	Michele	Sweet	Cleveland	OH	$ 72,000.00	1/2/1999

Customer sheet.

You can see that each column represents a different data type (called a field in database terminology), and each row represents a unique person (called a record in a database).

To turn this spreadsheet into a table, just select the entire range that represents your table (in the sample sheet, it's A1:F8—do include the header row). Then on the Ribbon click on the **Insert** tab, then find the Table group. Click on the **Table** button.

You are asked to verify the range of your table. You had the table selected to begin with, so that should be correct. The table does have column headers, so leave the "My table has headers" box checked. Click **OK**.

Your range now has been converted into a table. You can immediately see that it has been formatted with colors. The header row is one color. Alternating "banded" rows show different colors. The table looks professional.

Notice that your header row has a series of AutoFilter boxes for each column. You learned about these in the last chapter. (See Figure 30.2.)

Also notice that the Table Tools tab displays on the Ribbon, with several available options. We talk about some of them.

Figure 30.2

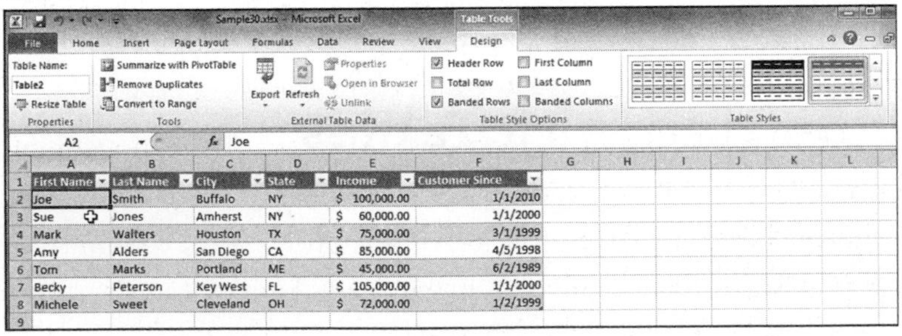

The table.

Table Styles

On the far right of the Ribbon, you can see the Table Styles gallery (see Figure 30.3). You can select from several different styles to make your table look appealing.

Figure 30.3

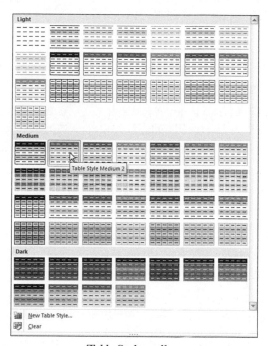

Table Styles gallery.

Notice that some of the styles have differently colored header rows. Some have banded row colors, and some don't. Some have borders between the cells, some don't. You can also create your own table-style format, but that's beyond the scope of this book. Select a table style that looks good to you.

If you change the theme for your workbook, doing so results in a completely different set of table styles that match the theme you choose. Click **Page Layout > Themes** to see how changing your theme changes all the table styles available to you.

To the left of the table styles gallery (on the Table Tools > Design tab) are the table style options. You can change whether you have a header row.

You can also turn on a Total Row (the check box is in the Table Style Options group). If this is on, Excel automatically provides totals for any rows containing numeric data. In this case, it provides a count at the bottom of the Customer Since column. Click this total row, and you'll see a drop-down box. You can change the function that's used here. (See Figure 30.4.)

Figure 30.4

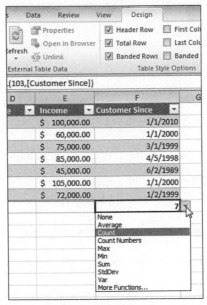

The Total Row.

Let's create a SUM for the Income column. Just click the total row under the Income column (in cell E9), and then pick **SUM** from the list of available functions. (See Figure 30.5.)

Figure 30.5

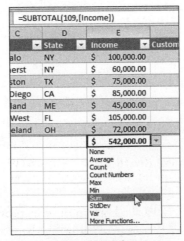

Total Row SUM function.

Going back to the table style options, you can turn row color banding on or off. Check boxes also enable you to create banded columns and to change the style of the first and last columns in the table. Feel free to experiment with these options. Remember, your table style might affect them, too.

- Header Row—Changes the style of the header row
- Total Row—Turns on the "total row" at the bottom of the table; a place where you can add automatic calculations like SUM or COUNT
- First Column—Changes the style of the first (leftmost) column
- Last Column—Changes the style of the last (rightmost) column
- Banded Rows—Changes the color of every other row, alternating in colors
- Banded Columns—Changes the color of every other column

Adding Rows and Columns to Tables

If you want to add columns to your table, just start typing in the column that's immediately adjacent to your table (on the right side). Excel expands the range of the table automatically to include the new column. In Figure 30.6, a Children column has been added to the table to indicate the number of children each customer has.

Figure 30.6

	E	F	G
	Income	Customer Since	Children
	$ 100,000.00	1/1/2010	0
	$ 60,000.00	1/1/2000	4
	$ 75,000.00	3/1/1999	3
	$ 85,000.00	4/5/1998	2
	$ 45,000.00	6/2/1989	1
	$ 105,000.00	1/1/2000	5
	$ 72,000.00	1/2/1999	3
	$ 542,000.00	7	18

Adding a column to a table.

TIP

You can also right-click a column header anywhere inside the table and select Insert to insert a column just to the right of the column you've clicked on.

If you want to add a new row to the bottom of your table records, just click in the bottom-right-most cell of the table (not counting the total row) and press the **Tab** key. (See Figure 30.7.)

Figure 30.7

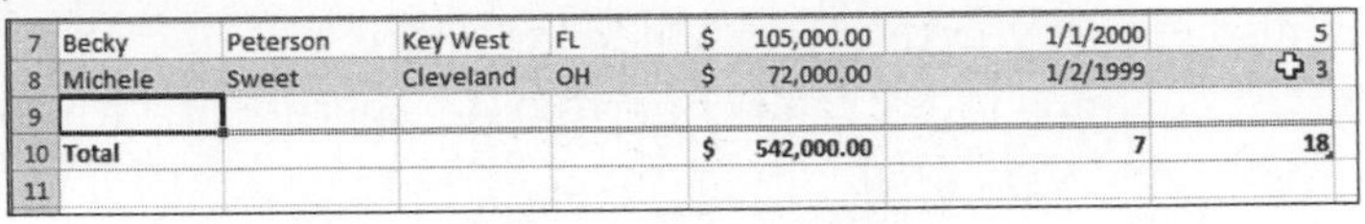

Adding a row to a table.

Excel automatically expands the size of the table by one row and inserts a blank row for you above the total row. If you want to manually expand the size of the table, you can click the corner marker in the bottom-right corner of the table (see Figure 30.8).

Figure 30.8

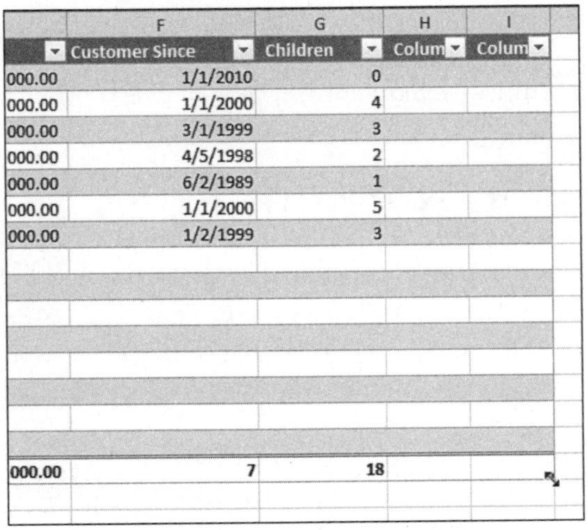

Manually expanding a table.

You can also click the **Resize Table** button on the Ribbon under Table Tools > Design in the Properties group. This will allow you to specify the complete range of the table, enabling you to change the number of rows and columns.

Table Formulas

One special thing about tables is that you can create formulas that work for entire columns, and you don't have to remember to AutoFill them down the column.

Let's say you want to figure a tax credit for each child in the family. For every child, the family gets a $2,000 tax credit. So you need to multiply the value in column G by 2,000. Start by inserting a new column called Tax Credit.

Click cell H2 to start the table formula. Type an equals sign (=) and then, instead of typing a cell number, click cell G2. (See Figure 30.9.)

Figure 30.9

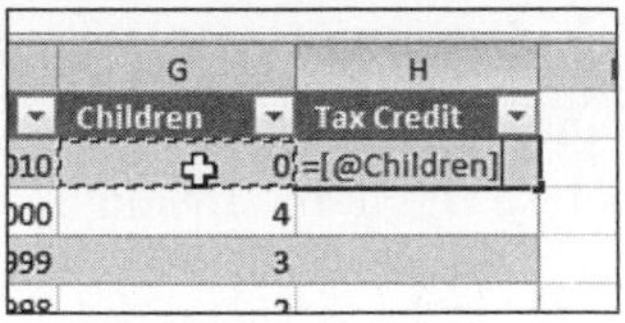

Column reference.

Instead of placing G2 in the formula, the equation now reads as follows:

    =[@Children]

This is called a *table column reference*. It means, "Get the value from the Children column in this same row." Finish the formula by typing in "***2000**" so that the whole formula reads:

    =[@Children]*2000

Press **Enter**. Excel copies the formula automatically to every row in this column (see Figure 30.10). This is one of the major benefits of using a table. Every cell has the exact same formula, and you don't have to worry about AutoFilling anything.

Figure 30.10

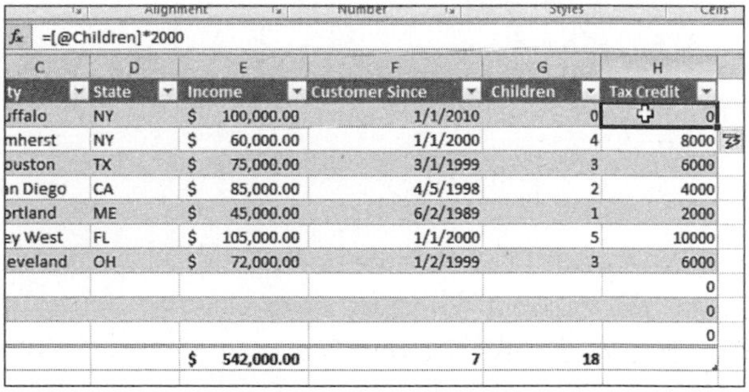

Column formula copied to each row.

Let's try another one. Now that you have the tax credit amount, let's add an "effective" income in the next column. This is essentially the income plus the tax credit.

Create the formula for effective income the same way. Start by typing the equals sign, click cell E2 (Income), type the plus sign, and then click cell H2 and press **Enter**. The final formula is:

    =[@Income]+[@[Tax Credit]]

Because I have spaces in the name of my Tax Credit column, Excel adds another set of brackets. Recall from our discussion on sheet tab names back in Chapter 22, if you want to refer to a different sheet in your formulas, and that sheet tab name has a space in it, you need to enclose the name inside of square brackets. Table column references work the same way.

The Least You Need to Know

- If your data has similar structure and form, use a table to maintain consistency.
- Table styles are a great way to add a professional look.
- Utilize table formulas to make sure that all the calculations in a column are the same for every row in a column.

PivotTables

In This Chapter

- Creating a PivotTable to make sense out of large tables of data
- Learning how to "pivot" different types of data to change the way you view information
- Creating a 3-D PivotChart

To "pivot" means to rotate something on an axis. In Excel, a PivotTable is a tool used to examine data from many different angles. PivotTables are useful for looking at large amounts of data in different ways.

Which stores had the best sales in the fourth quarter of last year? Which customers ordered the most of a specific product last month? Which employees had the most complaints registered against them from customers with purchases in more than two cities? Sounds crazy, but these are all questions you can answer easily with PivotTables.

PivotTables are widely underutilized. Most people don't know they exist or are afraid to use them. After using a PivotTable, however, you'll see that they're very powerful and easy to work with.

What Is a PivotTable?

PivotTables are used to create summaries of large amounts of data or collections of data that are difficult to comprehend. Whereas a spreadsheet full of data might look like a jumble of numbers at first glance, a PivotTable can make sense out of the mess.

PivotTables help you analyze data and reveal trends and relationships in that data that might not otherwise be apparent just by looking at rows and rows of information. You might have 10,000 rows of sales figures. After you load this data into a PivotTable, you might notice that the Chicago store, for example, is doing really well.

You can use PivotTables to format, filter, or hide data on a mass scale. This makes it easier to emphasize a point, such as which store has the highest quarterly sales. PivotTables enable you to analyze the data in a table without having to create manual functions and formulas. You can summarize a large amount of data in a small space with only a few clicks.

PivotTables enable you to perform cross-tabulation, which is summarizing multiple pieces of data in various ways. For example, you can quickly and easily show sales by product and store, or sales by store and year, or time worked by employees at each office. The possibilities are endless.

PivotTables make it possible to quickly and easily change the types of functions you perform on your data (SUM, AVERAGE, COUNT, and so on). This enables you to change the way you view your data on the fly. You can even quickly add groups and subtotals to your data.

Creating a PivotTable

Let's look at a simple sheet that contains store sales and expense information. Open the workbook Sample31.xlsx from the sample file on the book's CD. Although you can use a PivotTable with only a few rows, it's best to have a table with a lot of data. (See Figure 31.1.)

Figure 31.1

	A	B	C	D	E	F	G
1	Year	Quarter	Store	Manager	Sales	Expenses	Profit
2	2000	1	Buffalo	Davis	465	245	220
3	2000	1	Chicago	Adams	560	412	148
4	2000	1	Toronto	Williams	654	134	520
5	2000	2	Buffalo	Davis	546	238	308
6	2000	2	Chicago	Adams	467	235	232
7	2000	2	Toronto	Williams	759	354	405
8	2000	3	Buffalo	Davis	587	246	341
9	2000	3	Chicago	Adams	854	279	575
10	2000	3	Toronto	Williams	846	653	193
11	2000	4	Buffalo	Davis	546	345	201
12	2000	4	Chicago	Martin	597	325	272
13	2000	4	Toronto	Williams	585	643	-58
14	2001	1	Buffalo	Davis	522	147	375
15	2001	1	Chicago	Martin	568	465	103
16	2001	1	Toronto	Williams	645	125	520
17	2001	2	Buffalo	Jeffries	214	158	56
18	2001	2	Chicago	Jeffries	547	234	313
19	2001	2	Toronto	Davis	467	234	233
20	2001	3	Buffalo	Jeffries	562	254	308
21	2001	3	Chicago	Jeffries	568	235	333
22	2001	3	Toronto	Davis	594	214	380
23	2001	4	Buffalo	Jeffries	213	165	48

Sample table.

If you create your own sheet, be sure to turn the range into a table by clicking **Insert > Table** (for more information, refer to Chapter 30).

This table shows the year, quarter, store location, manager's name, total sales, expenses, and profit for each store. As you can see, it's a collection of numbers with no purpose. You can make sense out of this with a PivotTable.

Click somewhere inside the table range, and then click **Insert > PivotTable**. Either click the **PivotTable** button, or click the drop-down and then click **PivotTable**. There's also a PivotChart feature that we look at later.

You're asked which table or range you want to work with. Choose the table you already created, Table1. Next, select where you want the PivotTable to go: either a new worksheet or a region inside an existing worksheet. Let's put it in a new worksheet. Click **OK**.

The PivotTable Tools tabs displays on the Ribbon, and a new worksheet is created. Notice a region on the left that says, "To build a report, choose fields from the PivotTable Field List." On the right is the field list. Check which fields of data you want to appear in the PivotTable. (See Figure 31.2.)

Figure 31.2

Building the PivotTable.

Let's begin by summarizing the sales for each of the stores by year. Click the **Store** field (see Figure 31.3).

Figure 31.3

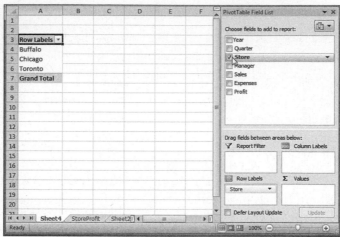

Store field as a Row Label.

The Store field displays in the PivotTable under a row label. Row labels and column labels enable you to compare values based on multiple criteria. Let's see sales by store by year.

To add the Year field as a column label, click the **Year** field (see Figure 31.4).

Figure 31.4

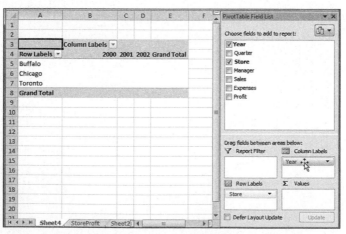

Year field in the wrong place.

Excel mistakenly thought that the Year field was the value data and put "Sum of Year" in the Values box (see Figure 31.5). That's okay. Click and drag it to move it up into the Column Labels box.

Figure 31.5

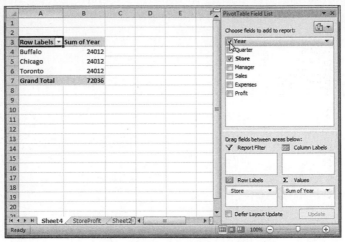

Year field as a Column Label.

That's much better. Now you can see the PivotTable taking form. You have stores as the row labels and the years as the column labels. Now you need to add the data. To track sales for each store, click the **Sales** box (see Figure 31.6).

Figure 31.6

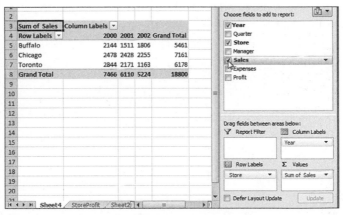

Sales as the value.

Notice that "Sum of Sales" has been placed in the Values box. This means that Excel is going to SUM up the sales for each of the stores for each year and then put that calculation on the PivotTable, which includes Grand Totals for each store and for each year.

You should appreciate Excel's capabilities at this point. Figuring out these numbers based on the original sheet would have taken a lot of manual calculations, along with sorting, filtering, and moving things around. Getting the same data from a PivotTable involves only a handful of easy clicks.

But you're not even close to finished yet ….

Working with PivotTables

Once you have your PivotTable built, there are several things you can do with them, such as change the calculation functions, and add more fields, filter and sort data, and so on.

Changing the Function

If you don't want to calculate the SUM of the sales from each city, you can easily change the function that's used. Click the **Sum of Sales** drop-down box in the Values box, and then click **Value Field Settings**.

In the Value Field Settings dialog box, you can easily change the type of field calculation to COUNT, AVERAGE, MAX, MIN, and lots more. Select **AVERAGE**. You can also give the field a custom name. Let's leave the name as "Average of Sales."

Notice that the PivotTable is now updated to the AVERAGE function (see Figure 31.7). You might also want to click the Decrease Decimal button on the Ribbon (Home > Number > Decrease Decimal) so that the values have a uniform number of decimal places.

Figure 31.7

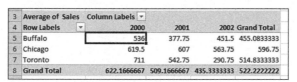

3	Average of Sales	Column Labels			
4	Row Labels		2000	2001	2002 Grand Total
5	Buffalo		536	377.75	451.5 455.0833333
6	Chicago		619.5	607	563.75 596.75
7	Toronto		711	542.75	290.75 514.8333333
8	Grand Total		622.1666667	509.1666667	435.3333333 522.2222222

AVERAGE function in PivotTable.

Click the **UNDO** button to go back to the SUM function.

Adding Fields

If needed, you can add more fields to the PivotTable. Let's say that, in addition to the Store field, you want to see Manager. Click the **Manager** box (see Figure 31.8).

Figure 31.8

		Column Labels			
Sum of Sales		2000	2001	2002	Grand Total
Row Labels					
⊟Buffalo		2144	1511	1806	5461
Davis		2144	522	1003	3669
Jeffries			989		989
Jones				357	357
Williams				446	446
⊟Chicago		2478	2428	2255	7161
Adams		1881		1223	3104
Davis				564	564
Jeffries			1860		1860
Martin		597	568	468	1633
⊟Toronto		2844	2171	1163	6178
Davis			1526		1526
Jones				226	226
Williams		2844	645	937	4426
Grand Total		**7466**	**6110**	**5224**	**18800**

Choose fields to add to report:
☑ Year ☐ Quarter ☑ Store ☑ Manager ☑ Sales ☐ Expenses ☐ Profit

Drag fields between areas below:
Report Filter | Column Labels: Year
Row Labels: Store, Manager | Σ Values: Sum of Sales

☐ Defer Layout Update | Update

Manager field added.

Notice that, in addition to totals for each store, you can see totals for each manager at each store. Again, it is difficult to get these numbers without a PivotTable.

As you can see from the data, some of the managers worked at multiple stores. If you want to flip this around (that is, pivot) the data so that the top level is the manager and the sublevels are the stores, click and drag the Manager item up so that it's above the Store item in the Row Labels box.

Notice in Figure 31.9 how the PivotTable has adjusted itself so that the top level of data is the manager and the sublevels are the stores.

Figure 31.9

Row Labels
Manager
Store

☐ Defer Layout Update

Move Manager above Store.

Collapsing Levels

You can collapse the main levels of the PivotTable if you don't want to see all the information at once. Perhaps you're interested only in Davis's sales. Click the boxes with the minus signs in them that are next to the manager names to collapse that level. (See Figure 31.10.)

Figure 31.10

3	Sum of Sales	Column Labels			
4	Row Labels	2000	2001	2002	Grand Total
5	⊞ Adams	1881		1223	3104
6	⊟ Davis	2144	2048	1567	5759
7	Buffalo	2144	522	1003	3669
8	Chicago			564	564
9	Toronto		1526		1526
10	⊞ Jeffries		2849		2849
11	⊞ Jones			583	583
12	⊞ Martin	597	568	468	1633
13	⊞ Williams	2844	645	1383	4872
14	Grand Total	7466	6110	5224	18800

Collapse levels.

The box now has a plus sign in it, which you can click again to expand the level.

Filtering and Sorting Data

After building your PivotTable, you can filter the data in it. Let's say you don't want to see Jones's and Martin's sales. Click the down arrow next to the Row Labels box in the PivotTable.

Now you see the Filter Data menu discussed in Chapter 29 (see Figure 31.11). Check off the data you don't want to see.

Figure 31.11

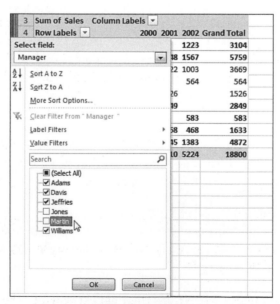

Filter Data menu.

Notice that the filter is applied, and the filter drop-down box next to Row Labels contains the funnel icon to indicate that a filter is active. (See Figure 31.12.)

Figure 31.12

Sum of Sales	Column Labels				Grand Total
Row Labels		2000	2001	2002	Grand Total
⊟ Adams		1881		1223	3104
Chicago		1881		1223	3104
⊟ Davis		2144	2048	1567	5759
Buffalo		2144	522	1003	3669
Chicago				564	564
Toronto			1526		1526
⊟ Jeffries			2849		2849
Buffalo			989		989
Chicago			1860		1860
⊟ Williams		2844	645	1383	4872
Buffalo				446	446
Toronto		2844	645	937	4426
Grand Total		6869	5542	4173	16584

Filter funnel.

TIP

Using the same technique as described above, you can filter the columns, too. You will also find options to sort both the rows and columns using the same drop-down box.

If you have multiple levels in your row labels, you can apply a filter or sort by clicking the level first and applying the sort/filter. For example, to sort the managers alphabetically, click a manager name first and then apply the A-to-Z sort. If you want to sort the stores, click a store name first and then apply the sort.

Report Filter

To filter the data (values) of the PivotTable, drag the field to the Report Filter box. Let's say you want to show only sales from the first quarter of each year. To do this, you need to filter the PivotTable based on quarter.

TIP

You can remove a field from the PivotTable by clicking and dragging it out of the boxes and back into the field list.

Click and drag the Quarter field from the field list down to the Report Filter box (see Figure 31.13).

Figure 31.13

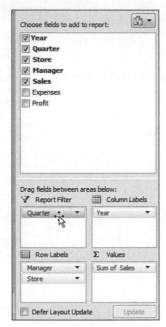

Report Filter box.

Notice that a Quarter Report Filter box displays starting at cell A1 in your sheet. (See Figure 31.14.)

Figure 31.14

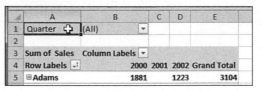

Report Filter by quarter.

Now click the drop-down box next to Quarter and choose the first quarter. To select multiple items (such as the first and second quarters), you have to check the **Select Multiple Items** box (see Figure 31.15).

Figure 31.15

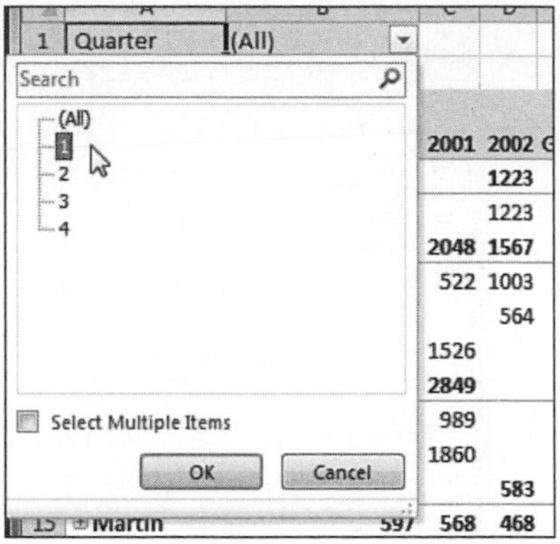

First quarter sales only.

Now out of all of the data in the main table, you see sales data for only the first quarter of each year, broken down by year, store, and manager. (See Figure 31.16.)

Figure 31.16

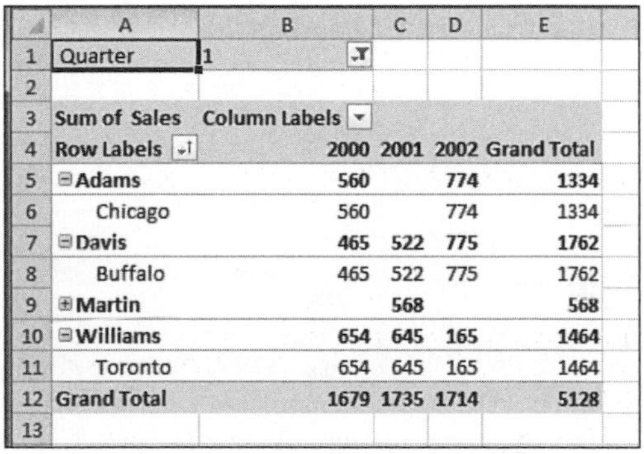

	A	B	C	D	E
1	Quarter	1			
2					
3	Sum of Sales	Column Labels			
4	Row Labels	2000	2001	2002	Grand Total
5	⊟Adams	560		774	1334
6	Chicago	560		774	1334
7	⊟Davis	465	522	775	1762
8	Buffalo	465	522	775	1762
9	⊞Martin		568		568
10	⊟Williams	654	645	165	1464
11	Toronto	654	645	165	1464
12	Grand Total	1679	1735	1714	5128
13					

First quarter sales results.

Pivoting the Data

You can quickly and easily move fields to different axes and filter locations to view the data from different angles, which is where PivotTables get their name.

Let's say you want to see the sales for each store, cross-referenced by each manager. In addition, you want to be able to quickly choose the year and quarter from a report filter.

First, let's move the Manager field to the Column Labels section.

Now move the Year field up to the Report Filter section. (See Figure 31.17.)

Figure 31.17

Move Year to Report Filters.

Notice how the data changes based on the new row and column criteria you specified. You can see each manager's sales based on the store. Some managers, like Davis, worked at multiple stores, with sales in two places. To limit the list to just 2002 sales, open the Year report filter (see Figure 31.18).

Figure 31.18

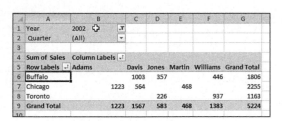

	A	B	C	D	E	F	G
1	Year	2002					
2	Quarter	(All)					
3							
4	Sum of Sales	Column Labels					
5	Row Labels	Adams	Davis	Jones	Martin	Williams	Grand Total
6	Buffalo			1003	357		446	1806
7	Chicago		1223	564		468		2255
8	Toronto				226		937	1163
9	Grand Total		1223	1567	583	468	1383	5224
10								

Sales by manager by store by year.

Slicers

New in Excel 2010 are Slicers, which enable you to quickly apply different filters to the PivotTable based on specific fields. Slicers don't really add any functionality that's not already in the PivotTable tools, but they make it easier for novice Excel users to work with your PivotTable.

For example, click the **Insert Slicer** button from the PivotTable Options tab.

Choose which field or fields you want Slicers for. Let's choose just the **Store** field (see Figure 31.19).

Figure 31.19

Insert Slicer field.

A Slicer box appears next to your PivotTable. If you click any of the data options, a filter is placed on the PivotTable showing just the selected data. As you can see, this isn't anything fabulous that you can't already do, but it's a nice, clean interface that someone who isn't as familiar with Excel can easily use (see Figure 31.20).

Figure 31.20

	A	B	C	D	E	F	G
1	Year	(All)	▾				
2	Quarter	(All)	▾				
3						Store	⫟
4	Sum of Sales	Column Labels	⫟			Buffalo	
5	Row Labels	Chicago	Grand Total				
6	Adams	3104	3104			Chicago	
7	Davis	564	564			Toronto	
8	Jeffries	1860	1860			(blank)	
9	Martin	1633	1633				
10	Grand Total	7161	7161				
11							
12							
13							
14							
15							
16							

Slicer buttons.

There's a Clear Filter button in the upper-right corner of the Slicer box. To get rid of the Slicer, click the edge of the box and click **Delete** to delete it like any other object in Excel. Don't forget to clear your filter first.

Adding Data to the Table

If you add or change data in your original table, Excel automatically expands the range of your table to accommodate it. That's one of the benefits of using a table (see Figure 31.21).

Figure 31.21

37	2002	4	Toronto	Williams	226	214	12
38	2003	1	Toronto	Williams	500	200	300
39	2004	1	Chicago	Jones	800	100	700
40							
41	⊹						
42							

Add data to table.

Because your PivotTable is based on the table and not a set range of cells, the data automatically updates when you add new records. However, you might have to manually recalculate the PivotTable. You can do this with the Refresh button on the PivotTable Options tab.

Formatting PivotTables

The options in the Design tab in the PivotTable Tools section of the Ribbon are similar to those you've seen throughout Excel so far. Notice a Styles gallery to change the look of your PivotTable.

There are options to show subtotals at the top or bottom of each group, or not show them at all. Subtotals appear when you have multiple levels for your row labels (see Figure 31.22).

Figure 31.22

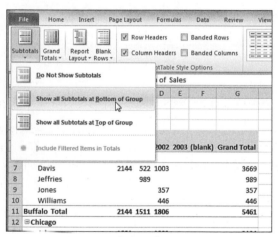

Subtotals.

You can decide whether to show Grand Totals for your columns and rows. You can also choose among various Report Layouts. You can decide whether to insert blank lines after each main row item.

Check boxes show row and column headers, as well as banded rows and columns, just like with table styles.

PivotCharts

When you have your PivotTable showing the data that you want to represent, you can convert it to a chart, for even more visual appeal. (See Figure 31.23.)

Figure 31.23

4	Sum of Sales	Column Labels ▼					
5	Row Labels ▼I	2000	2001	2002	2003	(blank)	Grand Total
6	Buffalo		2144	1511	1806		5461
7	Chicago		2478	2428	2255		7161
8	Toronto		2844	2171	1163	500	6678
9	(blank)						
10	Grand Total		7466	6110	5224	500	19300
11							
12				✥			

Data to chart.

In Figure 31.23, sales are organized by store by year. Let's turn that into a PivotChart. Click the **PivotTable Tools**, **Options** tab. Click the **PivotChart** button in the Tools section (see Figure 31.24).

Figure 31.24

PivotChart.

The Insert Chart dialog box appears. Select a 3-D Column chart.

The PivotChart looks similar to the 3-D charts you created in Chapter 20. Filter buttons are available for each axis and for the report filters. The PivotChart Tools tabs appear, which are almost the same as the regular chart toolbars (see Figure 31.25).

Figure 31.25

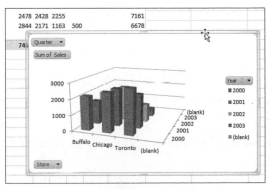

Final PivotChart.

Excel inserts the PivotChart as an object in the same sheet as your PivotTable, so click the **Move Chart** button (on the Design tab) and then move it to a new sheet (for more information, refer to Chapter 20).

The Least You Need to Know

- A PivotTable makes sense of large amounts of data.
- You can "pivot" the table in different ways by looking at different fields and values.
- PivotCharts can visually demonstrate trends in your data.

Miscellaneous

This part covers everything that didn't fit neatly into another part.

Chapter 32 covers reviewing. This includes the spell check, thesaurus, and dictionary, as well as the research, translate, and comments features.

Chapter 33 is about customizing the Excel interface. You learn how to customize the Quick Access Toolbar and create your own tabs and groups on the Ribbon. We also cover some of the more important settings under Excel Options.

Reviewing

In This Chapter

- Checking your sheets for misspelled words
- Using the thesaurus to find synonyms
- Researching a topic with a keyword search in Excel
- Translating words into other languages
- Inserting comments into your spreadsheets

This chapter covers spell check, the research function, the thesaurus, translation, and comments. Generally features like spell check and thesaurus are more suited to a word processing program, like Microsoft Word. However, you will find the need for these features even in Excel from time to time. Fortunately, most of these features are available in all of the Microsoft Office 2010 programs, including Word, Excel, and PowerPoint.

Spelling

When you've finished your masterpiece spreadsheet and you're ready to send it out for the world (or at least your boss) to see, you should spell-check it first. You can find the Spelling button on the Review tab of the Ribbon.

When you click the Review > Proofing > Spelling button, the spell checker starts. It searches your sheet for misspellings. The first misspelled word it found in the example sheet shown in Figure 32.1 is "Televison."

Figure 32.1

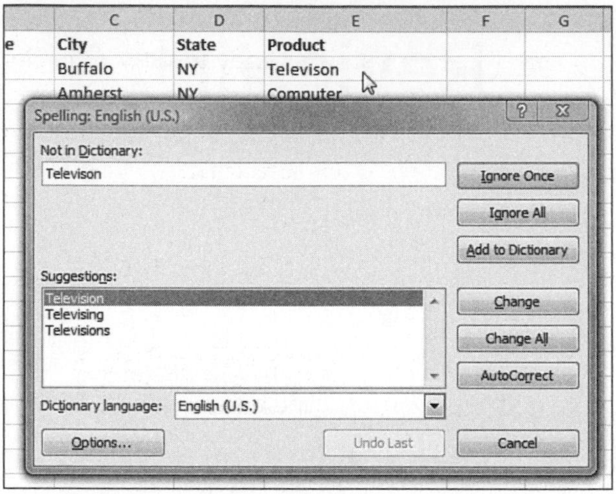

Misspelled word.

Yep, that's definitely spelled wrong. Now you have several options that are found on the right side of the Spelling dialog:

- **Ignore Once:** This option ignores the misspelled word this one time and continues with the spell check.

- **Ignore All:** This ignores all instances of a word if it finds it again in this spreadsheet. This is handy for words that might be proper nouns or words that you know are spelled correctly but aren't in Excel's dictionary.

- **Add to Dictionary:** This option enables you to add the word to your custom dictionary. Any words you add to the dictionary do not appear as misspelled again in any spreadsheets.

- **Change:** Change the word with the currently selected item from the list to the left. In Figure 32.2, you can see three alternate words listed: the correct spelling of *television*, *televising*, and *televisions*. Choose one and click **Change** to change just this word.

- **Change All:** This changes the current word with the selected word whenever it finds it in the spreadsheet.

> **WARNING**
>
> Be careful with the Change All option. Excel might change words that you aren't expecting, especially if it's a simple word. You might prefer to change words one at a time so you can see the exact changes as they're made.

Thesaurus

The thesaurus (say that 10 times fast) is a handy tool for replacing a word with another word that means the same thing. For example, in Figure 32.2, you will see several words to represent each of the customer's moods. We want to replace "Happy" with something else, but we're not quite sure what.

Click **Happy**, and then click the **Thesaurus**. The Research pane opens, and you can see a list of words that are synonyms for *happy* (see Figure 32.2).

Figure 32.2

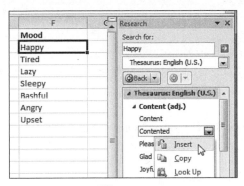

Thesaurus.

To make the replacement, simply click the word you'd like to replace *happy* with and then choose **Insert** from the drop-down menu. Now the word *happy* is replaced with *contented*.

You can also double-click a word to look up that word in the dictionary. Use the Back button to move back to the previous word. Just be careful that you know the word's meaning—you don't want to insert a word just because it sounds cool.

Dictionary

If you're not sure of a word's meaning, change the reference book type from the thesaurus to the Encarta Dictionary (see Figure 32.3). Use the drop-down menu just below the "Search for" word box. Under "All Reference Books" you should see the "Encarta Dictionary" option.

Figure 32.3

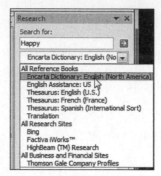

Dictionary.

This provides a clear definition of what *happy* means.

Research

While you have the Research pane open, you can also use it to look up other information, if you have an active Internet connection. For example, search for the keyword "Microsoft" and switch the research site to "Bing" using the same drop-down menu as before. Now click the green **Go** arrow (next to the keyword box). This brings up Bing search results for Microsoft.

You can search several other sites for information as well. These change from time to time as Microsoft updates its services. Feel free to explore them all.

Translate

If you want to translate a word into a different language, Excel offers the Translate button. Click a word, like "Tired," and then click **Translate**.

Choose Spanish from the list of languages, and the translation appears in the Research pane. All this work makes us *fatigado*.

Comments

If you want to put notes on your sheet, but you don't want to waste valuable space in an actual cell, or you want to make them really noticeable (or hidden), use comments.

Click the cell you want to add the comment to, and then click **New Comment** on the Review tab.

A comment box opens with your name in it (it's the name of the user currently logged in). Type a comment—you can delete your name, if you want to. (See Figure 32.4.)

Figure 32.4

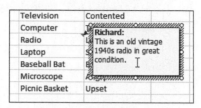

Enter your comment.

When you're done entering your comment, click on some other cell. All you see is a red marker in the upper-left corner of that cell to indicate that there's a comment in there.

To see the comment, hover your mouse over that cell, and it pops up. This is good if you want to include more information with a cell, but you don't want to take up a lot of space.

If you want the comment to always be visible, click the cell and click the **Review** > **Comments** > **Show/Hide Comment** button on the Ribbon. The comment remains visible even when you click off it. In fact, you can click and drag it to move it wherever you want, and it will stay there. (See Figure 32.5.)

Figure 32.5

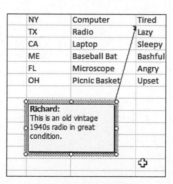

Move your comment.

NOTICE

The Comments section includes buttons to edit the comment, delete the comment, jump to the previous or next comment in the spreadsheet, and make all the comments in the entire sheet visible.

The Least You Need to Know

- Use the spell checker to examine your sheets for misspelled words.
- Employ the thesaurus to find synonyms for the words in your sheet.
- Insert comments into your spreadsheets to include additional information or draw attention to something.
- Use the Research tool to search for information on the web, and the Translate tool to translate words into different languages.

Customizing Excel

In This Chapter

- Adding the commands you use most often to the Quick Access Toolbar
- Creating your own Ribbon tab and group
- Using the Excel system options to change anything you want

Excel is highly customizable. You can take several actions to make using Excel more friendly. These include customizing the Quick Access Toolbar, the Ribbon, and some of the Excel options.

Customizing the Quick Access Toolbar

The Quick Access Toolbar (QAT) is that toolbar across the top of the Excel window. It's on the same level as the title bar, and it sits above the Ribbon tabs.

Normally, the QAT comes with just three commands: Save, Undo, and Redo. However, if you have a favorite command that you use often, you can simply add it to the QAT.

The easiest way to add a command to the QAT is to find it on the Ribbon. Then right-click on it and select **Add to Quick Access Toolbar**. In Figure 33.1, the Bold command is added to the QAT.

Figure 33.1

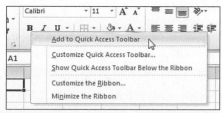

Adding the Bold command to the Quick Access Toolbar.

Now you can see the Bold command is right up there on the Quick Access Toolbar.

To take a command off the QAT, just right-click it and select **Remove from Quick Access Toolbar**.

You can also click the down arrow to the right of the QAT toolbar to display a menu with several of the most popular commands people like to add to the QAT, such as Print Preview and Sort.

Another way to add commands to the QAT is to right-click any command button and select **Customize the Quick Access Toolbar** to display the menu in Figure 33.2.

Figure 33.2

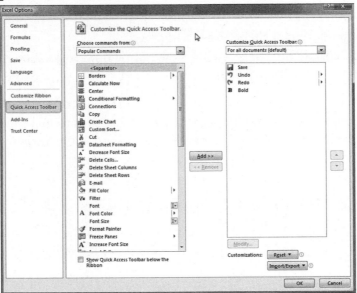

Customize the Quick Access Toolbar.

The Excel Options dialog box displays. You can find almost every command in Excel on the left side, where you can browse based on categories in the "Choose commands from" drop-down box.

When you find a command that you want to add to the QAT, just double-click it (or click it once and click the **Add** button).

You can also include separators on the QAT. At the top of the feature list on the left you'll see the <Separator> option. Double-click on that to add it to your QAT. It just breaks the buttons up a little bit so you can group like buttons together.

You also see a check box that, if enabled, shows the QAT below the Ribbon instead of on top of it. That's just a matter of personal preference. When you're done, click **OK** to have your changes take effect.

Customizing the Ribbon

New in Excel 2010 is the capability to customize the Ribbon. This isn't quite as easy as customizing the QAT, but it's not difficult. Right-click anywhere on the Ribbon and select **Customize the Ribbon**.

Using this feature, you can create your own custom Ribbon tabs and groups. This is a great way to put all the commands that you like to use on a regular basis in one place. Let's add our own tab to the Ribbon:

1. Click the **Home** tab (on the right side, under the "Customize the Ribbon" drop-down menu) and then click the **New Tab** button. This inserts a new tab and a new group. These are labeled "New Tab (Custom)" and "New Group (Custom)."

2. Select **New Tab**, click the **Rename** button (toward the bottom of the window), and give your tab a good name. The one in Figure 33.3 is Ricks Tab.

3. Click the up-arrow button (on the right of the window, as shown in Figure 33.3) to move it above the Home tab.

Figure 33.3

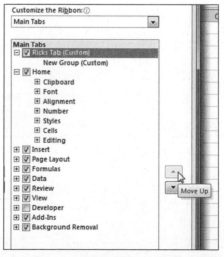

Ricks Tab.

4. Next, click **Custom Group** on and click the **Rename** button. Pick a symbol to represent the group, give the group a name. In Figure 33.4, it is named Ricks Group.

Figure 33.4

Ricks Group.

Now, with Ricks Group selected, you can go down the commands on the left and add them to the group. Add just a few (see Figure 33.5).

Figure 33.5

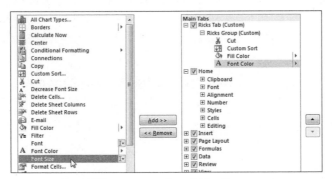

Adding commands to Ricks Group.

When you're done, click **OK**. You see Excel's main interface, and you can see Ricks Tab just to the left of the Home tab (see Figure 33.6).

Figure 33.6

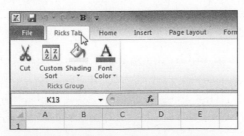

Ricks Tab displaying on the Ribbon.

Now that you're done experimenting with customizing the Ribbon, remove the tab. To do this, you go back into Customize the Ribbon and then right-click **Ricks Tab**. Select **Remove**.

Excel Options

Now let's take a look at some of the Excel program options. Click **File** and then click **Options**.

> **NOTICE**
>
> Excel offers many different configuration options. This discussion covers the more commonly used settings. Discussing all of them would take a very long time, and most people never use them, so just the important ones are covered here.

The General tab includes mostly user interface options that change the way Excel looks and behaves. (See Figure 33.7.)

The first option on the General tab says "Show Mini Toolbar on selection." That's the toolbar that pops up with font formatting options when you select text. It was a little annoying when Microsoft first added it to Excel 2007, but you can get used to it.

Figure 33.7

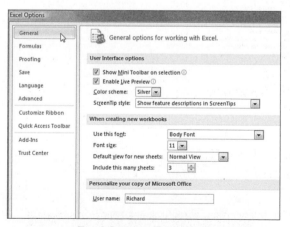

Excel Options, General tab.

The next option says "Enable Live Preview." If you have a slower computer, you can turn off Live Preview. Recall that Live Preview shows you how something will look if you choose an option that changes a font, color, and so on. If your computer bogs down when Live Preview runs, turn it off here by unchecking this option (or get a faster computer).

The next option says "Color scheme." This is the general look and feel for the Microsoft Excel window and interface. Blue is the old Office 2007 setting. Silver is the default Office 2010 setting. Black is kind of neat as well.

The next option is "ScreenTip style." ScreenTips are help windows that display whenever you hover over a command or menu button. You can change the way they behave here, by changing the option in the drop-down menu. The default is "Show feature descriptions in ScreenTips."

You find some options on this menu for creating new workbooks. You can change the starting font, font size, display view, and how many sheets are created. These are all located in the "When creating new workbooks" section. You can also change your default user name under the "Personalize your copy of Microsoft Office" section.

Skip the Formulas and Proofing tabs. The default options on those tabs are fine for most users.

On the Save tab, you can change the default file format that Excel uses when it saves a workbook (see Figure 33.8). If a lot of people in your office are still using Excel 2003 or earlier, you can change your default file format here so that you don't have to keep manually saving your workbooks in the older format (refer to Chapter 9 for details on how to do this). If half of your company uses Excel 2010 and half still uses Excel 2003, you're probably going to want to stay with the Excel 2003 file format so you can easily share documents back and forth without conversion.

Figure 33.8

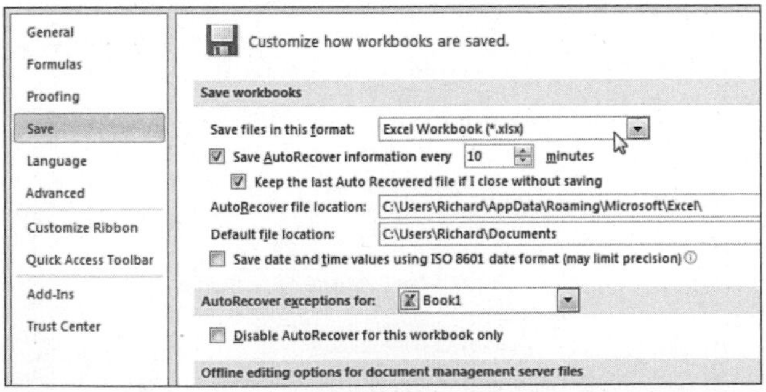

Excel Options, Save tab.

You can also find AutoRecover information on the Save tab. AutoRecover automatically saves your work every 10 minutes. If the power goes out or your computer locks up, Excel has saved a portion of your work, and the most you'll lose is the last 10 minutes worth. Generally, 10 minutes is fine for most users. You can change this value if you want, but if you make it too frequent, and you have a slow computer, you may be annoyed with how often Excel automatically saves your work. If you make it more than 10 minutes, you might lose a significant amount of work if there's a problem with your PC causing a lock up.

When restarting Excel after a power loss or lockup, Excel displays the Document Recovery task pane showing a list of documents that were not properly saved when Excel closed. You have the option of opening that file and making sure it's properly saved.

If you want to change the folder location where the AutoRecovery information is saved to, you can do so on the Save tab as well.

You may also find documents that were saved by the AutoRecover feature if you click on File and then Recent. Under the Recent Documents list, you may see files that say "when I closed without saving" under them. These are documents that you were working on, but something caused you to exit without properly saving them. You can open them and re-save them from this menu.

On the Save tab you can set your default file location. This is the folder where all of the documents you work on are stored, and where Excel first looks for any documents you are trying to open. Normally, it's set to your user documents folder, but if you'd like to use a different folder, feel free to specify it here.

Next, even though you're not yet an advanced user, let's take a quick look at the Advanced tab (see Figure 33.9). You can change some options here to make using Excel a little easier.

Figure 33.9

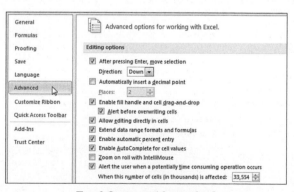

Excel Options, Advanced tab.

For example, the first option says after pressing Enter, move selection. You can change this from Down to Right, Left, or Up if you want. The default option is Down when you press Enter. This is just a matter of personal preference, but some people like Enter to move them to the right instead of down.

You can have Excel automatically insert a decimal point for you. If you like to type "100" and have that changed to "1.00," this is the option for you. It is called "Automatically insert a decimal point." This is useful for accountants who always enter *everything* in dollars and cents. Change this to 2 decimal places and then typing in "526" will give you "5.26" in the cell.

Look over the options on this menu. If you see something that you want to change, try it. If you're not sure what something is, click the Help button on top of the window or press F1 for the help system.

The Least You Need to Know

- You can add the commands you use most often to the Quick Access Toolbar so they're always ready for one-click access.
- You can customize the Ribbon and create your own tabs and groups, although modifying the built-in tabs isn't recommended.
- Look through the Excel options and change anything you understand that you feel needs changing.

What's New in Excel 2010

Excel 2007 was a complete redesign from previous versions, so we do not attempt to list everything that changed from Excel 2003 to 2007. This list of new and updated features is for those of you who previously used Excel 2007 and want to know what's been added or changed in Excel 2010.

New Features

- Microsoft has replaced the big round Office button with a new File tab, also called Backstage View. In some ways, this is a return to the Office 2003 File menu. See Chapter 9 for details.

- Sparklines enable you to see trends in columns of data without making a chart. Sparklines are essentially mini charts that exist in a single cell. See Chapter 21 for details.

- Slicers enable you to quickly filter PivotTable data to get fast, different views of your information. Slicers are covered in Chapter 31.

- The Screen Capture tool enables you to take anything you can see on the screen and quickly insert it as an image in your spreadsheets. Screenshots are covered in Chapter 19.

- It is now possible to easily customize the Ribbon. You can add your own tabs, groups, and buttons. We briefly discuss this in Chapter 33.

- Paste Preview allows you to see the results of a paste operation with different options. When you copy and paste something, the Paste command displays options with a live preview.

- Security features prevent untrusted macros from running. Specific workbooks can be designated as "trusted." This is great because you don't have to worry about getting an unsafe workbook from the Internet or a co-worker.

- A new version of Solver assists you in solving complex data analyses.

Improved and Updated Features

- Conditional formatting has been greatly enhanced, as have data bars. See Chapter 13 for all the details.

- Additional PivotTable and PivotChart formatting options have been added. See Chapter 31.

- Excel 2010 boasts faster performance and a larger sheet size than previous versions. Plus, support for 64-bit processors (running 64-bit versions of Windows) has been added.

- Improved accuracy has been added for some of the numeric and statistical functions. In some rare instances, Excel returned a wrong result, but a lot of these problems have been fixed in Excel 2010.

- Some of the more advanced functions have been renamed to be more intuitive. These functions are beyond the scope of this beginner book, but don't worry—the old function names you're used to still work.

- Image editing has been improved, along with new graphics options such as color saturation and artistic effects.

- More cell styles have been added.

- Some enhancements have been made to the VBA (Visual Basic for Applications) programming language.

- Co-authoring has been improved for better simultaneous editing of documents.

- The updated Equation Editor enables math geeks (and teachers) to create math equations and place them in spreadsheets.

- Excel Web App and Excel Mobile 2010 enable you to access your Excel data from anywhere you have an Internet connection.

Excel 2010 Function Reference

This appendix is not a comprehensive listing of all the functions available in Excel. Hundreds, if not thousands, of functions are available to choose from. However, the good old 80/20 rule applies: you'll use 20 percent of the functions in Excel 80 percent of the time.

This book shows you how to use the functions that enable you to accomplish the most common tasks in Excel.

This list is organized by the chapter each function appears in. If you'd like to learn more, you can easily refer to the appropriate chapter.

Chapter 6: Introduction to Functions

- SUM   Adds all the cells in one or more ranges
- AVERAGE   Calculates the average of the cells in a range
- COUNT   Counts the unique number of NUMERIC values in a range
- MAX   Calculates the largest value in a range
- MIN   Calculates the smallest value in a range

Chapter 23: Text Functions

- EXACT   Checks to see whether two strings are exactly the same
- CONCATENATE   Joins several text strings into one
- LEN   Calculates the length of a text string
- LEFT   Gives you the left N characters of a text string

- RIGHT   Gives you the right *N* characters of a text string

- MID   Gives you the middle *N* characters in a text string, starting at position *X*

- FIND   Returns the starting position of one text string inside another (case sensitive)

- SEARCH   Returns the starting position of one text string inside another (not case sensitive)

- LOWER   Converts a string to lowercase

- UPPER   Converts a string to uppercase

- PROPER   Converts a string to proper case

- SUBSTITUTE   Replaces existing text with new text in a string

- REPLACE   Replaces part of a text string with a different string

- TRIM   Removes spaces from the left and right sides of a string

Chapter 24: Date and Time Functions

- NOW   Returns the current date and time

- TODAY   Returns the current date

- YEAR   Returns the year portion of a date, such as 1999

- MONTH   Returns the month portion of a date, such as 12

- DAY   Returns the day portion of a date, such as 31

- HOUR   Returns the hour portion of a time, such as 12

- MINUTE   Returns the minute portion of a time, such as 60

- SECOND   Returns the second portion of a time, such as 59

- WEEKDAY   Returns the day of the week, from 1 to 7

- DATE   Returns a date value when given the three separate components (day, month, year)

- TIME   Returns a time value when given the three separate components (hour, minute, second)

- DATEDIF   An undocumented function that calculates the difference between two dates

Chapter 25: Logical Functions

- NOT   Changes TRUE to FALSE, and vice versa
- AND   Returns TRUE if all arguments are TRUE
- OR   Returns TRUE if any arguments are TRUE
- IF   Checks to see if a condition is met. If so, returns the TRUE argument; otherwise, returns the FALSE argument
- ISBLANK   Returns TRUE if a cell is empty
- ISERROR   Returns TRUE if a cell contains an ERROR message
- ISERR   Returns TRUE if a cell contains an ERROR message, excluding #N/A
- ISNA   Returns TRUE if a cell contains the #N/A error
- ISTEXT   Returns TRUE if a cell contains a text value (non-numeric)
- ISNONTEXT   Returns TRUE if a cell does not contain text
- ISNUMBER   Returns TRUE if a cell contains a numeric value
- ISLOGICAL   Returns TRUE if a cell contains a logical value (TRUE or FALSE)
- ISEVEN   Returns TRUE if a cell contains an even value
- ISODD   Returns TRUE if a cell contains an odd value
- IFERROR   Returns a specified value if an argument contains an error

Chapter 26: Lookup Functions

- VLOOKUP   Looks up a value in the left column of a table, and then returns the value in the same row from a column you specify. The table should be sorted in ascending order
- HLOOKUP   Looks up a value in the top row of a table, and then returns the value in the same column from a row you specify. The table should be sorted in ascending order
- LOOKUP   Returns a value from a one-row or one-column range

- MATCH   Returns the relative position of an item in a range that matches a given value in a specified order

- INDEX   Returns a value or reference of the cell at the intersection of a particular row and column

Chapter 27: Math and Statistical Functions

- SUMIF   Adds the cells in a range if they meet a specific criterion

- COUNTIF   Counts the number of cells in a range if they meet a specific criterion

- AVERAGEIF   Calculates the average of the cells in a range if they meet a specific criterion

- SUMIFS   Like SUMIF, but allows multiple conditions

- COUNTIFS   Like COUNTIF, but allows multiple conditions

- AVERAGEIFS   Like AVERAGEIF, but allows multiple conditions

- COUNTA   Counts the number of cells in a range that are not empty

- COUNTBLANK   Counts the number of empty cells in a range

- ROWS   Counts the number of rows in a range

- COLUMNS   Counts the number of columns in a range

- ROUND   Rounds a number to the specified number of digits

- ROUNDUP   Rounds a number up, away from zero

- ROUNDDOWN   Rounds a number down, toward zero

- MROUND   Returns a number rounded to the desired multiple

- CEILING   Rounds a number up to the nearest multiple

- FLOOR   Rounds a number down to the nearest multiple

- INT   Rounds a number down to the nearest integer

- TRUNC   Truncates any decimal portion from a number, returning just the integer portion

- MEDIAN   Returns the middle value from a range of values

- MODE   Returns the most common item from a range of values

- POWER   Returns a base number raised to a power
- SQRT   Returns the square root of a number
- QUOTIENT   Returns the integer portion of a division
- MOD   Returns the remainder of a division (modulus)
- ABS   Returns the absolute value of a number
- SIGN   Returns the sign of a number (negative, zero, or positive)
- RAND   Returns a random number between 0 and 1
- RANDBETWEEN   Returns a random number between two values
- PI   Returns the value of pi to 15 digits
- SIN   Returns the sine of a number in radians
- COS   Returns the cosine of a number in radians
- TAN   Returns the tangent of a number in radians

Chapter 28: Financial Functions

- PMT   Calculates monthly payments for a loan or investment
- FV   Calculates future values for a loan or investment
- RATE   Calculates interest rates for a loan or investment
- NPER   Calculates the number of periods for a loan or investment
- PV   Calculates the present value for a loan or investment

Shortcut Keys You'll Actually Use

A lot of Excel books give you pages upon pages of shortcut keys to show you *everything* that's available. This appendix shows you the shortcut keys you'll actually use on a daily basis. Consider Table C.1 a quick-reference guide to Excel and your keyboard.

Table C.1   Shortcut Keys

Key	Purpose
Arrow keys	Moves up, down, left, or right one cell
Home	Moves to the beginning of a row
End-Arrow key	Moves to the edge of the current sheet in that direction
PgUp	Moves up one screen
PgDn	Moves down one screen
Ctrl+Home	Moves to cell A1
Ctrl+End	Moves to bottom-right corner of the sheet
Ctrl+A	Selects all the cells in the entire sheet
Enter	Moves down one cell
Tab	Moves right one cell
Shift+Tab	Moves left one cell
F1	Opens Help
F2	Enters edit mode for current cell
Ctrl+C	Copies the selection
Ctrl+X	Cuts the selection
Ctrl+V	Pastes the selection
Ctrl+Z	Undo
Ctrl+B	Applies bold to the selected text
Ctrl+I	Applies italics to the selected text
Ctrl+U	Applies underline to the selected text
Ctrl+N	Creates a new workbook
Alt+Enter	Starts a new line in the current cell

Again, this guide is not comprehensive. There are dozens, if not hundreds, of additional keyboard shortcuts. However, these are the most popular ones and the keys you are likely to use every day. Feel free to tear this page out of the book and post it up on the bulletin board near your computer so you can glance over at it when you want to recall one of these shortcut keys.

If you want to use the keyboard with a particular feature, remember that you can always access it using the Alt-key tricks you use to navigate the Ribbon, as discussed in Chapter 3.

Index